Simple Lessons in Statistics for Psychology

Third Edition (Revised)

Jack Barnhardt

Wesley College

Dover, Delaware, U.S.A.

Updates for the third edition

- New chapter on statistical power
- Additional in-chapter examples
- Additional and revised end-of-chapter questions and problems
- New topics covered and expanded explanations of concepts

CONTENTS

Chapter 1
Introduction to statistics

The first question on your mind as you begin a statistics course may very well be: *Why on earth am I required to take a course in statistics?* It's a valid question, and there is a very good answer: Statistics are vital for the *communication* and *interpretation* of research results in Psychology. Without statistical procedures, researchers would not be able to clearly see what they found (including researchers in disciplines other than Psychology). Actually, they wouldn't even be able to tell if what they found should be called a *finding* at all!

The purpose of this book is to teach you about how these statistics work, and how to apply them to a variety of research situations.

The first part of the book presents various ways to summarize and describe the data collected so it can be effectively communicated to others (these are called *Descriptive Statistics*). The second part covers the theory and logic behind the type of statistic that allows the researcher to interpret their results (called *Inferential Statistics*). Finally, a number of specific inferential statistical tests are presented. You will see the particular test to use depends on the specifics of the research being carried out.

By the end of this book, you'll know how to clearly *communicate* your results, and how to choose and then use an inferential statistical test to help you *interpret* your results. Importantly, you will not only be able to use these tests, but you will have a deeper understanding of how they work.

The rest of this first chapter is devoted to some concepts and issues that will get you started on the way to learning all of the above. And don't worry: You can do it!

* * *

Let's begin by clarifying a very important distinction between two different groups relevant to psychology research: a *population* and a *sample*. The population is the group the experimenter wants to learn something about. If a researcher wanted to learn something about how 3rd graders interact with one another, his *population* would be all 3rd graders.

> The **population** is the entire group of individuals the researcher is interested in learning about. This group is usually far too large to study in its entirety.

Unfortunately, the population is far too large to study. Think about how many third graders there are, for example. But, thanks to inferential statistics, it is completely unnecessary to study the whole population. Instead, the research question (such as *Are 3rd graders more* *outgoing when they are outside or inside?*), is answered by investigating a group of individuals from whom we *can* obtain the data we need. These individuals are called the *sample*.

> A **sample** is a group of individuals selected from the population, from which the researcher collects data.

Depending on the result of the inferential statistical test, you may then generalize the findings you obtained in the sample to the population, essentially saying "*Yes, the result I found with my sample is indeed real. By real I mean that, if I could study the whole population, I'd find a similar result.*" Or, you may not say any of that, and instead conclude the result you found was due just *to chance*. You will learn a lot more about that later; for now all you need to know is that the sample is the group you actually study, and the population is the much larger group you hope to learn something about *from* your sample (which you could only do by statistically analyzing the results).

*   *   *

You may have learned in other psychology courses that sciences, such as Psychology, rely on *empirical* evidence. *Empirical* means based on observations–going out and collecting data. This is opposed to, say, coming to a conclusion based on what makes sense, or what is logical. To be sure, the empirical evidence does sometimes coincide with the logical conclusion you would have drawn without any empirical data. But often the data contradicts what you see as logical. When that happens, data always takes precedence over logic.

For example, you may think people wouldn't be more romantically attracted to someone if they happened to meet that person after chugging two energy drinks. However, the data suggest that may indeed be the case (though the effect is small).

It is fine to be skeptical about a research result such as the one in the previous paragraph. Just be careful about ignoring empirical evidence solely because it contradicts what you think makes sense.

*   *   *

Nevertheless, when you conduct research in Psychology, you're always dealing with *variables*. A *variable*, simply put, is something that varies.

> A **variable** is something that varies.

For example, let's say you decide to greet strangers and see how many of them respond back to you. You could say in this case you are making observations, but you could also say (and should say) you are *measuring a variable*. Since some people will respond back to you and some will not, then that's something that can vary, or take on different values. In this case, it can probably take on 2 values: 1) *responded* and 2) *didn't respond*.

See if you can think of 3 other variables.[1]

*   *   *

Greeting people to see how many of them respond back isn't a study in the true sense of the word (though you may casually refer to it as a study or even an experiment). But why isn't it? One reason is that you looked at only *one* variable. If you found that 40% of people responded back to you, your curiosity may have been satisfied to some extent, but you haven't learned much.

By contrast, in an actual research study, you always have at least 2 variables. Often, one is called the *independent variable* and the other the *dependent variable*. In the current example, you may go out wearing very nice clothing and see how many people respond back (let's say 60% of people responded back) and then right afterwards go out again wearing dirty, ratty clothing and do the same thing (and let's say 40% of people responded back under that condition).

You would have to do a statistical test to determine whether the 20% difference (60% vs. 40%) is real or just due to chance, but, if this test determined the difference is indeed real, you could justifiably conclude that *people are more likely to greet someone if they are dressed nicely.*[2] Now you've learned something!

> An important note, though: The statistical test can't tell you *why* people were more likely to greet you when you wore the nice clothing. For example, it may be the difference actually occurred because when you wore the nice clothing you were more confident—so the difference was caused by *confidence*, not by the clothing per se. The only thing the statistical test can tell you is whether the difference occurred for *some reason* (i.e., some *effect* on people's tendency to respond back when greeted), or instead occurred just *due to chance*.

In any case, in the current example the *type of clothing* you wore, nice vs. ratty, is the independent variable and *whether the subjects responded back* is the dependent variable.

---

[1] Usually, answers to questions like the one posed here will appear in a footnote. In this particular case, however, there are far too many possible answers to list all of them. But some are: *hair color, place of birth, weight, age, IQ, gender, GPA, # of video games owned, hours per week spent in car, type of car, handedness, birth order,* and *susceptibility to hypnosis.*

[2] You may have encountered the term *statistically significant.* That means the researcher decided the result is real (as opposed to being due to chance).

Let's look at another example to clarify the distinction between the independent and dependent variable. Imagine a new study, where one group of participants was given instructions verbally and another group was given instructions in writing. The independent variable would be *type of instructions given*. The *independent variable* is thus the variable that is in some way manipulated by the experimenter.[3]

> The **independent variable** is the variable that is manipulated by the experimenter, or otherwise used to create groups or conditions.

The *dependent variable*, on the other hand, is the variable you measure. So, in the current example, you may have wanted to see if the type of instructions given, verbal vs. written, influenced how well people performed on a test. In that case, the dependent variable is *scores on the test*.[4]

> The **dependent variable** is the variable that is measured or observed in a study. The point is to determine whether this variable depends on the independent variable.

The term *dependent variable* makes sense: You want to see whether test scores *depend* on instructions or, in the earlier example, whether the likelihood of people responding *depends* on the type of clothing worn.[5]

*   *   *

As the variables you named earlier may have demonstrated, variables can differ from each other in many ways. One fundamental way variables can differ is in the *scale of measurement* they are measured on.

There are actually four scales variables can be measured on. They vary in their level of sophistication (how much you can do with them statistically and such). We will examine them in order from the least sophisticated to the most sophisticated.

---

[3] See now why *type of clothing* was termed the independent variable in the previous example? The experimenter had control over that.

[4] See now why *whether people responded* was the dependent variable in the previous example? The experimenter had no control over whether people responded; she simply *measured* that variable.

[5] Notice the term *dependent* implies there is a cause/effect relationship between the variables. But be aware that even if there is little evidence that type of relationship exists, the terms *independent variable* and *dependent variable* are still normally used.

Nominal scale

Points along a nominal scale variable differ only in some *qualitative* way. For example, the variable *marital status* is nominal because all you can say about the different points on this variable (married, single, divorced, etc.) is that they are different. You can't even so much as put them into any meaningful order.

Another example of a nominal scale variable is *home state*. It is a variable because it can vary, of course: Different people have different home states. It's a *nominal* scale variable because all you can say about the different points (e.g., Delaware, New York, Texas) is that they are different.

Ordinal scale

If you're dealing with an ordinal scale variable, you *can* put the different points in order. An example of this is *class rank*. Another is *place finished* in a marathon. Notice in both cases there is an order (freshman, sophomore, etc., or finished first, finished second, etc.). However, you don't know what the "distance" between the points is. Take the fourth-, fifth-, and sixth-place marathon runners: Were there roughly equal distances between the three? Or were the fourth and fifth very close to each other and the sixth was way behind? Or perhaps the fifth and sixth were very close, and the fourth was way ahead. Ranking them as 1st, 2nd, 3rd, and so on, does not provide such information. Or, as is the case with class rank (Freshman, Sophomore, etc.) there isn't even a quantifiable distance or difference.[6] Either way, with an ordinal scale variable, all you know is the order.

Interval scale

With an interval scale variable, you can also put the points in order, but the intervals between the points are quantifiable and *equal*. An example of an interval scale variable is degrees Fahrenheit (°F). The same difference exists between, say, 4 and 5°F as between 5 and 6°F, and so on.

Ratio scale

A ratio scale variable is just like the interval scale, but with one important difference: On the ratio scale, there is a *true zero point*. At first, then, it may seem like the Fahrenheit scale is ratio—after all, there is a zero point: 0°F. You may have even been out on a 0° day and felt it for yourself. But, does 0°F really mean *zero* heat? Clearly not. Although 0°F is quite cold if you're not properly dressed, it is very far from zero heat! Thus, 0°F is not a *true* zero point.

---

[6] You may be thinking that you need a certain number of credits to be a sophmore, and a certain number to be a junior, and so on. True, but then your variable would be *number of credits*, not *class rank*.

The zero point on the Fahrenheit scale is instead an *arbitrary* zero point—chosen not because it really represents no heat, but for some other reason.

Ratio scale variables are very common, and most of the variables you will encounter in the rest of this book will be ratio scale variables. Some examples are *seconds, inches, grams,* and *pounds.* Notice in each of these examples, zero represents the complete lack of whatever each is measuring:

- Zero seconds means something truly took NO time to occur
- Zero inches means something truly has NO length
- Zero grams means something truly has NO mass
- Zero pounds means something truly has NO weight

Now that you know the distinction between the ratio and interval scales comes down to whether the zero on the scale represents a true zero, the next question is *why* that matters. What's the relevance of whether or not the zero point on the scale represents a true zero?

You can find the answer in the name of the scale: *ratio.* If there is a true zero point then you can form *ratios*:

A 10 second long video is twice as long as a 5 second long video.
(ratio is 2:1)
An 8 inch plant is 4 times as tall as a 2 inch plant.
(ratio is 4:1)
Something that is 2 grams has 10 times the mass of something that is 0.2 grams.
(ratio is 10:1)
A 150 pound person weighs 3 times as much as someone who weighs 50 lbs.
(ratio is 3:1)

Now try to form a ratio with an interval scale variable, like Fahrenheit:

A 2°F day is twice as warm as a 1°F day. If you look at a Fahrenheit thermometer, it does *look like* 2 is twice as far from 0° as 1° is (see below). But wait—is it really?

What's causing the confusion? The problem is that the zero point above is *arbitrary.* In other words, it does not represent the complete lack of heat.

But if we did put zero at the *true* zero (that is, at the point where there truly is no heat at all), it would look more like this:

Now we can plainly see, indeed, 2°F is not twice as far from the true zero as 1°F, and thus you *cannot* correctly say that 2°F is twice as warm as 1°F. Notice whether you can correctly form ratios all comes down to whether the zero on the scale is a true zero.

The following summarizes the four scales of measurement:

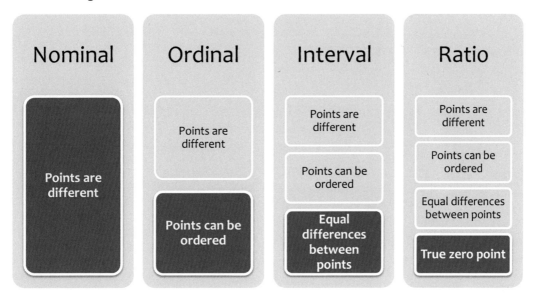

A couple quick notes before moving on. First, notice the name of each of the scales helps to clarify which is which:

> *Nominal* – differ only in *name*
> *Ordinal* – can be *ordered*
> *Interval* – equal *intervals* between points
> *Ratio* – can form *ratios*

Second, a note about the marathon runners mentioned earlier. If we measure their place finished (1st, 2nd, etc.), that is an ordinal variable, as previously discussed. But if instead we measured the time *it took them to complete the marathon* (180 minutes, 360 minutes, etc.), that is a ratio scale variable: A person who took 360 minutes took twice as long as one who took 180 minutes. The lesson from this example is: It's not what is being measured that determines the scale of measurement, but *how* it is being measured that matters.[7]

* * *

Now a bit about using formulas, because you will need to be able to handle them throughout this book. That requires two basic skills: correct use of the order of operations, and knowledge of what the symbols (aka the *statistical notation*) in the formulas mean. Other than that, all you need is a basic calculator.

So, be sure you can correctly use the order of operations. To test yourself, solve the formulas below. If you have any problems, consult a basic math book or other resource that reviews the order of operations.

Given g = 5 and a = 2, find *J* for the next two formulas. Solutions are below[8]

1) $$J = \frac{(g-a)^2}{a}$$

2) $$J = \frac{g-a^2}{a}$$

As for the statistical notation, you will learn many symbols as we go along. But it would be helpful to mention a few right now:

X:

This is a big one. *X* is used to designate a single *score*. The word *score* is used generically in statistics to mean whatever is being measured. Sometimes the word *score* fits perfectly, such as when you're looking at participants' test scores. But other times the word doesn't fit quite right, like if you were measuring participants' weight—but the term *score* is used anyway. If you were weighing mice, for example comparing those who ingested an

---

[7] Another example that illustrates this point: Although Degrees Fahrenheit is an interval scale since zero degrees isn't the true zero, *degrees Kelvin* (°K) is a ratio scale because zero Kelvin really is the true zero (that is the point at which there really is no heat whatsoever, called *absolute zero*). Both F and K measure temperature, but one is interval and the other ratio because of *how* they measure temperature.

[8] 1) 5-2 = 3; 3^2 = 9; 9/2 = 4.5   2) 2^2 = 4; 5 − 4 = 1; 1/2 = 0.5

experimental weight loss drug with those who did not, each mouse would get a score, where *score* is their weight (if mouse #4 weighed 20 grams, that mouse's score is X = 20).

Y:

If you were measuring two variables, for example if you also recorded the ages of those mice, you would designate that variable Y. If that mouse #4 was 8 months old, you may say his Y score is 8. So for mouse #4, X = 20 and Y = 8. But most of the time you are measuring only one variable, so you won't see Y again until much later.

N:

You will definitely be seeing a lot of this one. N, either uppercase or lowercase, refers to the *number* of participants. Depending on the context, it could refer to the number of participants in the whole experiment or only to the number of participants in a certain condition, or in a certain group. If there were 15 mice who took the drug, then we'd say n = 15 for that group.

Σ:

Σ is the uppercase Greek letter sigma. In statistics it means to *sum* whatever comes after it. For example, ΣX means *sum the X scores*.

*   *   *

Now, test your knowledge of some of the concepts above with a few exercises. Following are three sets of data. For each, find **1) ΣX 2) ΣX² 3) (ΣX)² and 4) (ΣX)² / N**

Data Set #1[9]

       X: 3,1,5,3

Data Set #2[10]

       X: 4,1,8,5,6,3

Data Set #3[11]

       X: 7,8,10,2,1,8

---

[9] $\Sigma X = 12$; $\Sigma X^2 = 44$; $(\Sigma X)^2 = 144$; $\Sigma X^2/N = 36$
[10] $\Sigma X = 27$; $\Sigma X^2 = 151$; $(\Sigma X)^2 = 729$; $\Sigma X^2/N = 121.5$
[11] $\Sigma X = 36$; $\Sigma X^2 = 282$; $(\Sigma X)^2 = 1296$; $\Sigma X^2/N = 216$

Questions and problems.

1) A college administrator wants to find out how students at her college feel about having fast food restaurants on campus. She constructs a survey and asks the registrar's office to supply a list of 25 randomly chosen students to take the survey. What is the *sample*, and what is the *population*?

2) In a research study you read about recently, some participants were given a drug which increased their heart rate and others were given a placebo. The researchers found participants who took the drug reported more anxiety than the placebo group. What is the independent variable in this study? The dependent variable?

3) For each of the following variables, indicate *nominal, ordinal, interval,* or *ratio.*

    a) Number of TVs owned

    b) Typing speed, in words per minute

    c) Score on an IQ test, where score is determined by the number of items answered correctly.

    d) Medal received (gold, silver, bronze)

    e) Coffee shop preference (Starbucks®, Dunkin' Donuts®, etc.)

    f) Volume of soda consumed per day, in ounces.

4) Write an equation, using statistical notation, for the following: *First, add up participants' scores, then square that value, then divide it by the number of scores. Finally, find the square root.* Let's call this made-up value Q (so begin with "Q =").

5) Find Q for the following set of scores: 4,1,6,7,3,2

6) Find Q for the following set of scores: 9,10,3,1,4,8

Answers to questions and problems.

1) The *sample* is the group of students (N = 25) who take the survey. The *population* is all the students who attend that particular college. The hope is, of course, the opinions of those in the sample reasonably reflect the opinions of the whole student body, the population.

> If you answered that the population was all college students, you were thinking along the correct lines, but notice the administrator seems interested in learning only about students at her college (*A college administrator needs to find out how students at her college feel ...*). Had the administrator been interested in how *college students* (in general) feel about something, then the population would have been *college students*. Remember, the population is the group the researcher is interested in learning about.

2) The independent variable is *whether or not participants got the drug*, and the dependent variable is *how much anxiety the participants reported*.

> When in doubt, first list the variables (here, *drug* and *anxiety*), and try to fit them into this sentence: *The researcher wanted to know if _____ has an effect on _____.* You will find one arrangement makes much more sense than the other. Here, we've got two possibilities: 1) *The researcher wanted to know if* the drug *has an effect on* anxiety, and 2) *The researcher wanted to know if* anxiety *has an effect on* the drug. See how #1 makes a lot more sense? Once you figure out which arrangement makes sense, the rest is easy: The one in the first blank is the independent variable (the one, potentially, *doing the affecting*) and the one in the second blank is the dependent variable (the one, potentially, *being affected*).

3) The scales of measurement are:

> a) Number of TVs owned: Ratio. Even if you weren't completely sure if there are equal intervals here, the fact that 1) zero TVs really means zero TVs and 2) you can form ratios (for example, if you own 2 TVs and your friend owns 1, you indeed own twice as many TVs as your friend- the ratio is 2:1), means it's a ratio scale variable.
>
> b) Typing speed, in words per minute: Ratio
>
> c) Score on an IQ test, where score is determined by the number of items answered correctly: Interval.

It could also be argued this is ordinal, depending on whether the increments have equal "distances" between them, but it is definitely not ratio, because a zero on an IQ test does NOT mean the total lack of intelligence. A gorilla, for example, is very intelligent (much more intelligent than something like a pillow, which indeed has zero intelligence), but a gorilla would nevertheless score a zero on some IQ tests. So, a zero on an IQ test does not (necessarily) mean zero intelligence. Also, someone who scores 100 on an IQ test is NOT twice as smart (twice as far from zero intelligence) as someone who scores 50:

0 ←true zero (<u>zero</u> intell.)   Zero on an IQ test →0 1 2

d) Medal received (gold, silver, bronze): Ordinal

e) Coffee shop preference (Starbucks®, Dunkin' Donuts®, etc.): Nominal

f) Volume of soda consumed per day, in ounces: Ratio

4)

$$Q = \sqrt{\frac{(\Sigma X)^2}{N}}$$

5) 9.39

	X
	4
	1
	6
	7
	3
	2
ΣX	23
ΣX, squared	529
$(\Sigma X)^2$ divided by N	88.17
square root of that	9.39

6) 14.29

	$\underline{X}$
	9
	10
	3
	1
	4
	8
ΣX	35
ΣX, squared	1225
$(\Sigma X)^2$ divided by N	204.17
square root of that	14.29

Chapter 2
Introduction to descriptive statistics

As previously discussed, psychological research is *empirical*, which simply means *data* is collected. Usually a psychological study produces not just *some* data, but tons of data. This chapter introduces you to ways for organizing all that data so you, and your audience, can make sense of it.

Consider a survey administered to 50 participants, where participants are asked to rate 25 items on a seven-point scale about their stress levels in various situations. This would actually be considered a small study, but even this would produce 1,250 numbers (25 items x 50 subjects = 1,250). Can you imagine trying to communicate the results of this study by showing all 1,250 scores?

It would look something like this:

The above is way too much data to take in. Results such as these must be *summarized* in some way so they can be better communicated to a larger audience, and so they can be better understood by the researchers themselves. In other words, we need to *describe* the results without actually showing all of them, and do so in a meaningful and accurate way. This is the goal of *descriptive statistics*.

> **Descriptive statistics** *summarize or describe a set of data to make it more easily communicated and understood.*

Our definition here refers to *data*, but the general concept of a description is obvioulsy not unique to statistics. Think about what you would do if you were assigned to describe or summarize a newspaper article for a political science class. Would you reproduce the whole article? Of course not—you'd give a short report of what it is basically about. If done well, your summary would give the gist of the article, and it would not mislead the readers or miss a vital aspect of the story. If the story was about a fellow student who was arrested by police, you would certainly report why they were arrested. And you wouldn't leave out the fact that the student was subsequently cleared of the charge, and the actual suspect was apprehended.

Unfortunately, even when you take great care in your summary (description), you usually lose information when you summarize/describe it. Actually, loss of information is inherent in the very definitions of the terms *summary* and *description*. This can all be conceptualized as a continuum, with the opposing qualities of *simplicity* and *comprehensiveness* at the ends:

Simplicity ━━━━━━━━━━━━━━━ Comprehensiveness

Any given description, or choice of descriptive statistics, falls somewhere along this continuum; the more simple your description, the less comprehensive it usually is, and vice versa. How you choose to describe the data depends on a number of factors, and so several methods of describing data will be presented.

*   *   *

Let's begin by describing the data above from the survey which asked participants to respond to 25 items on a seven-point scale regarding how stressed they become in various situations. We will arrange the results in something called a *frequency distribution*.

A frequency distribution can be arranged in table or graph format. Here is what the data above would look like when arranged in a frequency distribution table:

X	f	
7	100	(there were 100 7's in there)
6	123	(there were 123 6's in there)
5	150	(there were 150 5's in there)
4	165	(there were 165 4's in there)
3	169	(there were 169 3's in there)
2	150	(there were 150 2's in there)
1	124	(there were 124 1's in there)

Notice there are two columns in the table: one for the scores, labeled X, and another for how many times those scores appeared in the data set (the scores' respective *frequencies*). Frequency is typically labeled f.

It should be obvious the frequency table gives a much clearer picture of the data compared to the original group of numbers at the beginning of this chapter. However, a graph is usually even better. If we make a frequency graph of the same data, we get:

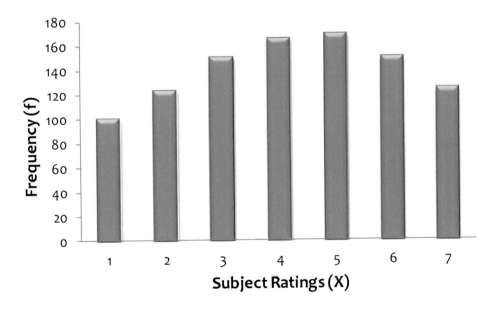

A frequency distribution graph is always arranged with frequencies on the Y-axis, and whatever is being counted, in this case participants' ratings, on the X-axis. You can see a frequency distribution gives a nice picture of the data—how many participants gave a rating of 1, how many gave a rating of 2, and so on. You cannot tell from the graph exactly what the frequencies are, like you can in the table, but the trade-off is that the graph is simpler.

Now a little more about variables. Begin by noticing the bars in the graph above do not touch. This is to indicate that the variable, *participant ratings*, is *discrete*. *Discrete* means the variable can only be whole numbers; subjects gave ratings of either 1 or 2 or 3 or 4 or 5 or 6 or 7. Another example of a discrete variable is *number of children*: You have either 1 child, or 2, or 3, etc. There's nothing in between those numbers (right?)[12].

However, many variables are not discrete, but are instead *continuous*. That means the variable can take on *any* value.

> A **continuous** variable can take on any value; it can be infinitely divided between points. A **discrete** variable only occurs in whole numbers; it cannot be divided between points.

You learned earlier that *seconds* (e.g., to complete a task) was a ratio variable. Well, it's also a continuous variable because an infinite number of values exist between, say, 10 seconds and 11 seconds. For example, something can take 10.231674987612029464 seconds to happen. That may look like a lot of decimal places and thus may seem like an *exact* measurement, but really this hypothetical event, let's say you timed how long it took a pencil to hit the floor when you dropped it, did not take *exactly* 10.231674987612029464 seconds. In other words, even that is a rounded number. It may have actually taken 10.2316749876120294641276755412009876445 seconds. But actually, even *that* is rounded. As a matter of fact, you can never know the exact measurement of something that is measured on a continuous variable. Do you know how tall you are, down to the trillionth of an inch? What about to the trillionth of a trillionth of an inch?

Surely, we usually can't measure as accurately as the examples in the previous paragraph suggest. For example, in timing the pencil, our instrument may only measure to the nearest whole second. That means, even though the event we were measuring may very well have taken about 10.231674987612029464 seconds, our instrument would read 10.

There is an important consequence of all this: If we time something and the stopwatch reads 10, that *really* means the event could have taken anywhere from 9.5 seconds to 10.5 seconds. How do we know that? Because, if the event took less than 9.5 seconds (e.g., 9.3, or even 9.499999999) the stopwatch would (or at least *should*) read 9, and if it took more than 10.5 seconds (e.g., 10.7, or even 10.500000001), the stopwatch would read 11. Thus, you would say the *real limits* of 10 are 9.5 and 10.5. That is, any time the measurement *you take* is 10, the

---

[12] Qualitative variables such as *type of fish* (flounder, bluefish, etc.) and *dwelling* (apartment, house, condo, etc.) are also discrete.

real measurement—the *true* amount of time the pencil took to fall—could actually be anywhere between 9.5 and 10.5[13].

> The **real limits** of an observed measurement represent the range within which the real measurement falls.

To find the real limits of your measurement, do the following:

Go halfway down to the next lower measurement you could take, which in this case is 9 since we could only measure to the whole second, and halfway up to the next higher measurement you could take, which is 11 here. 9.5 (halfway between 10 and 9) and 10.5 (halfway between 10 and 11) are thus the *lower* and *upper* real limits, respectively. It may help to visualize it:

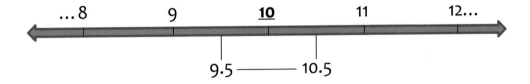

But say another instrument also timed that same pencil fall, but this one was a bit more precise and could measure to the 10th of a second, and you timed the pencil at 10.2 seconds. What are the real limits of 10.2? Since this instrument measures to the 10th of a second, the next lower measurement below 10.2 is 10.1, and the next higher measurement above 10.2 is 10.3. Halfway down to 10.1—halfway between 10.2 and 10.1—is 10.15. Similarly, halfway up to 10.3 is 10.25:

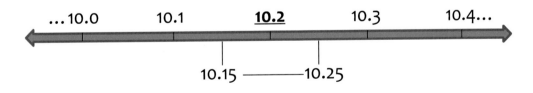

---

[13] This is assuming a continuous variable is being measured. If the variable is discrete, none of this applies. For example, when measuring *number of children*, 10 really means 10; it doesn't mean somewhere between 9.5 and 10.5!

What about an even more precise stopwatch, which timed the event at 10.231? What are the real limits of 10.231?[14]

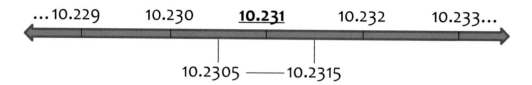

... 10.229   10.230   **10.231**   10.232   10.233...

10.2305 ——— 10.2315

Remember that real limits only apply to a continuous variable. You should also be aware that when a continuous variable is measured, the bars in the frequency distribution describing it should touch each other. This touching indicates visually that the variable is continuous. Note, for example, how the bar labeled 2 below stretches from the lower real limit of 2 (assuming the measurement is to the whole second) to the upper real limit of 2 (i.e., 1.5 and 2.5).

When the bars touch, the technical name for the graph is a *histogram*.

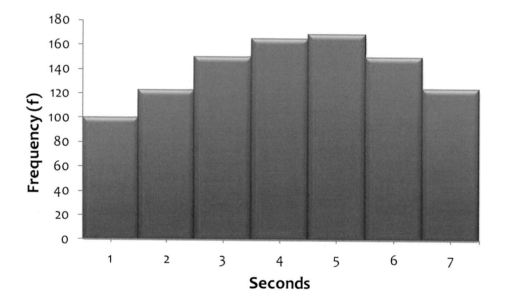

---

[14] The real limits of 10.231 are 10.2305 and 10.2315.

Another option to display frequency data for a continuous variable is a line graph:

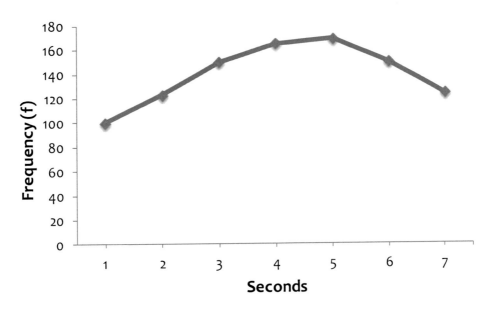

The rule is: If the variable is discrete, use a bar graph (bars don't touch); if the variable is continuous, use either a histogram (bars touch) or a line graph.

*   *   *

As previously discussed, descriptive statistics are used to summarize or describe a relatively large amount of data. But sometimes you want to better describe just a *single* score. For example, if you learned your classmate got a 15 on her quiz in History class (X = 15), you wouldn't know what that means. Did she do very well? Very poorly? More or less average?

You can see the problem that sometimes arises when an X score is reported but, fortunately, you have another option. You may have even heard of it before: a *percentile rank*. Instead of reporting her raw score, if your classmate instead told you her percentile rank was 92, or that she scored at the 92nd percentile, you'd now know something much more useful than her X score. Namely, you'd know that 92% of the other students who took the test scored the same or lower than she did.

> A **percentile rank** indicates the percent of scores from the same distribution that are the same or lower than a given score.

Pay close attention to the terminology—the same or *lower* than. Do not make the mistake of thinking of percentile ranks as necessarily meaning what percentage of people scored *worse*.

For example, if that classmate was at the 75th percentile for height, it does not mean 75% of people have a *worse* height than her. It means 75% of people are shorter than her, in other words, scored *lower* for height than she did.

The next chapters will present other ways to describe data. There is more than just one way to describe data for many reasons. For example, several aspects of the data can be described, certain descriptive statistics are unduly biased in certain situations and so another should be chosen, and different audiences expect data to be presented in different ways. You will be learning about several such *descriptive statistics*.

Questions and problems.

1) When you summarize a data set, you _____ (lose or gain) information. However, you also _____ (complicate or simplify) the data.

2) Create a frequency distribution table of the following data set:

4,2,3,3,1,5,5,5,3,3,3,3,1,2,4,5,5

3) Sketch a frequency distribution graph of the same data. Assume those values represent the *number of children* of a sample of parents.

4) Indicate whether each of the following variables is *discrete* or *continuous*.

     a) Number of TVs owned

     b) Typing speed, in words per minute

     c) Typing speed, in time took to type a given paragraph, in seconds

     d) Medal received (gold, silver, bronze)

     e) Coffee shop preference (Starbucks®, Dunkin' Donuts®, etc.)

     f) Volume of soda consumed per day, in ounces.

5) Usain Bolt ran the 100m sprint in 9.77 seconds. His actual time in that race was somewhere between _____ and _____ seconds. (That is, what are the real limits of 9.77 sec?)

6) What if a more accurate timer was used, and the result for that race for Mr. Bolt was 9.772 seconds. What are the real limits of that measurement?

7) Say Mr. Bolt has 6 Olympic gold medals. What are the real limits of 6?

8) You received 12 parking tickets last year, which puts you at the 80th percentile for tickets received last year. What does it mean that you are at the 80th percentile in this case?

Answers to questions and problems.

1) lose; simplify

2)

X	f
5	5
4	2
3	6
2	2
1	2

3)

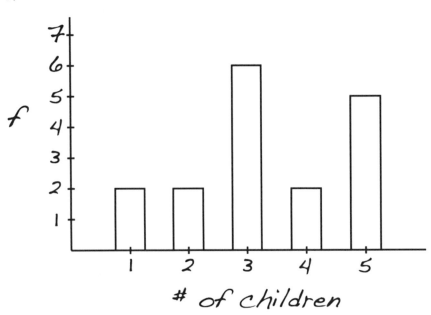

4)   a) Number of TVs owned: *discrete*

       b) Typing speed, in words per minute: *discrete*

       c) Typing speed, in time to type a given paragraph, in seconds: *continuous*

       d) Medal received (gold, silver, bronze): *discrete*

       e) Coffee shop preference (Starbucks®, Dunkin' Donuts®, etc.): *discrete*

       f) Volume of soda consumed per day, in ounces: *continuous*

5) The real limits or 9.77 are 9.765 and 9.775. In other words, Mr. Bolt's actual time in that race was somewhere between 9.765 and 9.775 seconds.

6) The real limits or 9.772 are 9.7715 and 9.7725. In other words, Mr. Bolt's actual time in that race was somewhere between 9.7715 and 9.7725 seconds.

7) The real limits of 6 in this instance are 6 and 6. Or you could say real limits just don't apply here. In other words, the measurement of 6 in this case really means exactly 6, since *number of gold medals* is a discrete variable (not a continuous variable like *time to complete the 100m sprint*).

8) Having a percentile rank of 80, or being at the 80th percentile, for *tickets received last year* means 80% of drivers received the same number or fewer tickets last year than you did.

Chapter 3
Central tendency

To begin the discussion of central tendency, let's think back to the survey results we looked at in the previous chapter, where participants rated 25 items on a seven-point scale and we described those results in a frequency distribution.

Another way we could describe those results is to report a measure of *central tendency*. A measure of central tendency is meant to capture, or represent, the so-called *center* of the distribution–where scores *tend* to fall.

One way to do this is by calculating the *average* rating for each item:

Item #	Average rating
1	3.21
2	5.14
3	6.77
25	1.88

Or, since all the items were asking about the same basic thing (stress), you may instead just calculate the overall average across all the items. In either case, what we're talking about here is a measure of central tendency you probably already know about: the *mean*.

> The **mean** is the average: the sum of all the scores, divided by the number of scores.

As an exercise and review, write down the formula for the mean, using appropriate statistical notation (see the *Introduction to statistics* chapter if you need help). The symbol for the mean of a sample is M.[15]

The mean is no different than the average you have surely calculated many times before. Let's now discuss a statistic called the *weighted mean*.

---

[15] The solution is $M = \Sigma X/N$. First, you add up the scores (ΣX), then you divide by the number of scores ($/N$).

The weighted mean is the overall mean across multiple samples. For example, if you had two samples, and the mean of the first sample (M_1) was 70 and the mean of the second sample (M_2) was 80, then the weighted mean would be the midpoint between 70 and 80 (75)— but *only* if the number of subjects, n, was the same in the two samples.

Samples often do not have the same n, however, and the weighted mean is thus not simply the midpoint between the two sample means. In those cases, the weighted mean is always *closer to the mean of the sample with the larger n*.

> The **weighted mean** is the overall mean across multiple samples. The amount of influence that each of the samples has on the weighted mean, that is, their weight, depends on the respective sample sizes.

Let's do a couple examples.

Example 1.

Sample 1	Sample 2
M = 16	M = 20
n = 12	n = 8

Before doing the calculations, you need to be able to estimate the weighted mean. Why would you want to estimate it before calculating it? Estimating not only helps to see if the answer you ultimately calculate makes sense, but it has the added benefit of helping you gauge your *understanding* of the weighted mean. Being able to correctly estimate it is an encouraging sign that you have a good understanding of what it is. By contrast, you could calculate something by plugging the appropriate numbers into a formula without really *understanding* what it is you've just done. You should always be able to do 2 things: 1) find an answer, and 2) understand what that answer means.

In this case, we begin our estimation by noting the midpoint between 16 (the mean of Sample 1) and 20 (the mean of Sample 2), which is 18. Next, we note which sample has more weight. In this case, that's Sample 1 because it has a larger n. Thus, the weighted mean is pulled toward the mean of Sample 1.

Visually:

$M_1 = \underline{\textbf{16}}$		
$n = 12$		

$\underline{18}$

$M_2 = \underline{\textbf{20}}$
$n = 8$

The weighted mean is closer to M_1 because M_1 comes from more scores ($n = 12$) as compared with M_2 ($n = 8$). The weighted mean is therefore between 16 and 18.

Go ahead—estimate the weighted mean of the following two samples:

Sample 1	Sample 2
$M = 50$	$M = 100$
$n = 22$	$n = 38$

Answer: The midpoint between the means is 75, but, since Sample 2 has more weight (has a larger n), the weighted mean will be pulled toward it. Therefore, the weighted mean will be somewhere between 75 and 100.

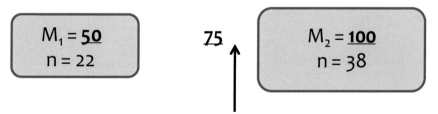

The weighted mean is between 75 and 100.

* * *

Now let's do actual calculations, which means using a formula. There are a number of formulas for the weighted mean, M_w, but here is the easiest one to work with in this application (next page):

$$M_W = \frac{\Sigma X_1 + \Sigma X_2}{n_1 + n_2}$$

It appears from the formula that we need to know the scores to find the weighted mean. After all, according to the numerator of the formula, we must add up all the scores from each sample (notice the ΣX's). But, we don't have to actually do that. Instead, we can calculate ΣX if we know M and n.[16]

Examining why this shortcut works is a useful exercise. Consider a simple case where we have two scores: X = 6, X = 10. The sum of the X scores, ΣX, is thus 16. Now pretend you don't know the scores, but instead were only told the mean is 8 and n is 2. You could still figure out ΣX by pretending every score is equal to the mean of 8: X = 8, X = 8. Now you can plainly see that ΣX is 8 + 8 = 16, just as if we added up the actual scores of 6 and 10. Importantly, ΣX will be 16 for *any* combination of 2 scores whose mean is 8 (0 and 16, 9 and 7, and so on). Try it with any numbers you wish: If the mean of the 2 numbers you choose is 8, then they will add up to 16.

This method of pretending all the scores are equal to the mean and then adding them up will always work, but it would be tedious if you had many scores instead of just two. For example, if M = 20 and n = 13, then you could find ΣX by pretending all 13 scores are X = 20 and adding them up:

20 + 20 + 20 + 20 + 20 + 20 + 20 + 20 + 20 + 20 + 20 + 20 + 20 = 260

However, a simple formula will make it much easier:

$$\Sigma X = M * n$$

$$\Sigma X = 20 * 13 = 260$$

Try using it to find ΣX for the following two samples (call them ΣX_1 and ΣX_2).[17]

Sample 1	Sample 2
M = 30	M = 18
n = 8	n = 13

---

[16] And we will always know these values. Actually, we will always know everything there is to know about our sample. Why wouldn't we?

[17] $EX_1 = 30 * 8 = 240$; $EX_2 = 18 * 13 = 234$

Since you already found ΣX_1 and ΣX_2, you may as well finish up and find the weighted mean of the two samples above. The answer immediately follows, but try first to do it on your own.

Remember the formulas:

$$M_W = \frac{\Sigma X_1 + \Sigma X_2}{n_1 + n_2}$$

$$\Sigma X = M * n$$

Solution:

$$\Sigma X_1 = M_1 * n_1 = 30 * 8 = 240$$

$$\Sigma X_2 = M_2 * n_2 = 18 * 13 = 234$$

$$M_W = \frac{\Sigma X_1 + \Sigma X_2}{n_1 + n_2} = \frac{240 + 234}{8 + 13} = \frac{474}{21} = \mathbf{22.57}$$

Is that answer plausible? To find out, let's see if it is consistent with how we would estimate it:

> The midpoint between the means, 30 and 18, is 24. However, the sample with the mean of 18 has more weight, so the weighted mean will be pulled toward it. Therefore, the weighted mean should be somewhere between 18 and 24. Clearly, 22.57 is consistent with that estimate.

More practice problems for the weighted mean can be found at the end of this chapter. The discussion will now turn to some important things you need to know about the mean in general.

* * *

Although the mean is a widely used and simple way to describe the central tendency of a data set, it is not perfect. Notably, scores far from the mean have more influence on the mean than scores closer to it. This works against what you are trying to do by reporting central tendency in the first place (which is *to capture, or represent, the center of the distribution–where scores tend to fall*).

So you can better see why this is an issue, consider the following set of History quiz scores for a sample of 6th graders:

Student	X
Fred	3
Joe	4
Sarah	1
Jessica	2
Amanda	5
Monet	6
Stephanie	40

The mean of those scores is 8.7: (3+4+1+2+5+6+40) / 7 = 8.7.   But let's compare the influence of Monet's score with the influence of Stephanie's score by seeing what the mean would have been without each of them in turn.

First, Monet: If Monet was absent that day, the mean would have been 9.2, about ½ point different than it was with her there (9.2 was found by computing the mean without Monet, X = 6, included). But now Stephanie: If instead Stephanie was absent that day, the mean would have been 3.5, over 5 points different from what it was with her score included. So as you can see, Stephanie's score had a much larger impact on the mean.
By the way, since Stephanie's score was so different from the others, her score (or Stephanie herself) is called an *outlier*.

> An **outlier** is a score that lies substantially outside where the majority of the scores fall.

We could summarize all of the preceding by stating that *the mean is unduly influenced by outliers.*

Now, it could be argued that the outlier, in this case Stephanie's score of 40, *should* bring the mean up or down substantially. After all, the student did in fact score a 40, so why not include that value in your measure of central tendency?   Not a bad argument, but think about what we're trying to do: communicate the typical/central score as accurately as possible. In this case, it is difficult to argue 8.7 accurately captures the typical score in the distribution 3,4,1,2,5,6,40.   If you look closely you can see all but *one* score is below 8.7. Furthermore, the score closest to the mean is actually a full 30% below it! It is safe to say someone who was told the mean of the scores was 8.7 would be left with a pretty inaccurate impression of the results.
This demonstrates that, in some situations, the mean is an unacceptably biased measure. As such, it is not always an appropriate measure to use. But fortunately measures of central

tendency exist that are not so influenced by outliers (i.e., not so potentially biased). One such measure is the *median*, which is the score that divides the distribution in half.

> The **median** is the score that divides the distribution exactly in half; half the scores are above the median and half are below it.

Given this description of the median, how would you go about actually *finding* it, given a set of scores like 5,2,4,1,7,8,9?

Did you say something like this?: *First, put the scores in numerical order (lowest to highest or vice versa), then find the score in the middle.* If you did, you've got it![18]

Note: If there are *two* scores in the middle (EX: 5,10,6,2), then find the mean of the middle two. The median of 5,10,6,2, (2,5,6,10 put in proper order), is thus 5.5.

And what is the median of the data set we examined earlier?:

Student	X
Fred	3
Joe	4
Sarah	1
Jessica	2
Amanda	5
Monet	6
Stephanie	40

Step 1- **Put the scores in numerical order** (lowest to highest or vice versa)

1,2,3,4,5,6,40

Step 2- **Find the score in the middle**

1,2,3,$\boxed{4}$,5,6,40

The median is 4. An advantage of the median is that it avoids being overly influenced by outliers. It does so by not taking into account the values of the scores directly in its calculation, like the mean does. Instead, the median only takes into account the *positions* of the scores in the distribution. True, the positions of the scores are based on their values (when you put them in order to find the median), but the values themselves don't go into the calculation.

---

[18] The median of those scores is 5.

An example may help to clarify. The median of 1,2,3,4,5,6,**40** is the same as the median of 1,2,3,4,5,6,**100**. The *value* of the outlier, 40 or 100, didn't matter; the median is 4 either way. And if we added another outlier to the first set: 1,2,3,4,5,6,**40,85**, the median would now go up to only **4.5.** Notice it only changed a little bit (and also notice, had we added 500 in there instead of 85, the median still would have only changed to 4.5). For contrast, calculate the mean for the 3 data sets above, and note how it changes.[19]

∗　∗　∗

Another situation where the median is usually a better choice is when the distribution of scores is *skewed,* even when there are not one or two clear outliers, as above. In this context, *skewed* simply means not symmetrical (asymmetrical).

Following are two skewed distributions. Notice the asymmetry; the right and left halves are not mirror images of each other.

A

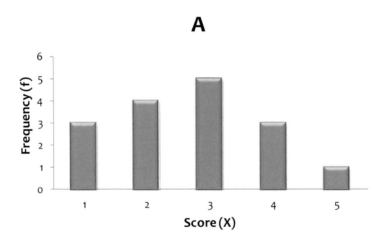

---

[19] 1,2,3,4,5,6,**40**: M = 8.71; 1,2,3,4,5,6,**100**: M = 17.29; 1,2,3,4,5,6,**40,85**: M = 18.25; 1,2,3,4,5,6,**40,500**: M = 70.13.

B

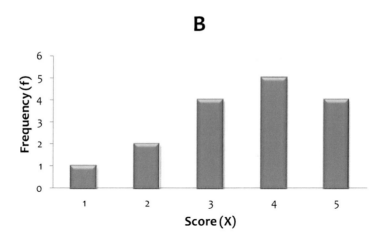

Let's contrast those with a normal distribution. You've probably seen the normal distribution before. It's also called the *bell curve*. Notice it is symmetrical.

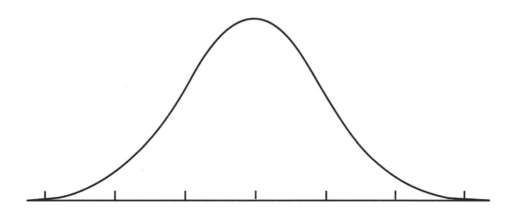

When the distribution is normal, the mean and the median are the same. But when the distribution is skewed, as in the two bar graphs labeled A and B, the mean and the median are different.

Distribution A's mean is 2.69 and its median is 3. Notice there are more scores toward the left side (lower scores) and fewer scores toward the right side (higher scores). This is called a ***positively skewed*** distribution.

Distribution B's mean is 3.56 and its median is 4. You can see in that distribution that fewer scores are toward the left side (lower scores) and more scores are toward the right side (higher scores). This is called a ***negatively skewed*** distribution.

> In a **positively skewed** distribution, there are more scores toward the lower end than the upper end. In a **negatively skewed** distribution, there are more scores toward the upper end than the lower end.

Since the mean and median are different when the distribution is skewed, the researcher must decide which measure is the best one to report. The general rule is: When the distribution is skewed, the median is the best choice.

> When the distribution is substantially skewed, the median is usually the best choice of central tendency to report.

But notice that is only a general rule, meaning the median is only *usually* the best choice. Why isn't it clear-cut? Again, think about what we're trying to do here: *communicate the typical/central score as accurately as possible.* What would you do if the distribution was only slightly skewed, so the mean and median were almost exactly the same? Which would you report? This is an example of when your audience may be the determining factor. If the mean and median (and mode, for that matter, explained soon), are basically the same, go with the one most people will be familiar with. Many are familiar with the median, and maybe even the mode, but everyone knows the mean. Think of the mean, therefore, as your go-to/default measure of central tendency, and only choose another measure when there is a compelling reason to do so.

*   *   *

The last measure of central tendence you need to know about is the *mode*. The mode is perhaps the most simple—it's just the most common score. With that definition in mind, pick out the mode in the following distribution of scores[20]:

X	f
4	3
3	7
2	21
1	6

Do the same here:

3,3,4,5,6,6,6,6,6,6,6,6,6,7,8[21]

---

[20] The mode is 2.
[21] The mode is 6.

And in this graph:[22]

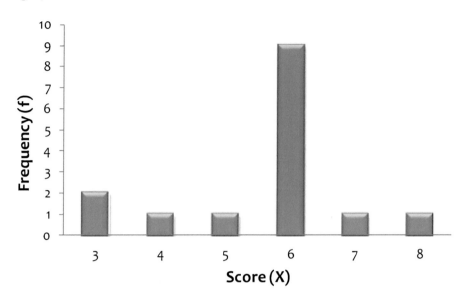

Finally, consider this distribution:

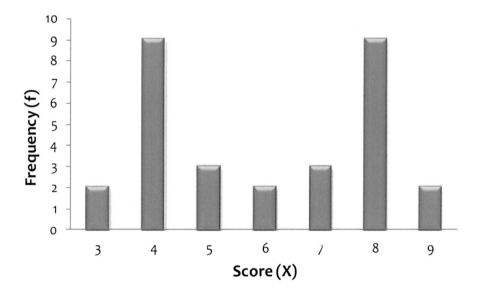

_____

[22] 6 (Did you notice that is a frequency distribution graph of the scores right before it?)

That last distribution has *two* modes: 4 and 8. This is called a *bimodal* distribution. In this case you would simply report both modes. You do this because it would be misleading to present the mean or the median, even when the distribution is symmetrical as above. Look at the graph: The mean and median are both 6, but see how they miss the mark when it comes to reporting where scores tend to be (i.e., the purpose of central tendency)?

To be sure, reporting that the mean is 6 would not be an outright lie, but, then again, hardly anyone scored 6 or right around 6. So if you were to report that the mean is 6, you'd actually be reporting as your measure of central tendency a score which people tended to *not* get!

Finally, what about the influence of outliers on the mode? Before answering, think about what the mode is for a minute. Now, would you say the mode is *very affected, somewhat affected,* or *not at all affected* by outliers?[23] It is actually *not at all* affected by outliers. This is basically a good thing, but, on the other hand, the mode is incomplete in the sense that other scores (ones that are not the most common) are completely ignored: The mode of 2,4,7,7,7,7,7,9,10 is 7, but the mode of 1,1,7,7,7,7,7,7,12,19,21,25 (arguably a very different looking distribution) is also 7.

If two distributions look very different, and yet have the same value on a statistic (e.g., the same mode), you know that statistic is missing something important and, thus, either a different one needs to be reported or an additional statistic needs to be included (more on that later), or both.

*   *   *

It should be apparent, though, that *none* of the measures of central tendency is perfect, in the sense of being completely free of bias. Neverthless, don't lose sight of the fact that they all define the center of the distribution in some way:

- The **mean** defines the center of the distribution as the mathematical center, where different scores carry different weights depending on how far they are from the mean.
- The **median** defines the center of the distribution as the point at which half of the scores are above it and half the scores are below it.
- The **mode** defines the center of the distribution as the most common score.

With all these options, the researcher must decide which one most accurately describes the data—which is the least biased. Competence and thoughtful judgment are vital, as is true with the use of any statistic. Just as when you are asked to summarize an article, a movie, or

---

[23] Throw in a score of 100 to any of the examples in this section and see what happens to the mode.

an event, you must use your judgment and your knowledge of both the material and of your audience to guide you.

Although reporting a carefully selected measure of central tendency goes a long way in summarizing your findings, it leaves out a very important aspect of the data: its variability. As a matter of fact, these two aspects of the data are both so vital that researchers usually report both a measure of central tendency and a measure of variability when summarizing a research finding.

In the next chapter, you will learn about another aspect of a set of data—*variability*—as well as several ways to measure it.

Questions and problems.

1. Fill in the blanks: When the data forms a normal distribution, the _____ is probably the best measure of central tendency to report. However, when the data is skewed, the best choice is likely the _____. Finally, when there are one or more scores that stand out as being much more frequent than others you should probably report the _____.

2. You gave a test to a class of 2nd graders ($N = 10$). The scores came out normally distributed. However, there was one child absent that day, so you gave her the test when she returned. She scored extremely high. Which measure of central tendency will be affected the most by adding her into the distribution? Which measure is likely to be affected the *least* by this outlier? Explain your answers.

3. Select the best measure of central tendency for the following set of data and report its value. You may want to sketch a frequency distribution to help with your decision.
   X: 2,2,2,3,4,4,4,5,8,12

4. Select the best measure of central tendency for the following set of data and report its value. You may want to sketch a frequency distribution to help with your decision.
   X: 4,4,5,5,6,6,6,7,7,8,8

5. For the following samples, a) *estimate* the weighted mean (without doing any calculations), then b) *calculate* the weighted mean:

   Sample 1
   M = 20
   n = 6

   Sample 2
   M = 100
   n = 90

6. Calculate the weighted mean of the following *three* samples:

   Sample 1
   M = 41
   n = 6

   Sample 2
   M = 62
   n = 12

   Sample 3
   M = 80
   n = 19

NOTE: The formula for M_W when there are three samples is the following:

$$Mw = \frac{\Sigma X_1 + \Sigma X_2 + \Sigma X_3}{n_1 + n_2 + n_3}$$

7. For the following samples, a) *estimate* the weighted mean (without doing any calculations), then b) *calculate* the weighted mean:

You took two samples. One had 10 subjects and the second had 8. The mean of the first was 23 and the mean of the second was 55.

8. Calculate the weighted mean:

There are three samples with means of 12, 14 and 21, with sample sizes of 5, 2, and 12, respectively.

Answers to questions and problems.

1) mean; median; mode(s)

2) mean: The mean is the mathematical center of the distribution, and uses the values of the scores themselves in the calculations. Therefore, outliers have the largest effect on the mean. Mode: The mode is the most common score. This will be totally unaffected by the addition of any extreme scores (outliers). EX: In the distribution 2,4,4,4,4,4,4,4,8, the mode is 4. If we add an outlier: 2,4,4,4,4,4,4,4,8,**132**. The most common score, the mode, is still 4.

3) Since the data is skewed, (and since no score really stands out as being much more common than others) the *median* (which is 4) is probably the best choice because it will not be as biased by outliers as the mean.

4) Since the data is symmetrical (but not bimodal), the *mean* (which is 6) is the best choice because that's what most people will know about and understand, and because it shouldn't be overly biased. (Plus, the mean, median, and mode are all 6, so you really have your pick of any of them—but again, more people know about the mean.)

5) a) weighted mean estimated: The two means are 20 and 100, but the sample with the mean of 100 is larger (N of 90 vs. 6), so the weighted mean will be pulled closer to it. Therefore, the weighted mean would have to be somewhere between 60 (the midpoint of the two) and 100. (NOTE: Since the second sample (with M = 100) is so *much* bigger, the weighted mean should be pretty close to 100).

b) weighted mean calculated:

M_1	20	M_2	100
N_1	6	N_2	90
ΣX_1	120	ΣX_2	9000

$$\frac{9120}{96} \quad M_W = \ \mathbf{95}$$

6)

M_1	41	M_2	62	M_3	80
N_1	6	N_2	12	N_3	19
ΣX_1	246	ΣX_2	744	ΣX_3	1520

$$\frac{2510}{37} \quad M_W = \mathbf{67.84}$$

7) a) weighted mean estimated: The two means are 23 and 55, but the sample with the mean of 23 is larger (N of 10 vs. 8), so the weighted mean will be pulled closer to it. Therefore, the weighted mean would have to be somewhere **between 39** (the midpoint of the two) **and 23**. NOTE: Since the first sample (with M = 23) is only a *little* bigger, the weighted mean should only be slightly below the midpoint of 39.

b) weighted mean calculated:

M_1	23	M_2	55
N_1	10	N_2	8
ΣX_1	230	ΣX_2	440

$$\frac{670}{18} \quad M_W = \mathbf{37.22}$$

8)

M_1	12	M_2	14	M_3	21
N_1	5	N_2	2	N_3	12
ΣX_1	60	ΣX_2	28	ΣX_3	252

$$\frac{340}{19} \quad M_W = \mathbf{17.89}$$

Chapter 4
Variability

Another aspect of the data that is important to describe, in addition to its central tendency, is its variability. A simple question should clarify what is meant by variability: Which is more variable, the heights of the blades of grass on a lawn that hasn't been mowed in a week, or the heights of the blades of grass on a lawn that was just cut? Here is a visual representation.

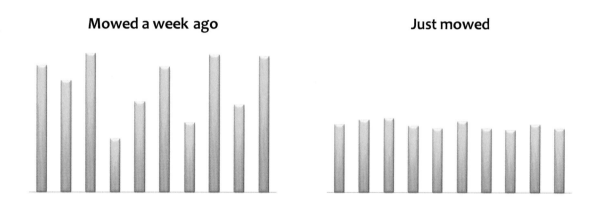

If you think the heights of the blades of grass on the lawn that hasn't been mowed in a week is more variable, then you just demonstrated a basic understanding of variability[24]. By the end of this chapter you will have a much *better* understanding, know more about the issues surrounding variability, and know a few ways to quantify (measure) variability. But you're off to a good start if you knew the answer to the question above.

If you didn't, consider the fact that the heights vary quite a bit in the diagram on the left, but in the right one the heights are much more similar to each other. That means there is more variability in the left one (and thus less variability in the right one).

Making general comparisons like this is useful. But how could we objectively *measure* the variability of the data in distributions/samples like these? Looking at it is one thing, quantifying it is another.

To start, you'll need the actual data—pictures aren't going to cut it. So, following are the heights (in millimeters) for the samples of grass we took from our two lawns. We can tell

---

[24] You may have also noted that the central tendency of the grass height also changed after mowing. The mean, for example, would be reduced.

these are samples because no lawn is just 10 blades of grass! So think of the whole lawns as the *populations* of scores, where scores are the heights of the individual blades. The 10 blades we picked and measured from the lawns make up our *samples*.

Here are the heights of our sample of 10 blades from the *unmowed* lawn:

| 84 | 74 | 92 | 35 | 60 | 83 | 46 | 91 | 58 | 90 |

And the heights of our sample of 10 blades from the mowed lawn:

| 45 | 48 | 49 | 44 | 42 | 47 | 42 | 41 | 45 | 42 |

* * *

Now that we have actual data, not only can we measure the variability, but we also have a *choice* in how we measure it. It turns out we have 3 options when describing the variability, just like we did with central tendency. They are:

1. The Range
2. The Interquartile Range
3. The Standard Deviation

Each will now be discussed in turn.

The Range

The range is simple, and you may even be able to guess what it is. It is the difference between the highest score (X_{MAX}) and the lowest score (X_{MIN}). That makes the formula:

$$Range = X_{MAX} - X_{MIN}$$

There is just one complication that sometimes presents itself when it comes to calculating the range. The complication occurs whenever you are dealing with a continuous variable. This applies to the current example since *height in mm* is a continuous variable[25].

In this case, the two scores we would use to find the range of the unmowed lawn (92 and 35, the highest and lowest scores) are really only estimates of those blades' heights. Just because your measurement of the highest blade was 92mm does not mean that blade was

---

[25] discussed in the *Introduction to Descriptive Statistics* chapter

exactly 92.0000mm; it could be anywhere from 91.5mm to 92.5mm. Same goes for your lowest blade; its height, measured at 35mm, could be anywhere from 34.5mm to 35.5mm. Fortunately, it's relatively easy to account for this. All you need to do is take the real limits into account (remember those?) by subtracting the lower real limit (LRL) of the lowest score (X_{MIN}) from the upper real limit (URL) of the highest score (X_{MAX}). That makes the formula for the range a bit different when you're dealing with a continuous variable. Here it is:

$$Range = URL_{XMAX} - LRL_{XMIN}$$

> The **Range** is calculated by subtracting the lowest score from the highest score: $URL_{XMAX} - LRL_{XMIN}$

With that information in mind, find the range of heights for the *unmowed* lawn, and for the *mowed* lawn.[26]

Although it's easy to calculate, the range is often a terrible measure of variability. In the example you just did it was probably fine, but what if, in your mowed lawn, you had one blade of grass which was 97 mm high? That would make the Range 97.5 – 40.5 = 57, making it seem like the variability of the mowed lawn was about the same as that of the unmowed lawn. But was it? Not really—even with that one blade sticking way up it would be misleading to say the two lawns have roughly the same variability. So, when you have outliers like that, the range can be very misleading.

But on a positive note, the range is very easy to understand. Remember, a major reason for describing data is to communicate your findings to others, so the range can be a good choice if your audience is unsophisticated in statistics.   If you said the range of scores was 11 points, they'll know what you mean. And even if they don't, all you have to tell them is "A range of 11 means the highest score and the lowest score are 11 points apart" or "A range of 11 means the highest score is 11 points higher than the lowest score", and they'll be fine.

Our next two measures of variability aren't quite as simple, but they are less susceptible to bias than the range.

---

[26] The highest score is 92 (URL = 92.5) and the lowest is 35 (LRL = 34.5), so 92.5 – 34.5 = 58. The range is 58. The highest score is 49 (URL = 49.5) and the lowest is 41 (LRL = 40.5), so 49.5 – 40.5 = 9. The range is 9.

The Interquartile Range

The Interquartile Range (IQR) is usually a better choice than the range because the IQR is not as sensitive to bias from outliers. To find IQR, you take the score at the 75th percentile and subtract from it the score at the 25th percentile.[27]

The score at the 75th percentile is denoted Q3 and the score at the 25th percentile is denoted Q1. So...

$$IQR = Q3 - Q1$$

> The **Interquartile Range** is equal to the score at the 75th percentile minus the score at the 25th percentile.

Just like the range, the interquartile range is a subtraction between two scores. The key difference is that those scores are more carefully chosen for the IQR, in order to avoid undue bias from outliers.

To find the IQR, you put all the scores in the distribution in order, find the one at the 75th percentile and the one at the 25th percentile, and subtract the two.

Let's find IQR for the following distribution of scores (assume a discrete variable)[28]:

7   7   8   10   12   15   17   21   25   29

The score at the 75th percentile (Q3) is 20
The score at the 25th percentile (Q1) is 8.5
Therefore, IQR = 20 – 8.5 = **11.5**

Now let's add an outlier at the high end:

7   7   8   10   12   15   17   21   25   29   **300**

---

[27] Remember, percentiles refer to the percentage of scores lower than a given score. So, 75% of scores are lower than Q3 and 25% of scores are lower than Q1.
[28] If the variable was continuous, you'd have to take into account the real limits, just as with the range. Since it's discrete, you don't have to do that.

The score at the 75th percentile (Q3) is 23
The score at the 25th percentile (Q1) is 9
Therefore, IQR = 23 – 9 = **14**

Notice adding that outlier had relatively little impact on the IQR. But it would have a huge effect on the range, which would go from 22 to 293. So, just as the median isn't very sensitive to outliers, the IQR isn't either, and for the same reasons.

Even if you have no idea how Q3 and Q1 were found—and you shouldn't have any idea—you *should* see why they would not change very much when an outlier is present in the distribution. If you're not sure, think back to the score at the 50th percentile (that is, the median).

What is the Median for the first set of data?[29] Now what is the median for the second set of data?[30]

See how with both the median and the IQR, the addition of an outlier had only a small effect? That's what makes the IQR usually a better choice than the range. Actually finding Q3 and Q1 is very time-consuming, and is beyond the scope of this book. Therefore, we will settle for knowing everything about the interquartile range except how to do the calculations to find Q3 and Q1.

The Standard Deviation

The standard deviation, abbreviated s or *SD*, or σ if you're dealing with a population, is the most useful and widely used of all the measures of variability.

The standard deviation is basically the average distance that scores fall from the mean. The word *basically* is used because, mathematically, that's not *exactly* accurate, but it's close enough.

> The **standard deviation** *is how far, on average, scores in the distribution fall from the mean.*

---

[29] There are two middle scores here (12 and 15), so the median is 13.5.
[30] The median is 15.

There are two formulas for the standard deviation. One is called the *conceptual* formula because you can see by looking at it (very carefully) what standard deviation actually is. The other formula is called the *computational* formula because, although you cannot tell by looking at it how on earth it ends up giving you standard deviation, it is often easier to use for computing the standard deviation than the conceptual formula.

We will begin with the conceptual formula:

$$S = \sqrt{\frac{\Sigma(X - M)^2}{N - 1}}$$

Note the similarity between this formula and the formula for the mean. To make the comparison easier, the square and square root (and the *minus 1* part) have been eliminated from the standard deviation formula below.

$$M = \frac{\Sigma X}{N} \qquad \text{vs.} \qquad S = \frac{\Sigma(X - M)}{N}$$

← the standard deviation formula with some parts removed for comparison to the mean formula **(don't actually use this!)**

You can now see that the two formulas are similar. The main difference is, while the mean is the average *score*, the standard deviation is the average *difference between the scores and the mean* $(X - M)$. Notice that fits pretty well with our definition of standard deviation (*how far, on average, scores in the distribution fall from the mean*).

But back to the actual formula. To make working with it more manageable, we can break the process into several smaller steps. Following is an overview of the steps, which we'll then go through with some actual data. Read each step below, then note where that step is found in the conceptual formula (next page).

Step 1: Subtract the mean from each score in the distribution. $(X - M)$

Step 2: Square each of the values you end up with in Step 1. $(X - M)^2$

Step 3: Add all those numbers together. $\Sigma(X - M)^2$

Step 4: Divide that by N − 1.

Step 5: Find the square root ($\sqrt{}$) of that number.

Conceptual formula:

$$S = \sqrt{\frac{\Sigma(X - M)^2}{N - 1}}$$

We will now use the conceptual formula to find s for some sample data:

12   14   9   16   7   2

Step 1. In this step you must subtract the mean from each score, so begin by finding the mean:
M = ΣX/N = 60/6 = **10**

You'll need to set things up in columns to keep everything in neat order, so arrange the scores into a column, labeled X since they are scores, then subtract each one from the mean in a column labeled $X - M$:

X	X – M	
12	12 - 10 = 2	
14	14 - 10 = 4	
9	9 - 10 = -1	(M = 10)
16	16 - 10 = 6	
7	7 - 10 = -3	
2	2 - 10 = -8	

The $X - M$ values are called *deviation scores* because they are a measure of how far each score deviates from the mean. For example, X = 12's deviation score is 2 because it is 2 points above the mean and X = 7's deviation score is -3 because it is 3 points below the mean.

You should take a minute to make sure these deviation scores add up to 0. If they don't, you have made a mistake and you must go back and fix the mistake before proceeding.

Step 2. Square each of the deviation scores from Step 1. Again, arrange a column, this time labeled $(X - M)^2$.

X	X-M	$(X-M)^2$
12	2	4
14	4	16
9	-1	1
16	6	36
7	-3	9
2	-8	64
	0	

You now have *squared deviation* scores. Note all of these scores are positive.[31]

Step 3. Sum those squared deviation scores:

X	X-M	$(X-M)^2$	
12	2	4	
14	4	16	
9	-1	1	
16	6	36	
7	-3	9	
2	-8	64	
	0	130	(SS)

You have just found something called **SS**, short for *Sum of Squares*, which in turn is short for *the sum of the squared deviations*. See why this is called the *sum of the squared deviations*?[32]

Step 4. Divide SS by N – 1.

X	X-M	$(X-M)^2$	
12	2	4	
14	4	16	
9	-1	1	
16	6	36	
7	-3	9	
2	-8	64	
	0	130	/5 = 26

---

[31] Some more advanced calculators will indicate a negative number when you square negative values, depending on how you enter the data. Regardless, make sure all the squared deviations are positive.
[32] Because you found deviation scores, then squared them, then summed them, that value is called the sum of the squared deviations. Since that is a mouthful, the term *sum of squares* (SS) is used instead.

When you divide SS by N – 1, in this case 130 divided by 5[33], you now have what's called the *variance*, denoted s^2.

Step 5. Find the square root of the variance.

$\sqrt{26}$ = **5.10**

To summarize:
The sum of squares (SS) = 130
The variance (s^2) = 26
The standard deviation (s) = 5.10

For describing data, which is what we're doing here, the standard deviation is more useful than variance or sum of squares, and thus the only one we truly needed to mention here. However, there is a more advanced inferential statistic that uses sum of squares and variance, which you will encounter later. And as you can see, if you work step-by-step, you can't help but find SS and s^2 along the way when finding standard deviation anyway.

*   *   *

Since we are using standard deviation to describe data, it's very important to understand how to interpret the number we just found: What does *standard deviation* = 5.10 mean, exactly?

Well, it means that, *on average, scores varied from the mean of the distribution by 5.10 points.* Some scores fell closer to the mean than 5.10 points, and some fell further than 5.10 points from the mean, but the *average* distance that scores fell from the mean was 5.10. Looking back at the data, does that sound about right, keeping in mind the mean is 10?:

12	14	9	16	7	2
(deviated by **2**)	(deviated by **4**)	(deviated by **1**)	(deviated by **6**)	(deviated by **3**)	(deviated by **8**)

*   *   *

Now let's use the computational formula. You may be wondering why, if you can calculate standard deviation with the conceptual formula, you need to learn a second formula. The reason is that the conceptual formula is very difficult to use when the mean is not a whole number, as it was (conveniently enough) in our previous example. And because of the

---

[33] N is 6, so 6 – 1 = 5. You can tell N is 6 because there are 6 scores (12,14,9,16,7, and 2).

rounding that would be involved in such a case, the conceptual formula may yield a significantly inaccurate result. [34]

The computational formula is:

$$S = \sqrt{\frac{\Sigma X^2 - \frac{(\Sigma X)^2}{N}}{N - 1}}$$

You can see we need to find ΣX^2 and $(\Sigma X)^2$, but the mean, M, plays no part here, which is why this formula works well with an uneven mean. How the computational formula gets you the average distance that scores fall from the mean (i.e., the standard deviation) without even factoring in the mean is an example of the amazing power of mathematics.

Let's find the standard deviation, s, for the following set of scores, using the computational formula.

5   1   8   4   5   2

First, arrange the scores into a column. This will make it easier to find $(\Sigma X)^2$ and ΣX^2. Then create other columns as illustrated below.

X		X		X^2
5	To find $(\Sigma X)^2$, we add up the X values, and then square that number:	5	To find ΣX^2, we square all the X values and then sum those squared values:	25
1		1		1
8		8		64
4		4		16
5		5		25
2		2		4
		$25^2 = 625$		135

---

[34] The reason for learning the *conceptual* formula is that working through problems with it gives you a much better feel for what standard deviation actually is. The computational formula does not do that.

With that information, and N (which we can see is 6 by counting the X scores), we can now just plug numbers into the formula to find the standard deviation, s:

$$S = \sqrt{\frac{\Sigma X^2 - \frac{(\Sigma X)^2}{N}}{N - 1}}$$

$$S = \sqrt{\frac{135 - \frac{625}{6}}{5}}$$

$$S = \sqrt{\frac{135 - 104.17}{5}}$$

$$S = \sqrt{\frac{30.38}{5}}$$

$$S = \sqrt{6.17}$$

$$S = 2.48$$

If you are feeling especially ambitious, go ahead and use the conceptual formula to find s for this same set of scores, and see if you come up with 2.48. Remember, the conceptual formula often requires more rounding than the computational formula; this can affect the outcome, so your answer may be different.

If you round everything to 2 decimal places (including rounding the mean to 4.17) you should end up with s = 2.27 using the conceptual formula. If you're curious, a statistical program that doesn't round at all finds the standard deviation of those scores to be 2.48327740429189. The computational formula, not surprisingly, came closer to that than the conceptual formula.

A note about rounding:

Throughout this book, you may find your answers differ slightly from the ones provided. This is probably due to differences in the method used for rounding. To avoid this issue, you could *always round to two decimal places*—not just in your final answer, but in intermediate steps as well.

For example, if you were to solve the equation below without rounding anywhere, you'd get 37.144125 (rounded to **37.14**). But if you were to round *each step* to 2 decimal places, you'd get:

$$\left(\frac{12.33*2.41}{4}\right) * \mathbf{5} = \left(\frac{29.64}{4}\right) * 5 = 7.41 * 5 = \mathbf{37.15}$$

In this particular case, the difference was small (37.14 vs. 37.15), but the more steps there are, the greater discrepancy will result from different methods of rounding. So, again, *always round every step to two decimal places* so your answers will match the answers provided, if you do everything correct.

*   *   *

You have now learned the basic ways a researcher can describe their results: creating a frequency distribution, reporting a measure of central tendency, and reporting a measure of variability.

The next chapter discusses a way to better represent a single score (as opposed to summarizing multiple scores) as something called a *z score*. You will see the *z* score has other uses, as well.

Questions and problems.

1. Explain why the range is often a bad choice for describing a distribution's variability.

2. Explain how the interquartile range (IQR) overcomes the problem you described in #1 above.

3. You asked a sample of 35 students how many books they purchased for fall semester. The score at the 25th percentile was 2 and the score at the 75th percentile was 6. What is the interquartile range (IQR) for your data set?

4. Which of the following is the best definition for standard deviation?
    a. How far scores are from the mean
    b. The average difference between scores and the mean
    c. The distance between the scores and the mean
    d. How far, on average, scores fall from each other

5. Find the standard deviation of the following sets of scores. Start by finding the mean. If the mean is a whole number, use the conceptual formula. If the mean is not a whole number, use the computational formula.
    a. 5,1,8,9,2
    b. 5,6,7,6,6
    c. 12,13,15,17,12
    d. 14,11,6,3,18,6,4,2
    e. 2,9,4,5,1,3,4,6,10
    f. 10,8,11,3,2,1,14,3,11

Answers to questions and problems. (Remember that all answers in this book are based on rounding each step, and the final answer, to 2 decimal places. Your answers may differ if you round differently).

1) The range is often a bad choice because it is calculated from the highest and lowest scores, which are often much lower or higher than most scores. Therefore, this statistic can be very misleading. You could also mention that it does not take into account most of the scores in the distribution.

2) The interquartile range is based on the scores that fall at certain percentile ranks (25th and 75th) and so it is only somewhat influenced by the extreme high and low scores (just like the median is only somewhat influenced by extreme scores).

3) IQR = 4

4) You can cross off options *a* and *c* since neither mention anything about an average distance or difference, which is an essential aspect of the standard deviation (that is, that it represents some sort of *average*). Option *d* says that standard deviation is a measure of how far scores fall from each other on average, which is wrong. As you can tell from the definition offered in this chapter, as well as from the calculations you perform, standard deviation measures how far, on average, scores fall from the mean. So the answer is *b* (*The average difference between scores and the mean*).

5) Standard deviations are:
   a. 3.54
   b. 0.71
   c. 2.17
   d. 5.73
   e. 3.02 (computational formula)
   f. 4.80 (computational formula)

Chapter 5

Z scores

Our discussion of z scores will begin with Jim, who just informed his parents he scored 105 on his spelling test. Naturally, Jim's parents want that to be a high score. But maybe it's a low score. Perhaps it's a more-or-less average score? Wait... what on earth *should* his parents conclude?

The fact that you cannot answer that question demonstrates that the raw score (here, X = 105) is often not very informative. To know how Jim did on his spelling test, we need to find out where he falls in the distribution, that is, how he scored *relative to others who were measured*. To do that, we need some more information—two more pieces of information, to be exact.

One thing you need to know is the *average* (mean) score on the spelling test Jim took. If you were told the average was 90, you'd have a better idea of how well he did. But, believe it or not, you'd still only be half way there. Even though you know Jim is 15 points above the mean, you still only have a very vague idea how he did relative to everyone else.

That may sound odd, but look at the distribution below and try to mark where Jim (X = 105) falls in it:

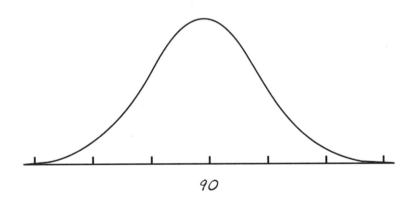

90

Not sure where to put him, are you? Although you know he's higher than 90—on the right hand side of the distribution, above the average—you don't know how *much* higher. He might be only a little above 90 if the distribution looked like the following (next page).

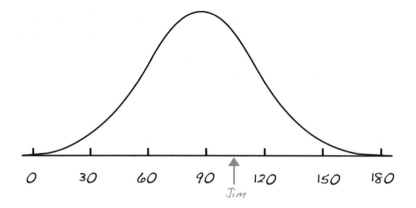

... or *way* above 90, if the distribution looked like this...

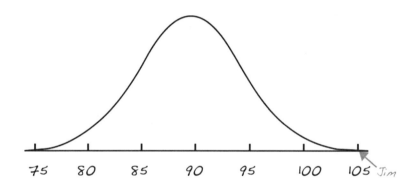

...or something in between, like this:

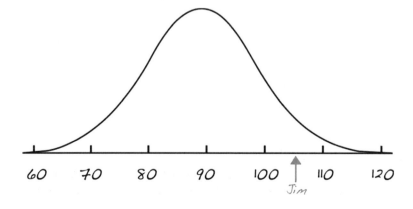

The piece of information that was missing earlier, which is essential in determining where Jim falls in the distribution, is the amount of *variability* in the distribution. You can see by checking the values on the X axes how much more variable the scores were in first distribution relative to the second, for example.

Importantly, for any given score and mean, like 105 and 90, more variability means the score is closer to the center of the distribution, and less variability means the score is further from the center of the distribution[35]. Take another look back at those distributions, because very soon you'll need to be able to sketch them yourself.

When sketching a distribution, the convention is to label the tick marks according to the standard deviation, σ. Thus you can infer that σ is 30 in the first distribution, in the second distribution σ is 5, and in the last distribution σ is 10.

*   *   *

Using these principles, label the X axes on the distributions below and mark where Jim would fall in each (recall his score is X = 105 and the mean is M = 90). See the end of the chapter for the solution.

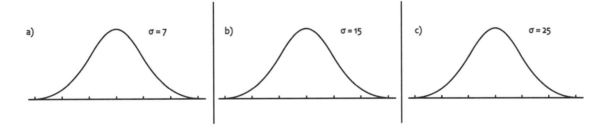

We can now see that the location of a person's score within a distribution is influenced by three factors:

1- Their raw **score**

2- The **mean** of the distribution their score came from. Knowing this tells us how many points above or below the mean their score is.

3- The **standard deviation** of the distribution their score came from. With this final piece of information, we can tell exactly *how far* the score is from the mean (i.e., from the center of the distribution).

---

[35] Since the distribution is normal (we'll always assume that is the case), the mean, median, and mode are right in the center. However, from now on we'll always use the mean as our reference point.

As you may have guessed, we can't *only sketch* out the distribution and eyeball where the score falls (though it is quite useful to do that). We must also, or instead, calculate *exactly* where the score falls. We do this by converting the raw score (*X* score) to something called a *z score*. We do that with a simple formula:

$$Z = \frac{X - \mu}{\sigma}$$

Notice the formula corresponds exactly with our list of the factors which influence where a score falls in a distribution:

1- **X** is the **score.**

2- **μ** is the **mean** of the distribution the score came from.

3- **σ** is the **standard deviation** of the distribution the score came from.

By converting a raw/*X* score into a *z* score with the formula above, we can tell exactly where the score falls in the distribution. Fortunately, *any* raw score can be converted to a more meaningful *z* score, as long as the mean and standard deviation are known.

> The **z score** *takes into account the raw score, and the mean and standard deviation of the distribution the score came from. It reveals exactly where a score falls within a distribution.*

To clarify what is meant by *knowing exactly where a score falls*, let's use *z* scores again, this time to evaluate *Hank*, Jim's cousin from North Dakota. Hank took a different spelling test, and scored **87**. The mean of the distribution of scores for that test is **83**, with a standard deviation of **1.5.**

Again, we want to not only see where the *X* score falls in the distribution by sketching it all out (which requires knowing the mean and the standard deviation), but we also want to convert that *X* score to a *z* score. In this case, the sketch has been started for you. But finish the sketch that follows by appropriately numbering the X axis and then indicating where Hank's score is.

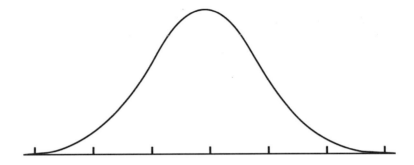

(See answer at the end of the chapter.)

Next, find Hank's z score by applying the z score formula:

$$Z = \frac{X - \mu}{\sigma} \quad \text{\tiny 36}$$

*   *   *

One of the great things about z scores, since they tell you the exact location of a score within a distribution, is that they allow you to compare scores from different distributions. Let's take advantage of that and find out who seems to be the better speller, Jim or Hank. We'll assume Jim came from *Distribution A* from earlier, where μ is 90 and σ is 30.

Looking at the *raw* scores, we see Jim's was higher—he scored 105 vs. Hank's 87. Not only that, but Jim was 15 points above the mean while Hank was only 4 points above the mean. It's looking pretty good for Jim. But let's see what happens when we convert the raw scores into z scores:

Jim: $\quad Z = \frac{105 - 90}{30} = +0.50$

Hank: $\quad Z = \frac{87 - 83}{1.5} = +2.67$

That's right—it turns out Hank is the better speller. You know this because he has a higher z score. Z scores are *universal* or *standard* scores, meaning, for one thing, they are directly

---

[36] (87-83)/1.5 = 4/1.5 = + 2.67

comparable. Again, whoever has a higher z score, scored higher and whoever has a lower z score, scored lower.[37]

Note a z score can be either positive, when the score is above the mean, or negative, when the score is below the mean. Keep in mind the larger the z score, whether positive or negative, the further out in the distribution the score falls. Conversely, the smaller the z score, the closer to the center of the distribution the score falls. For each of the following, note which z score is further from the center of the distribution:

- z = +1.23 vs. z = -1.98
- z = -4.12 vs. z = -1.51
- z = 0.23 vs. z = -0.01[38]

In this case, since we converted both Jim's and Hank's score to a universal, or standard, z score, we have in effect put them both into the same distribution: a *distribution of z scores*:

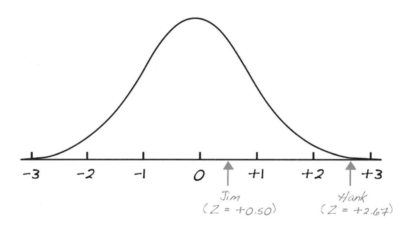

---

[37] Note *higher* and *lower* do not necessarily mean better and worse (after all, sometimes a high score is a bad thing). Also note, even when high scores are indeed 'good', someone with a higher z score is not necessarily better than someone with a lower score. In our Jim vs. Hank example, it could be that, even though Hank scored higher (had the higher z score), Jim is actually a better speller. Seems odd, but what if the other people who took Hank's test were all really bad spellers and the others who took Jim's test were excellent spellers. Perhaps Jim's z score of +0.50 among great spellers is more impressive than Hank's z score of +2.67 among bad spellers. However, analyzing that possibility would require a much more thorough analysis and a lot more information. But, going by what we DO know (the scores, the population means, and the population standard deviations), it seems Hank is the better speller, based on the fact that his score is higher in the z distribution than Jim's.

[38] z = -1.98; z = -4.12; z = 0.23

You can see above an advantage of the z score is that it allows us to compare scores which come from different distributions. Without a z score, or some other standard score, scores from different distributions would not be so directly comparable.

The z distribution is called universal, or standard, for a good reason: *Its mean and standard deviation are always the same.* Specifically, the mean is always 0, and the standard deviation is always 1. This is an inevitable consequence of the way z scores are computed, so it will always hold true.

> *The mean of the distribution is always **0** and the standard deviation is always **1**.*

One last point: z scores, also by virtue of the way they are computed, are in what's called *standard deviation units.* So...

- A z score of +2.50 means the score is 2.5 standard deviations above the mean.
- A z score of -1.00 means the score is 1 standard deviation below the mean.
- A z score of +3.88 means the score is 3.88 standard deviations above the mean.
- A z score of -1.75 means the score is _____ standard deviations _____ the mean.[39]
- A z score of 0.00 means the score is _____.[40]

Notice, unlike an X score, a z score tells you exactly where in the distribution the score is. If someone tells you a student's quiz grade is 8, you don't know how she did. But if you were told her z score is +3.10 you sure do.

* * *

Let's work through another problem for good measure:

Who is bigger: *Harley*, a 93 lb 5th grader, or *Jacob*, a 5'2" (62") high school freshman?

Assume the following:

Harley's distribution: μ = 95, σ = 10

Jacob's distribution: μ = 67, σ = 5

---

[39] 1 ¾ (or 1.75); below
[40] at the mean (or equal to the mean)

First, sketch the distribution for each person to get a feel for where they fall:

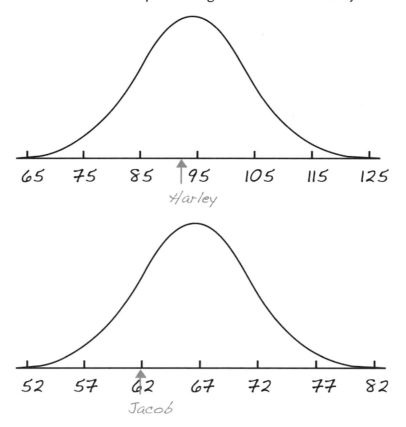

Although they are both below the mean, it appears Harley is a bit bigger since he's further to the right of his distribution than Jacob is in his. But you should convert each of their raw scores into z scores to get a more accurate picture of the situation:

Harley: X = 93, μ = 95, σ = 10

$$Z = \frac{93 - 95}{10} = \frac{-2}{10} = -0.20$$

Jacob: X = 62, μ = 67, σ = 5

$$Z = \frac{62 - 67}{5} = \frac{-5}{5} = -1.00$$

Sure enough, just as the sketches suggest, Harley is bigger. His z score is -0.20—in other words, he is only 0.2 standard deviations below the mean. Meanwhile, Jacob's z score is -1.00, meaning he is a full (1.00) standard deviation below the mean. Therefore, *Harley is bigger.*

You could also put them both on one distribution (the z distribution) after you've converted their raw scores to z scores, to see things even more clearly:

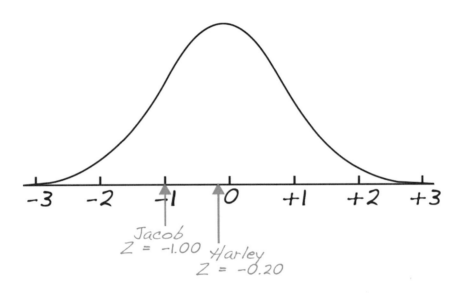

Let's consider one more question similar to the ones we've been asking (a question that, you will soon see, is more relevant in inferential statistics than questions like the ones we've been asking in this chapter). The question is: Who is more *unusual*: Harley or Jacob?

Try to answer that question without any further guidance. Look at the distribution above and see if you can figure out who is the more unusual of the two (in terms of the measures being considered).

Did you say it's Jacob, because he falls further out in the distribution than Harley? If so, then you are already on your way to understanding an important aspect of inferential statistics: The further out a score (or any "result") falls in the distribution, the more unusual it is, meaning the less likely it is to have occurred just by chance. If you didn't understand all of that—or any of it—don't worry. This will all make sense very soon!

In either case, you should note in this chapter we used z scores for two descriptive purposes:

1. to better represent a raw score
    o For example, Hank's raw score of 87 (X = 87) was essentially meaningless, but converting it to a z score (z = + 2.67) tells us quite a bit.

2. to compare scores that come from different distributions
   - For example, knowing Hank's and Jim's raw scores on their two different spelling tests ($X = 87$ and $X = 105$) didn't shed any light on who was the better speller, but converting their X scores to z scores ($z = +2.67$ and $z = +0.50$) sure did. Same goes for trying to compare Jacob and Harley.

You are now finished with the descriptive statistics portion of the book. The remainder will focus on inferential statistics. First, several chapters will explain the key concepts behind inferential statistics, and how they work. After gaining this understanding, you will then learn how to apply inferential statistics to help answer research questions, beginning with using the z score (yep, the z score can be used for both descriptive and inferential purposes).

Questions and problems.

1. If you took a test online that tests knowledge of history, and you scored X = 217 on it, what advantage would there be in first converting that raw/X score into a z score before reporting your score to others?

2. To convert your X score into a z score, what other information would you need?

3. Assume the mean GPA of students at your college is 2.25, with a standard deviation of 1.1. Joe's GPA is 2.50. What is Joe's z score?

4. Now assume the mean GPA of students at your college is 2.25, but the standard deviation is 0.5. Joe's GPA is still 2.50. What would Joe's z score be under these conditions?

5. What is more *unusual* (i.e., further from mean) in Springfield, an 80-degree day in October or a 50-degree day in August? Assume the following parameters. October: $\mu = 58$, $\sigma = 10$; August: $\mu = 82$, $\sigma = 12$.

Answers to questions and problems.

Mid-chapter problems:

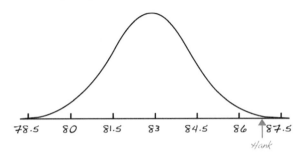

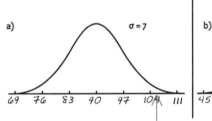

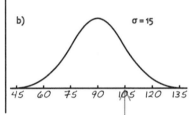

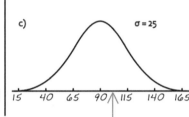

End-of-chapter problems:

1) Converting your raw score of X = 217 to a z score would be adventageous because a z score tells others whether you scored above or below the mean (based on whether the z score was positive/+ or negative/-), and also how far, in standard deviation units, how far from the mean you scored.

2) In addition to your X score (217), you'd also need to know the population mean on the test (μ), and the standard devation of scores on the test (σ). For example, if the population mean on the test were 250, with a standard deviation of 20, then your z score would be:

$$Z = \frac{X - \mu}{\sigma} = \frac{217 - 250}{20} = \frac{-33}{20} = -1.65$$

(meaning you scored 1.65 standard deviations below the mean)

3) Joe's z score is z = + 0.23.

4) Joe's z score is z = + 0.50.

5) The z score of the 80-degree October day is + 2.20. The z score of the 50-degree August day is -2.67. That makes the August day 2.67 standard deviations from the mean and the October day only 2.2 standard deviations from the mean. Thus, that August day was more unusual (further from the mean).

Chapter 6
Introduction to inferential statistics

This chapter marks the transition from descriptive statistics to inferential statistics. You will see that inferential statistics serve a very different purpose than descriptive statistics.

This chapter will present you with an introduction to the general strategy of inferential statistics. Then, you'll move on to some important concepts which inferential statistics rely on, and which you'll need to understand in order to grasp inferential statistics overall. Finally, you'll learn to use several inferential statistical tests.

Let's start from the beginning.

As you know, researchers in Psychology seek to learn about behavior, and to do so, they must engage in *empirical* research—make observations and collect data.

But what do they do with the data after they collect it (other than summarize it, of course)? In other words, what exactly are researchers looking for in all that data they collect? The answer is simple: They are looking for *relationships*.

That may be a surprisingly short answer, but all you need to do is open a research publication in Psychology and you will immediately see that it's true. Research in psychology is all about discovering relationships among variables. Look at the titles of some research studies in Psychology below (all of which happened to be published by undergraduate students):

1) *Changes in Parents' Stress as Their Children Become Adolescents: A Validation of the Stress Index for Parents of Adolescents* (Wheatley & Wille, 2009)[41]

2) *Perceiving Mood in Color: The Effects of Mood States on Reaction Times* (Duncanson, 2009)[42]

3) *Complex Environmental Enrichment and Spatial Reference Memory in Middle-Aged Mice* (Koke & Petro, 2009) [43]

4) *The Influence of Perceived Familial Emotional Support in Childhood on Adult Health-related Behaviors* (Maldonado & Vaughn, 2013)[44]

---

[41] Wheatley, M.K. & Wille, D.E. (2009). Psi Chi Journal of Undergraduate Research, 14(3).
[42] Duncanson, H. (2009). Psi Chi Journal of Undergraduate Research, 14(2).
[43] Koke, V. & Petro, M.S. (2009). Psi Chi Journal of Undergraduate Research, 14(1)
[44] Maldonado, A. & Vaughn, A.A. (2013). Psi Chi Journal of Undergraduate Research, 18(20).

To be sure, some of those titles are complex. Nevertheless, if we take a closer look we can see, in all cases, it is apparent the researchers were looking to see if a *relationship* exists between variables. Let's break down each one:

1) *Changes in parents' stress as their children become adolescents...*

   These researchers investigated the relationship between the variables **stress** (of the parents) and **age** (of the children). It's unclear from the title whether the authors found an increase or a decrease in parents' stress as their children aged (*became adolescents*), but they evidently found some sort of a change (i.e., a relationship between stress of the parents and age of the children).

2) *... The effects of mood states on reaction times*

   These researchers investigated the relationship between the variables **mood** and **reaction time.** In this case, they manipulated the participants' moods to see if the change in mood affected those participants' reaction time.

3) *Complex environmental enrichment and spatial reference memory...*

   Looks like these researchers wanted to see if there is a relationship between the **complexity** of the environment the mice grew up in and the **memory** abilities of those mice. They found that as the complexity of the environment increased, the memory ability of the mice increased.

4) *Influence of Perceived Familial Emotional Support in Childhood on Adult Health-related Behaviors*

   Here, student researchers investigated whether children's **perceived familial emotional support** (which must be how much support the subjects felt they got from family members when they were kids) is associated with their **health-related behaviors** (eating, exercise, etc.) as adults.

Although all psychological research comes down to the investigation of relationships, these relationships can come in many forms. For example, in #2 above, it is evident from the title that the authors investigated a cause-effect relationship (i.e., whether mood *affects* reaction time) while in #1 there isn't necessarily a cause-effect relationship between a parent's stress and their child's age.[45] But in all cases, the researchers were looking for, and evidently found, relationships between the variables they were studying.

---

[45] Always remember that inferential statistics can determine only *whether* a relationship exists; they cannot reveal the *nature* of the relationship—that is, whether it exists because one variable is affecting the other, or for some other reason.

*　*　*

Consider each of the following research studies:

> 1. *Influences of scent pleasantness on pain sensitivity.* These authors are investigating the relationship between what two variables?

> 2. *The impact of perfectionism on work attitudes.* These authors are investigating the relationship between what two variables?

> 3. *Is the left half of the brain better with language?* These authors are investigating the relationship between what two variables?[46]

*　*　*

Fortunately, no matter what the nature of the relationship you're investigating happens to be, there is a statistical test that allows you to figure out whether there actually *is* a real relationship.

Before we get to what is meant by *real*, let's clarify what is meant by *relationship*. Actually, we could do a pretty good job of defining it with a single word: *difference*. For example, if there is a *difference* between how on-time buses are when the weather is nice and how on-time they are when the weather is bad, then there is a *relationship* between the variables *weather* and *bus timeliness*—probably the better the weather, the more on-time buses are.

In some instances you may instead use the word *effect*: Weather has an *effect* on bus timeliness. Or even if you had a situation where the cause and effect wasn't clear, such as if you discovered a relationship between *weight* and *reading ability* among children, you'd still say there is some *effect* at play.[47]

Now, that word *real* you saw earlier: What does it mean to say a relationship, or difference, or effect, is *real*? You may be asking "Real? As opposed to what?" The short answer is "As opposed to not real," but clearly that is not satisfactory. Actually, a more meaningful answer to that question represents one of the most important concepts to understand in inferential statistics, and indeed in research. So continue to read carefully!

---

[46] 1. scent pleasantness; pain sensitivity. 2. Level of perfectionism; work attitude. 3. Brain side (even though only the left side is mentioned, it is necessarily being compared to the right side); language ability.

[47] This relationship is probably a result of the fact that, as children age, they gain weight, and also as they age, their reading ability improves. Notice this results in a relationship between *weight* and *reading ability*, but not because gaining weight *causes* one to become a better reader (or because becoming a better reader *causes* one to gain weight); it occurs because both of those variables are related to a third variable, *age*.

As it turns out, there will always *seem* to be a relationship between the variables when you first look at the results. For example, consider the study mentioned above which looked at the relationship between *mood states* (happy, sad) and *reaction time*. Believe it or not, regardless of whether mood has an effect on reaction time (i.e., regardless of whether there is a relationship between those two variables), the average reaction time of the sad group will *always* be different than the average reaction time of the happy group.

That may be counterinuitive—after all, if mood doesn't affect reaction time, shouldn't the reaction time for the participants in a sad mood be the same as the reaction time for the participants in a happy mood? So think of it this way instead: If the average reaction time for the happy group was 427 milliseconds, would you expect the average reaction time for the sad group to be *exactly* 427 milliseconds? That is, would you expect *no* difference whatsoever?

The answer is clear: *No, there will always be some difference.* So let's summarize: Even if mood had no effect on reaction time, you'd still never expect the averages to be exactly the same. Instead, what is sure to happen is that there will be *some* difference between the means, even if it is just a small one, such as 427 ms vs. 432 ms.

Therefore, since we know there will always be some difference, the question is not *Is there a difference?* (The answer to that is always *yes*). The question is: Is the difference *real*? By *real*, we mean the difference occurred because there really is a relationship between mood and reaction time. Now, you may be asking why *else* a difference would occur. This will be discussed a bit more, but, briefly, the other possibility is that the difference was just a chance occurrence.

So, when a researcher refers to an *effect of mood states on reaction time*, or to the *changes in parents' stress as their children become adolescents*, or to any other relationship between variables, they must have performed a statistical test on the data they collected in order to see if the relationship was real. This type of statistic is referred to as an *inferential statistic*.

> *Inferential statistics* *make it possible to determine whether there is probably a real relationship between the variables being studied, or whether the apparent relationship (difference/effect) is just due to chance.*

Since this is such an important and fundamental concept, it's important that you can think of it in another way. Specifically, if you have determined with an inferential statistical test that a relationship is real, what you're also saying is that you would expect to find that relationship if you were somehow able to study the whole population. Conversely, if you conclude that a relationship between variables does not exist (the difference was just a chance occurence), you're saying that you would *not* expect to find the effect if you were somehow able to study the whole population. Note the use of the word *expect* (and *if*, and *would*). We could never actually study the whole population, so inferential statistics are all about making an educated and informed conclusion (*inference*) about the population.

The specifics of how that is accomplished will depend on the situation you find yourself in. The procedure will differ depending on the kind of data being collected, on how complex your study is, and on other factors. However, the same basic question is always asked: *Is there a relationship between the variables being studied?*

> *The fundamental question that inferential statistics answer is: Is there a relationship between the variables being studied?*

Let's start with a somewhat ridiculous, but simple, research question, to clarify these ideas:

Are men taller than women?

First, the question above indicates that we are studying the relationship between what two variables?[48]

Since we're asking about men and women *in general*—not just a particular group of men and women—then to answer our question with absolute certainty we'd have to somehow obtain heights for every man and every woman in the world (the whole *population*). As discussed previously, such a feat is impossible since populations are far too large to study in their entirety, but it's also unnecessary.

For the current example, let's say we collected height data from a statistics class, and found that the men in class were, on average, 5' 8", and the women in class averaged 5' 5" tall. Should we conclude from that finding that men are taller than women?[49]

It is tempting to conclude from our result that men are taller than women, since 5' 8" is obviously taller than 5' 5". But how do you know that the 3-inch difference observed wasn't just a chance occurrence? After all, it could be, just by chance, our sample included some unusually tall men and/or some unusually short women. If that was the case, it could mean that the difference we found wasn't real but just due to random chance. Researchers refer to random, unknowable forces that affect experiments as *sampling error*. More specifically:

---

[48] The variables are *gender* and *height*. If you thought it was men and women, remember: Those are the levels of the variable. Men, for example, isn't a variable. Gender is the variable, and men is one of the *levels* of it (women is of course the other level).
[49] Ignore for now that such a sample could be biased--- assume instead that our sample nicely represents the population.

> *Sampling error* is the difference that inevitably exists between the result that was obtained from the sample(s) and the result that would have been obtained from the whole population.

The existence of sampling error can easily be confirmed by doing the following:

> Take a group of people and divide them randomly into two equal groups. For example, you could have people pick slips of paper out of a hat, where half the slips have "A" printed on them and the other half "B". You then measure these people on some variable, for example the number of letters in their hometown. Since the groups were created *randomly*, there should be no difference between the average number of letters in Group A's hometowns and the average number of letters in Group B's hometowns. But imagine that you've just finished calculating Group A's mean, and it's 7.21. Do you expect that when you find Group B's mean, it will work out to exactly 7.21? Of course not: There *will* be a difference. Since it's absurd to think that two randomly formed groups will differ "for real", then the difference you will inevitably observe must be due to sampling error.

On that note, let's refine the question above (*Should we conclude from that finding that men are taller than women?*) with your new-found terminology:

> Is the difference that we observed between men's and women's heights due to sampling error, or is it real?[50]

In this particular example, going through a statistical procedure to decide whether the 3-inch difference we found is likely just due to sampling error seems a bit ridiculous since we already know that men are generally taller than women. However, in actual research, unlike in an example from a textbook, you *don't* already know the answer. After all, if you already knew the answer, why would you do the research? Research is for answering questions that don't currently have answers!

For that reason, in actual psychological research the researcher must always determine whether the research finding represents:

> **a)** A *chance* occurrence that only *looks* like it may be a real finding (i.e., the difference you observed is within the range of what you'd expect to find due to sampling error).

> **b)** A *real* finding (i.e., the difference you observed *is bigger* than what you'd expect to find due to sampling error).

Inferential statistics are used in order to choose between *a* and *b*. Put another way:

---

[50] Speaking of terminology, recall another way to say a result is real is to say it's *statistically significant*.

> *Inferential statistics* are used to determine if the results obtained are *a)* within the range of what would be expected due to sampling error (chance) or *b)* outside that range and therefore represent a real relationship between the variables.

*   *   *

We can now see more clearly why the word *inferential* is used. It's because you study a sample, and from it you *infer* something about a population. Namely, you infer whether **a)** the effect does not exist in the population (i.e., whatever you found in the sample was just sampling error) or, **b)** the effect *does* exist in the population (the effect you found in the sample is real).

The overall procedure used in inferential statistics to make that "a/b" determination is as follows:

> **Step 1)** Determine the probability that your result was due to chance/sampling error.

> **Step 2)** Decide whether that probability is **a)** high enough to conclude your result was indeed just chance or, alternatively, **b)** low enough to conclude your result probably was *not* just chance and must therefore be real.

*   *   *

Does this all sound like a strange approach to take? Statistical nonsense? Unnecessarily complicated? Not at all. In fact, it's just what *you* may find yourself doing when trying to figure out whether something occurred just by chance (you may use the expression *just a coincidence*), or instead something real caused it to happen.

Find that hard to believe? Circle one of the options in brackets in the paragraph below and let's see if you use the same basic logic laid out above in assessing the following scenario:

> You are in a jewelry store in a large shopping mall, and there is a man next to you looking at the display case. After looking at the jewelry you decide to go get a pretzel, and as the cashier in the pretzel place is ringing you up, you notice the same man has just entered. *What do you think?* [a) chance OR b) not just chance (something more/real is happening)] Next, you go to the bookstore. You're browsing around at books and see, you guessed it, that same guy browsing down the aisle from you. *What do you think?* [a) chance OR b) not just chance (something more/real is happening)] Finally, you go to your car to leave and, sure enough, there's the guy again. *What do you think?* [a) chance OR b) not just chance (something more/real is happening)]

If you're like most people, you circled *a) chance* for the first item, and circled *b) not just chance (something more/real is happening)* for the last. But no matter what you decided to circle, as you ran into the person more and more times, you started to feel more and more like it was not simply due to chance. Right?

One way to characterize what you did—not literally, but in principle—is this:

> First **(Step 1)**, you considered the probability that the man being there was just chance. Then **(Step 2)**, if you felt that probability was **a)** sufficiently high, such as you probably did the second time you saw him, you concluded it indeed *was* just chance. If, on the other hand, you felt the probability of the man being there just by chance was **b)** very low, such as when you saw him for the 4th time at your car, you concluded it probably *wasn't* just chance. And if it's not just chance, it's got to be something else. In this case, that *something else* probably made you uncomfortable. Thankfully, determining that your result is probably not just chance *in research* makes you happy![51]

*   *   *

Surely, you would not literally calculate any probabilities in instances like the one in the mall. In fact, for most people the word *probability* wouldn't even come to mind. But, on some level, you decided that nothing was going on when the man first re-appeared because you felt one re-appearance was *likely to have occurred just by chance* ("just a coincidence" you may have said to yourself). Similarly, you made the decision later that something *was* going on because you felt the man's multiple re-appearances were *very unlikely to have occurred just by chance*. And always, if you decide something is *not* just chance, then you are also—by definition—saying that there must be some other, *real*, cause.

This is a good time to remind you that inferential statistics cannot identify what the cause of the result *is*. They only identify whether or not the result was probably due to chance/sampling error. In the mall analogy, your analysis of the probabilty of seeing that guy multiple times only answered whether it was a coincidence or not. It did not, for example, help in figuring out *why* he was following you.

Hopefully you have not found yourself in a situation like that one, but other examples abound. Read through the following scenarios, paying special attention to how they all follow the same basic logic being discussed.

1. *You come home and see facing you a blue pickup truck on the street. Your cousin, who lives in the next state over, has a blue pickup. Same make and model. Do you conclude that your*

---

[51] Because, of course, that means your result is real. Would you ever see a headline that read *Psychology Researcher Thought He Found Coffee Drinkers Have Lower Levels of Anxiety, but the Difference was Probably Just Chance?*

cousin has come for a surprise visit? Probably not, because it seems fairly likely this is just coincidental (chance). You walk around to the back and see that the license plate is from your cousin's state. Then you notice a sticker on the window from the same college your cousin attends. NOW do you conclude that your cousin has come for a surprise visit? Probably so; the chances all those things were just a coincidence is pretty small, so therefore your cousin probably is in fact paying you a surprise visit.

2. *You move to a new place, and on the first day the mail comes at around 10:00am. Is this the normal mail time? You probably don't assume so at first, but after a few days of the mail coming at that time, you assume it can't just be a coincidence that it came at about 10:00 a few days in a row, so that must be the regular time, and you expect it to more-or-less always come around 10:00. You doubt it was just a coincidence the mail kept coming at about 10:00; it happened for a reason.*

3. *You open a window to let in a cool breeze and a little while later notice a fly. Did the fly come in through the window (i.e., there is a problem with the screen)? Perhaps not, because you realize it could easily just be a coincidence that a fly would appear after you open a window. You shut the window and kill the fly. The next day the same thing happens- you open the window and another fly appears. Now you're really thinking about taking a close look at that screen. It's becoming unlikely that the apparent connection between you opening the window and a fly appearing is just chance. Certainly, if this happened a third or fourth time, you'd be confident there's an issue with the screen.*

4. *You're meeting a person for coffee who you just met for the first time a few days ago. She shows up late. Do you conclude that it could have just been a fluke occurrence, or do you conclude that she is just one of those people who is usually late? If you have already concluded that she is just one of those people, you may have jumped the gun a bit. But after the same thing happens several times, such a conclusion is probably warranted.*

*   *   *

To recap, the logic used in inferential statistics is similar to everday common sense, where you first determine the probability of something being just chance, and then, if you feel that probability is sufficiently high, you conclude it indeed *is* just chance. If, on the other hand, you feel the probability of something being just chance is very low, you conclude it must *not* be chance, so instead it must *mean something*, that is, the mail really *does* come at 10:00am, or flies really *are* coming in through the window, or your new friend really *is* one of those people, or your cousin really *did* come to visit.

The difference between the everyday examples and the inferential statistics used in research is, in the latter, you determine actual probabilities rather than just have a feeling about them. You also, importantly, set a specific probability as the criterion for deciding whether something is *likely* chance and so isn't real, or *very unlikely* chance and so is real. Although you are more careful, precise, and "scientific" in inferential statistics than you are in everyday situations, the same logic is applied.

The next question we must tackle is a very important one: *How?* *How* could some statistical procedure possibly determine how likely it is (that is, the probability) that your result was due to chance/sampling error?

An explanation of how we can do that is complex and involves understanding a number of concepts (and chapters!). But the very short answer—just to provide a bit of framework for moving forward—is this:

> We create a frequency distribution that shows *what would happen if* we conducted our study an infinite number of times and the only thing affecting the outcomes is chance/sampling error (i.e., if there was no relationship between the variables we're studying). Then, we actually conduct our study and see where the result falls within this distribution. The location of our result tells us the approximate *probability that the result was due to chance/sampling error.*

Didn't get all that? Don't worry. As stated above, that is just meant to be a preview to provide some context moving forward. There is much to learn. Let's begin by getting into how we could possibly know what would happen *if* we did something (e.g., conducted a study) an infinite number of times without actually having to do it. The key principle at work here is called *the law of large numbers*, the focus of the next chapter.

Chapter 7
The law of large numbers

In the last chapter, you were introduced to inferential statistics. At the end of the chapter, you were told that a mathematical phenomenon called *the law of large numbers* was essential for you to understand. Your goal for this chapter should be to understand this law and, by the end of the chapter, to understand how it underlies inferential statistics.

This law will be explained thoroughly, but it is basically this: As the number of trials increases, the closer the observed outcome matches the outcome predicted by the laws of probability.[52]

> *The law of large numbers*: As the number of trials increases, the closer the observed outcome matches the predicted (expected) outcome.

The term *expected* can be confusing because it refers not only to the exact outcome predicted by probability theory, but also to the variability *around* this prediction. For example, you would predict, and therefore *expect*, heads to come up 50% of the time if you flipped a coin 10 times. But at the same time you also *expect* some variability from this prediction. Though your best guess is that heads will come up 50% of the time—what you *expect*, so to speak—you are not surprised if it doesn't turn out exactly like that.

What you always need to determine in research is whether your result is *outside the expected range*, or *different enough from the expected*, for you to conclude something other than chance is at play (i.e., there is some effect). This is what inferential statistics are for. And this should all sound familiar from the last chapter.

Let's go back to the coin-flip situation for an example. In that case, the predicted/expected outcome when flipping coins is that they will come up heads 50% of the time. However, if you were to flip a coin only 10 times, you would not be at all surprised to find substantial deviations from this prediction. What if you flipped the coin 10 times and it came up heads only twice—20% of the time instead of the expected 50%? Would you conclude the coin is unfair—that something *other than chance* must have produced such a difference from the expected?

---

[52] In this context the outcome predicted by the laws of probability is called the *expected* outcome. Examples will follow immediately to clarify.

Of course not. You probably recognize, either from your experience or just intuitively, that heads coming up 20% of the time when you flip it only 10 times is within the limits of what you could attribute to chance.

But say you flipped the coin *100* times and it came up heads 20% of the time. Such a result would be highly suspicious (that is, very unlikely to have occurred by chance) and you almost certainly have an unfair coin. So, what is the difference between those two situations?[53]

Following this, you could also say that for a small number of trials, you *expect* a substantial difference between the observed and the expected outcome, but for a larger number of trials you expect *less* difference between the observed and expected outcome. Sounds like the law of large numbers!

*   *   *

How about some real data? Ideally we'd use actual coins, but performing a large number of coin tosses would take a very long time. Instead, we're going to look at coin-flip results from a website which allows you to toss virtual coins. The computer uses a randomizer algorithm to decide whether a virtual coin lands on heads or tails. The computer assigns the correct 50/50 probability to each individual toss and, being a computer, it can do many, many tosses very, very quickly.[54]

Below are the results of several samples of 10, 100, 1,000, and 10,000 tosses to demonstrate the law of large numbers in action. Remember, the law of large numbers states that, as the number of trials (tosses) increases, the closer the observed outcome will be to the expected outcome. Of course the expected outcome is 50% heads.

The results displayed on the following tables are from virtual coin tosses which, as explained above, are just as valid as actual coin tosses. In each case, five samples were done in order to get a better feel for what the results look like—to create at least a little bit of a *distribution* of results instead of just one result.

First up are samples of **10** tosses.

	Sample 1	Sample 2	Sample 3	Sample 4	Sample 5
Heads	8	4	4	6	7

---

[53] The two situations differ in the number of tosses that occurred. By the end of this discussion you should have a good grasp on *why* the number of tosses plays such an important role in determining whether a coin is fair.

[54] Although the coins aren't real, the data you are looking at is real because it's the result of a random, 50/50 process, just like real coin tosses.

Next are samples of **100** tosses.

	Sample 1	Sample 2	Sample 3	Sample 4	Sample 5
Heads	56	53	44	52	44

Now samples of **1,000** tosses.

	Sample 1	Sample 2	Sample 3	Sample 4	Sample 5
Heads	495	521	511	462	485

Finally, samples of **10,000** tosses

	Sample 1	Sample 2	Sample 3	Sample 4	Sample 5
Heads	4945	5019	5007	5165	5021

Do you notice a trend in the results displayed in those tables? Are you thinking something to the effect of: *As the number of flips increased, the closer the actual number of heads matched the expected result of 50%?* If you missed that, take another look.

Either way, you definitely won't miss it when we convert the results above into percentages:

10 tosses (**N = 10**)

	Sample 1	Sample 2	Sample 3	Sample 4	Sample 5
Heads	80%	40%	40%	60%	70%

100 tosses (**N = 100**)

	Sample 1	Sample 2	Sample 3	Sample 4	Sample 5
Heads	56%	53%	44%	52%	44%

1,000 tosses (**N = 1,000**)

	Sample 1	Sample 2	Sample 3	Sample 4	Sample 5
Heads	49.5%	52.1%	51.1%	46.2%	48.5%

10,000 tosses (**N = 10,000**)

	Sample 1	Sample 2	Sample 3	Sample 4	Sample 5
Heads	49.45%	50.19%	50.07%	51.65%	50.21%

Look above and confirm which of the following statements are accurate by checking the respective boxes:

☐ When we did only 10 tosses, the percentages of heads varied from 40% to 80%.

☐ When we increased to 100 tosses, the range in percentages of heads was less: 44% to 56%.

☐ With 1,000 tosses, the range in the percentages was even less: 46.2% to 52.1%

☐ Finally, when we did 10,000 tosses, the range was smaller still: 49.45% to 51.65%[55]

And just for fun, here are the results for 5 samples of 1,000,000 (1 Million) flips (**N = 1,000,000**)

	Sample 1	Sample 2	Sample 3	Sample 4	Sample 5
Heads	499,282	499,772	500,401	499,790	500,455

---

[55] You should have checked all the boxes (all the statements were accurate descriptions of the results). Also note *range* was used instead of standard deviation only because we can easily see the range without any calculations. However, you can be sure that the standard deviation of the means also got smaller as the number of flips increased from 10 to 100 to 1,000, and so on.

Converted to percentages...

	Sample 1	Sample 2	Sample 3	Sample 4	Sample 5
Heads	49.93%	49.98%	50.04%	49.98%	50.05%

The variability with 1,000,000 was tiny: The percentages of heads varied only from 49.93% to 50.05%. The focus here was implicitly on the *range* as the measure of variability. But, to be sure, just as the range decreased as we increased the number of tosses (i.e., sample size, N), so did all measures of variability: the interquartile range, sum of squares, variance, and standard deviation.

> *As the sample size increases, the less variability there is in the sample results.*

*   *   *

The focus so far has been on the fact that, as sample size increases, the variability of the results decreases. But, you also should know, regardless of the sample sizes, the *mean* of all the sample results will *always* be close to the expected outcome.

Let's illustrate. Look again at the results for N = 10:

	Sample 1	Sample 2	Sample 3	Sample 4	Sample 5
Heads	80%	40%	40%	60%	70%

As mentioned earlier, there is a lot of variability in our samples when N is so small. But now let's focus on the overall *mean* of all 5 samples: (80% + 40% + 40% + 60% + 70%) / 5 = **58%**

You're probably thinking that 58% is not the expected outcome—50% is. Good. But if we increase the number of samples from a very modest 5 to a larger number of 5,000, we can see how close the overall mean gets to 50%—and 5,000 isn't even close to the type of large number the law of large numbers refers to. A table with 5,000 cells would take up too much space, so the following shows just part of the table (next page):

N = 10

	Sample 1	Sample 2	Sample 3	Sample 4	Sample 500	Sample 1,000	Sample 5,000	Mean of all 5,000 samples
Heads	30%	60%	50%	40%	10%	60%	30%	**49.92%**

What do you expect would happen if we repeated the process, but we increased N from 10 to 100? Let's see:

N = 100

	Sample 1	Sample 2	Sample 3	Sample 4	Sample 500	Sample 1,000	Sample 5,000	Mean of all 5,000 samples
Heads	49%	46%	52%	52%	45%	44%	59%	**49.96%**

Just as expected! The *means of individual samples* were much less variable when N was increased to 100, but in both cases the *overall mean* across all 5,000 samples was very close to the expected 50%.[56] So, N affects the variability across sample means, but not the overall mean of all the samples. Take another look at those last two tables and make sure you see all this.

And remember, these results came from an actual random number generator. They are not convenient numbers being made up to illustrate the point. But see how the law of large numbers came through? It always does.

*   *   *

Now let's convert those tables into frequency graphs: How many times 0% heads came up, how many times 10% heads came up, how many times it came up as 20%, 30%, and so on up to 100%. Creating a picture should help to clarify the points just made. Plus, you will soon see

---

[56] Technically, those percentages for the individual sets are not means; they are the percent of the times heads came up. But we will usually be dealing with means, so we're calling them that for simplicity.

you're always using a distribution in inferential statistics, so it's vital you become comfortable in dealing with them.

First, for the N = 10 samples:

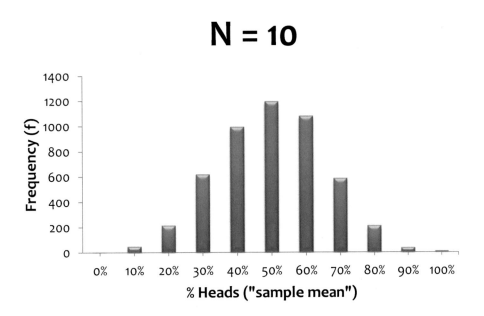

N = 10

Notice the overall average of all 5,000 samples of N = 10 is 50% (OK, 49.92%). Actually, we knew that already from the table above. But also notice in the graph the *variability* in the distribution, in other words the extent to which sample means *varied* from 50%.

As you can see, many samples were 40% or 60% heads, a decent number were 30% or 70% heads, even some 20%s and 80%s. 10% or 90% heads were very rare, and 0% or 100% heads were virtually non-existent.

Now let's look at the frequency graph for the N = 100 samples[57] (next page).

---

[57] Try not to be distracted by the fact that there are more bars in this next graph. That's just because there are more possible outcomes if you flip a coin 100 times (0% heads, 1%, 2%...99%, 100%) than if you flip it only 10 times (0%, 10%, 20%...90%, 100%).

N = 100

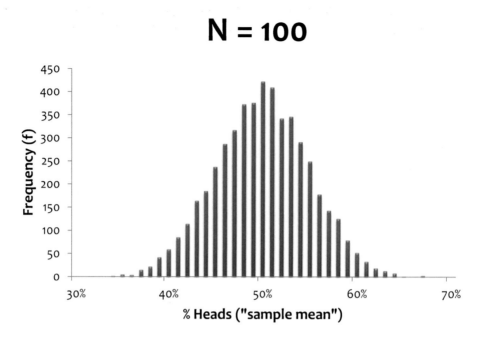

Notice, as with N = 10, the overall average of all the samples of N = 100 is also very close to 50% (49.96%). Also notice in both cases the shape of the distribution is normal. But what's notably different is the *variability* in the distributions.

Specifically, see how much closer the sample means in the N = 100 graph generally are to the overall mean of 50%? Even 40% or 60% heads, which were quite common when N was 10, are rare with an N of 100. And 30% or 70% heads were also not uncommon when N was 10. But when N was increased to 100, barely any of the samples came out less than even 40% or greater than 60% heads. As for samples where heads came up less than 30% or more than 70% of the time—also *none*.

There is nothing wrong with characterizing the differences in variability in this way, but a more direct and objective way is to simply find the *standard deviation* of the distribution. So, given what you've read so far, which distribution should have a smaller standard deviation, one in which the samples are N = 10, or one with samples of N = 100? If you answered N = 100, you are correct. One thing we can count on is that *the larger the sample size, the smaller the standard deviation of the distribution.*

Recognize the shape of the distributions, by the way? If you didn't see it before, here's the distribution of sample means for N = 100 from above, made into a line graph:

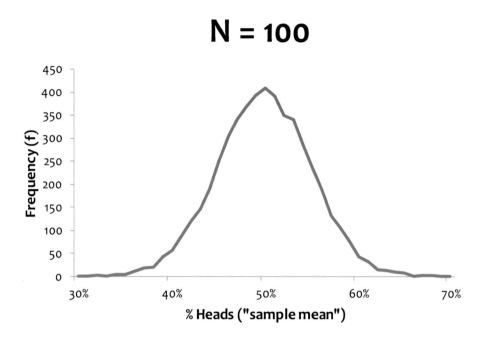

Yep, that's the normal distribution. It's not *perfectly* normal because we graphed only 5,000 samples, which as mentioned earlier is not a large number of the magnitude referred to in *the law of large numbers*. You can imagine, though, if we were able to approximate the normal distribution with just 5,000 samples, then a truly large number (like infinity) would be spot on, including a mean of *exactly* 50%. One more thing about the difference between our distribution above and the ones we actually use in research:

Since the distribution actually consists of an *infinite* number of samples, there is no result that *never* occurs (or has a frequency of zero). So above when we had an N of 100, we never got a sample where heads came up less than 30% of the time (or more than 70% of the time). But that's because we only did 5,000 samples. Had we done an infinite number of samples, every result, from 0% heads to 100% heads, would have occurred. Those results (0% or 100% heads) would not have occurred as often as, say, 10% or 90% heads (which would be quite rare themselves, by the way), but they will happen occasionally.

So, with an infinite number of samples, our distribution would be perfectly normal, where all sample means (even 0% and 100% heads) occur:

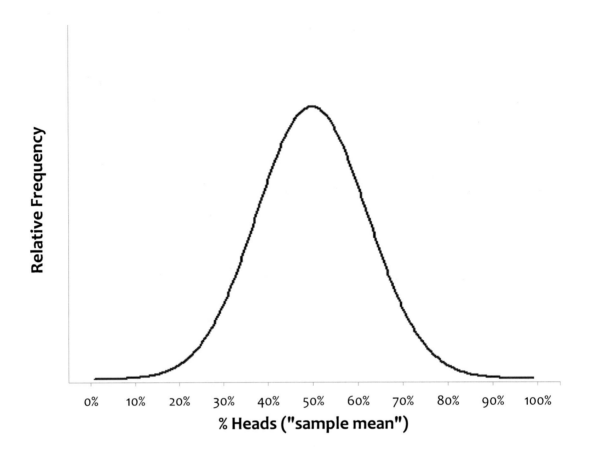

A very important thing to remember is the distributions you're looking at describe what the distribution of results would look like *if the coin is fair*. Put differently, it's what the distribution would look like if there is *no effect*, that is, if *only chance* is at play. For that reason we refer to this distribution as the *Null Distribution.*[58]

> The **Null Distribution** *is what the distribution of results would look like for a given N, over a large number of samples, if there is no effect.*

---

[58] *Null* basically means *nothing*. Here, the *Null* Distribution is what would happen if there was *no* effect—if *nothing* (other than chance) is affecting the outcome. Later you'll see the Null *Hypothesis* states that there is *no* effect.

One final point before moving on to the next chapter: The null distribution is not literally created the way we've done it here where actual data was collected. Remember the computer actually did create, for example, 5,000 samples of N = 10 and N = 100 coin flips. But this was only done in order to explain how things work. In practice, it would never actually happen.

But hopefully you can see that it doesn't *need* to be done. Put simply, we don't have to create a null distribution with actual data because we can trust that the law of large numbers will always hold. That is, we know what would happen *if* we flipped a coin 10 times, recorded how many times it came up heads, and repeated that an infinite number of times: It would look like that earlier graph titled *N = 10*. Since we know that, we don't have to actually create all those samples in order to construct that graph (the null distribution).

So what *do* we actually do? We take *one* sample of N = 50 flips, or whatever sample size we choose, and see where it falls within the null distribution.

You will learn in the next chapter, among other things, how to create the null distribution with just a couple pieces of information. You'll also learn, of course, *why* we do all this, that is, how it's vital to inferential statistics.

Chapter 8
The logic of inferential statistics

In the last chapter, we constructed the null distribution. As you know, the null distribution is the distribution that would result if you repeated your study a very large number of times (e.g., flipped a coin 50 times, recorded the result, and repeated that a large number of times), and nothing determined the outcomes except chance, that is, there was *no effect*. Recall, though, that in the last chapter we created the null distribution with actual data— results from many, many coin flips on a computer.

In research, however, you do not construct the null distribution in this way. Instead, you construct it from just a couple pieces of information. Those pieces of information allow you to know what the null distribution would look like *if you did* construct it from real data. Recall you can get away with this, so to speak, because of the law of large numbers.

Therefore, if we were to test an actual coin to determine if it is fair or not, we would not bother with obtaining all that data from a computer simulation to create the null distribution. Instead, we would simply create the null distribution based on those couple pieces of information we have about the population and/or our sample.

We will do that, but let's move away from coins. Coin flipping was a convenient way to introduce several concepts, but in most research there are more than only two possible outcomes (i.e., heads and tails). For example, if your dependent measure is a typical Likert rating scale, then there are 7 possible outcomes.[59] Or if your dependent measure is reaction time, measured in milliseconds, there are hundreds of possible outcomes.

Therefore, we will now switch to a different example that better resembles a real research situation where there are more than only 2 possible scores, but that is also tangible and simple.

Let's pretend that someone has accused a casino of using fixed dice—a charge they deny— and we have been hired to test the dice. That doesn't sound like research, but it is. Our research question is: *Are the dice fair?* And we are going to take a research-based approach, using inferential statistics to answer it.

The strategy used in answering research questions like this one was laid out in previous chapters. Recall that strategy consisted of two steps:

---

[59] You may know, in a typical Likert scale, subjects can give a rating of 1,2,3,4,5,6, or 7.

Step 1) Determine the probability that your result was due to chance/sampling error.

Step 2) Decide whether that probability is **a)** high enough to conclude your result was indeed just chance or, alternatively, **b)** low enough to conclude your result probably was *not* just chance and must therefore be real.

Step 2 is actually very simple (all it requires is comparing two numbers to each other), and we'll get to that later. Our focus now is on Step 1- *determining the probability that your result is due to chance/sampling error.*

This is where the null distribution is essential. To determine the probability that the result is due to chance/sampling error, we need to create a null distribution so we know what it would look like if only chance/sampling error was at play (that is, if there was no effect).

To create any distribution, you need to know its shape, mean, and standard deviation. The shape and mean are easy here: The shape is *normal* and the mean is 7.[60] However, the standard deviation of the null distribution, called the standard error, σ_M, needs to be calculated. The formula is:

$$\sigma_M = \frac{\sigma}{\sqrt{N}}$$

The standard deviation, σ, of individual dice rolls (i.e., *scores*) is 2.4.[61] As you can see from the formula, the only thing we need now is to decide on N, the number of times we plan to roll the dice. Let's go with N = 50 rolls. That would make the standard deviation of the null distribution, the standard error:

$$\sigma_M = \frac{\sigma}{\sqrt{N}} = \frac{2.4}{\sqrt{50}} = \mathbf{0.34}$$

So, the null distribution for N = 50 dice rolls would:

a) be a **normal** distribution

b) have a **mean** of **7**

c) have a **standard error** of 0.34 (2.4 / √50)

---

[60] The possible rolls of two dice are 2,3,4,5,6,7,8,9,10,11, and 12. So the average of a large number of rolls would be 7. And remember the null distribution is not a distribution of the individual scores (dice rolls in this case). It is a distribution of the *means* of samples of dice rolls. Those will always form a normal distribution, even when the distribution of the individual scores isn't normal.

[61] You are not expected to have figured out this number.

Take a look at the following sketch, noting especially the scaling on the X axis. Do you see where that scaling came from? (Hint: If not, see *b* and *c* above.)

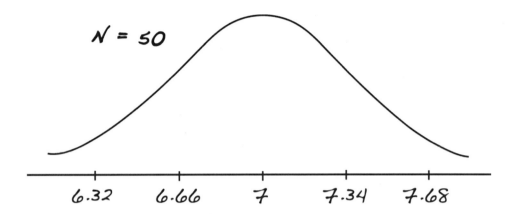

Now that we've established what the null distribution looks like, we can see where our actual result falls within it. Where our sample falls within the null distribution tells us how likely it is our result (our sample mean, in this case) occurred only by chance. The further out to the left or right of the distribution our result falls, the less likely it was due to chance; the closer to the center of the distribution it falls, the more likely our result was due to chance.

> *Where a result falls within the null distribution tells you the probability that the result was due to chance/sampling error. The further from the center of the distribution it falls, the less likely it is that the result was just chance.*

* * *

So, let's get our actual result—in other words, roll the dice 50 times. Remember we're rolling two dice, so each score could be anywhere between 2 (both came up 1) to 12 (both came up 6). Here are the results from our 50 rolls:

12	6	5	5	3	11	4	6	7	10
8	8	10	4	2	8	9	3	12	6
10	3	2	8	11	7	8	11	12	11
11	10	8	4	6	5	3	12	12	11
11	4	11	9	2	11	5	3	4	12

The sample mean (the mean of the above 50 rolls), is 7.52. We will now estimate where 7.52 falls within the null distribution for N = 50. In the sketch that follows you can see that our result of 7.52 is marked about halfway between 7.34 and 7.68.

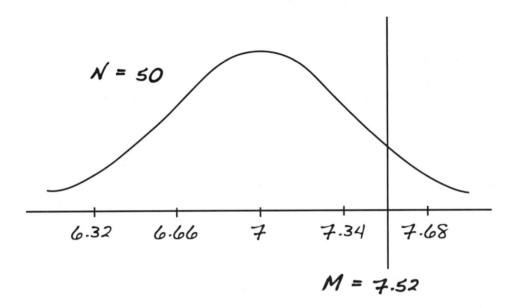

Be careful not to lose sight of what the above sketch is: It is a graph of what it would look like if you rolled the dice 50 times, recorded the mean of those 50 rolls, repeated that process a *large number* of times with dice known to be fair[62] (arranging the results into a frequency distribution), then, finally, rolled your actual dice 50 times and marked where the mean of those 50 rolls fell within the distribution. Again, it was not created by literally rolling dice known to be fair a large number of times. It was created based on three things we know, and can count on because of the law of large numbers—namely, that the null distribution for N = 50 dice rolls:

    a) is a **normal** distribution

    b) has a **mean** of **7**

    c) has a **standard error** of 0.34 (2.4 / √50)

After constructing the null distribution, we evaluate whether the result of our study (a sample mean of 7.52) falls either **a)** *not* way out in a tail[63], indicating the result is not *very*

---

[62] Also recall this is called the *Null* Distribution, meaning what it would look like if there is *no effect* (that is, if only chance is at play / if the dice are fair).

[63] The left and right ends of the normal curve, where the line starts to get close to the x-axis, are called the *tails* of the distribution.

unlikely to have occurred if the dice were fair, and so we should conclude that, indeed, the dice are fair, or **b)** way out in a tail of the distribution, indicating the result is *very unlikely* to occur if the dice were fair, and so we should conclude they are not fair. Take another look at that logic, and recall, as demonstrated in an earlier chapter, it is the same logic you've used in your everyday life, probably without realizing it.

*   *   *

So, what do you think: *Is our result way out in one of the tales of the distribution, and thus very unlikely to have occurred by chance, indicating our dice are fixed?* Probably not. Although 7.52 is not very close to the center of the distribution, it's not quite "way out" in a tail, either. We therefore would conclude the dice in question are fair.

So, if a casino patron alleged the dice used at his table were fixed, and we were given those dice to test (using standard research and statistical protocol), our conclusion would be in favor of the casino: The dice seem fair. Put differently, we must conclude from our result that the only thing at play in determining the dice's behavior is *chance*. We would only have concluded the dice were fixed if our result (M = 7.52) was *very unlikely* to have occurred by chance, that is, way out in the tail of the null distribution, and so something *other than chance* was very likely at play.

If you're asking where the cutoff is between what you'd call *very unlikely* and what you would not call *very unlikely* (what constitutes *way out* in a tail), then you're asking a great question. Actually, determining such a cutoff—a precise borderline between what we consider very unlikely and what we don't—is essential. Actually, that's the Step 2 you've read about, and will learn about in more detail soon. For now, the goal is for you to understand the logic behind inferential statistics.

*   *   *

Toward that goal, let's consider how things would be different if we got the same result (M = 7.52), but only had a sample size of 10. Well, the null distribution would still be normal, and would still have mean of 7—after all, 7 is still the expected result regardless of how many times we roll the dice.[64] However, the standard error (the standard deviation of the null distribution) *would* be affected. Look again at the formula for standard error, σ_M:

$$\sigma_M = \frac{\sigma}{\sqrt{N}} = \frac{2.4}{\sqrt{10}} = 0.76$$

---

[64] Remember the term *expected* here means the result predicted by the rules of probability, that is, what you'd *expect* if there is no effect (if only chance determines the outcome).

The standard error was not only affected when we went from N = 50 to N = 10 rolls, it was affected in a predictable way. Specifically, by decreasing N, standard error increased. This is a mathematical certainty, and you should be able to understand it two different ways.

For one, you can simply see that if you plug a smaller number into the denominator of the standard error formula (where N goes), a larger result will occur: 2.4 divided by $\sqrt{10}$ gives you a larger number than 2.4 divided by $\sqrt{50}$.

More importantly, however, is a conceptual understanding. Think about it like this: If you were to do samples of only 10 dice rolls, the means of those samples would fluctuate more than if you did samples of 50 dice rolls. In other words, samples of only 10 would come out, on average, further from M = 7 than samples of 50, which would come out closer to 7, on average[65]. This would result in a larger standard deviation of the distribution (called standard error) created by N = 10 rolls than by N = 50 rolls.

> Fill in the blanks: If you did a large number of N = 10,000 rolls, you know the means would tend to come out _____ (*very close* or *very far*) to the expected M = 7, resulting in a _____ (*very large* or *very small*) standard error.[66]

*   *   *

N is 10 in our current example, so the null distribution would have a standard deviation of 0.76 (that is, standard error = 0.76). With our result marked, things would look like the following:

---

[65] You saw this previously with coin flips.
[66] very close; very small

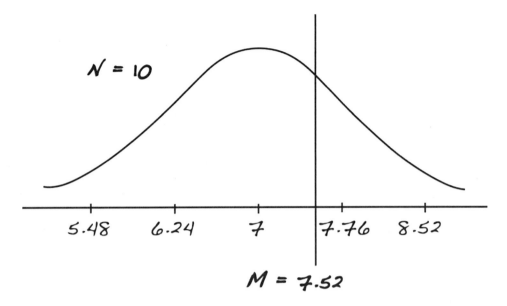

$N = 10$

5.48   6.24   7   7.76   8.52

$M = 7.52$

Notice our sample mean of 7.52 is closer to the center of the distribution—more likely to occur by chance—when we roll the dice only 10 times relative to when we roll them 50 times (just compare the last two figures). This is because, when we only roll 10 times, we expect more variation than when we roll 50 times[67]. When N was 50, standard error was 2.4 / $\sqrt{50}$ = **0.34**. When N was 10, standard error was larger: 2.4 / $\sqrt{10}$ = **0.76**.

What would happen if we did 500 rolls (increased N to 500): Would the standard error increase, putting M = 7.52 closer to the center, or would standard error decrease, putting M = 7.52 further out into a tail?

Fill in the blanks: If we increased N to 500, the standard error would _____, putting M = 7.52 _____ into the tail[68].

Let's sketch it. Again, the null distribution would be normal, and would still have a mean of 7. As for the standard error (next page):

---

[67] Recall from the last chapter, the smaller the number of coin flips, the more variation there was from the expected 50% heads result. The variation was due, of course, to sampling error.

[68] decrease; further. But please note this is a hypothetical question--if we actually increased N to 500, there's no reason to think we'd still get a mean 7.52 like we did when N was 50. As a matter of fact, *if* the dice were indeed fair, increasing the number of times we roll them (increasing N) would make our mean get closer to 7.

$$\sigma_M = \frac{\sigma}{\sqrt{N}} = \frac{2.4}{\sqrt{500}} = 0.11$$

We now label the distribution accordingly (mean of 7, standard error of 0.11), and mark where our result falls:

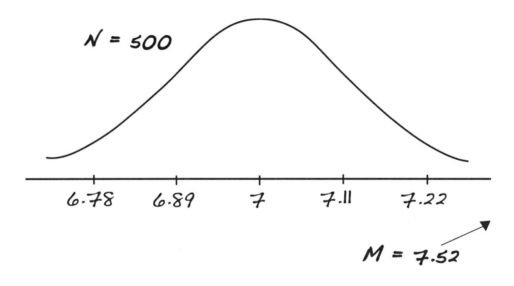

* * *

It is plain to see rolling our dice and coming up with M = 7.52 means different things depending on how many times we roll them (that is, it depends on N). Specifically, the larger N, the more unlikely that specific result is. A mean of 7.52 when you roll the dice 10 times is relatively likely to occur by chance, but that same mean of 7.52 when you roll the dice 500 times is much less likely to occur by chance. Again, that is because, when you roll 500 times, you expect less sampling error, so your result should be closer to the expected 7. And that's just what *will* happen if the dice are fair.

Now, is M = 7.52 *so* unlikely that we would conclude the dice were fixed had we got that result? Answering such a question requires a statistical test, which will of course rely heavily on N. But either way, remember for now we're not worrying about the exact point at which we call something *very unlikely*.

For now, it's more important that you understand the basic strategy in inferential statistics: Create a null distribution so we know what it would look like if there was no effect (that is, if only chance was responsible for the results), then see where our result falls within that distribution so we can determine the probability that our result was due to chance.[69]

The next step is to decide what to make of such a probability, that is, Step 2:

> Step 1) Determine the probability that your result was due to chance/sampling error.

> **Step 2)** Decide whether that probability is **a)** high enough to conclude your result was indeed just chance or, alternatively, **b)** low enough to conclude your result probably was *not* just chance and must therefore be real.

In the next chapter, with that cleared up, you will know everything you need to know in order to actually use inferential statistics in a research setting.

---

[69] which we can do with absolute confidence because of the law of large numbers

Questions and problems.

1) Sketch the null distribution if we decided to do 2,000 rolls of the dice ($\mu = 7$, $\sigma = 2.4$). Label where a sample mean of 6.9 would fall.

2) Sketch the null distribution if we decided to do 3,000 rolls of the dice ($\mu = 7$, $\sigma = 2.4$). Label where a sample mean of 6.9 would fall.

3) Which of the previous two results (sample means) is less likey to occur, the result in #1 or the result in #2, and why?

4) Sketch the null distribution if we decided to do 1,000 rolls of the dice. Label where a sample mean of 7.1 would fall.

5) Sketch the null distribution if we decided to do 1,000 rolls of the dice. Label where a sample mean of 7.2 would fall.

6) Consider two studies, A and B, in which the experimenter drew samples from the same population. Therefore, the population mean is the same across the two studies, as is the standard deviation. Let's say the population mean, μ, is 21. Given the information below, indicate which result is less likely to occur by chance:

Study A: M = 18, N = 20

Study B: M = 16, N = 20

7) Consider studies A and B again (where the population mean (21) and standard deviation are still the same across the studies). Given the information below, indicate which result is less likely to occur by chance:

Study A: M = 18, N = 30

Study B: M = 18, N = 20

8) Again, consider studies A and B. In both, the population mean and standard deviation are the same, *as are the sample means*. If Study A has fewer subjects than Study B, which result is less likely to occur?

9) One more: The population mean and standard deviation are the same across the two studies, *as are the sample sizes*. If Study A's mean is closer to the population mean, which of the two results is less likely to occur?

Solutions to questions and problems.

1)

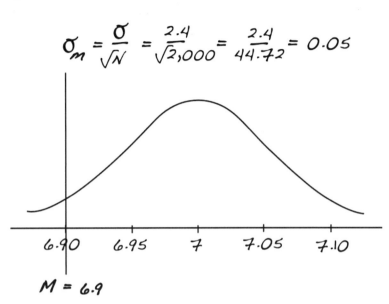

$$\sigma_m = \frac{\sigma}{\sqrt{N}} = \frac{2.4}{\sqrt{2,000}} = \frac{2.4}{44.72} = 0.05$$

| 6.90 | 6.95 | 7 | 7.05 | 7.10 |

M = 6.9

2)

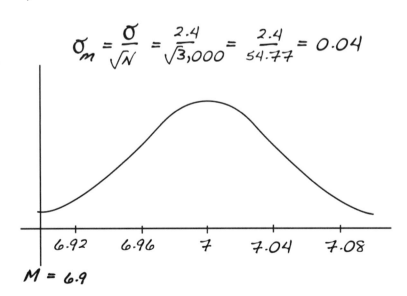

$$\sigma_m = \frac{\sigma}{\sqrt{N}} = \frac{2.4}{\sqrt{3,000}} = \frac{2.4}{54.77} = 0.04$$

| 6.92 | 6.96 | 7 | 7.04 | 7.08 |

M = 6.9

3) The result from #2 is less likely to occur. The reason can be explained several ways. For one, it's further out in the tail of the null distribution than the result from #1, meaning it is less likely to have occurred by chance. You could also have known #2 was less likely without reference to a sketch because N was larger, making standard error smaller, making a given result like M = 6.9 further from the expected mean of 7 (further from center of null distribution = less likely to occur by chance). You could even focus on the fact that, since N was larger in #2, you'd expect the mean to be closer to 7 than in #1. But it wasn't, so it's less likely to occur.

4)

$$\sigma_m = \frac{\sigma}{\sqrt{N}} = \frac{2.4}{\sqrt{1,000}} = \frac{2.4}{31.62} = 0.08$$

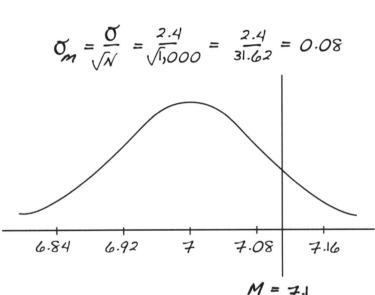

M = 7.1

5)

$$\sigma_m = \frac{\sigma}{\sqrt{N}} = \frac{2.4}{\sqrt{1,000}} = \frac{2.4}{31.62} = 0.08$$

6.84   6.92   7   7.08   7.16

M = 7.2

6) Study B's result is less likely to have occurred by chance. Note you do not need to know the population standard deviation, σ, to answer this question. Think about it: Even though you can't calculate standard error (since you don't know σ), you *do* know, since the samples are the same size and came from the same population, that the standard error would be the same in both cases. Thus, with that equal, whichever sample mean is further from the population mean is less likely to occur. *(If you'd like, you can work it all out with sketches and formulas if you just pick a standard deviation, σ, at random... how about 5?)*

7) Study A's result is less likely to have occurred by chance. This time, even though you again cannot calculate the standard error, you do know, since Study A has a larger sample size, N, the standard error will be smaller in that study. Again, you can sketch it if you'd like. (You can make up your own standard deviation this time.)

8) Study B's result is less likely to have occurred by chance.

9) Study B's result is less likely to have occurred by chance.

Chapter 9
Using inferential statistics

In the last chapter, you learned how to determine where within the null distribution a study's result fell. You also learned the reason for doing so, namely so you could ultimately know the probability the result was due to chance. In this chapter, we will get to that last part, and finish discussing the process of deciding whether or not a study's result is real. You will learn how to perform an inferential statistical test using a statistic you are familiar with: the z score.

Let's jump right back to the dice we were testing earlier. You've already learned to figure out where the result from our sample (M = 7.52) falls within the null distribution. Now, you will learn to figure out the exact probability that result was due to chance (based of course on where it falls within the null distribution), so you can decide whether the result was simply due to sampling error, or was instead real.

To recap, you already know that, to construct the null distribution, you need three pieces of information:

1. Its **shape**. No problem—we always assume the null distribution is **normal**.
2. Its **mean**. The mean of the null distribution is the result you expect if nothing is at play except chance, in this case meaning the dice are fair. As discussed, this expected result is a mean of **7**.
3. Its **standard error**. Standard error, σ_M, is the standard deviation, which is **2.4**, divided by the square root of N, which is **50**:

$$\sigma_M = \frac{\sigma}{\sqrt{N}} = \frac{2.4}{\sqrt{50}} = \frac{2.4}{7.07} = 0.34$$

After constructing the null distribution with that information, we indicate where our result fell (see next page). You'll recall our result was **M = 7.52** (the average of our 50 rolls was 7.52).

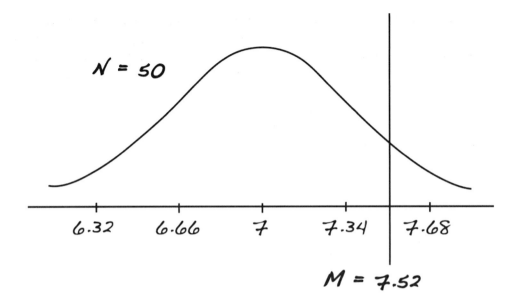

$N = 50$

6.32   6.66   7   7.34   7.68

$M = 7.52$

The sketch tells us the same thing it did previously. It gives us a feel for how far out into a tail our result fell, and thus also a feel for how likely it is the result occurred by chance—the further out into a tail, the less likely it is that the result occurred by chance (and thus the more likely it is that the result is real/significant).

Now is the new part, where we will be much more precise about *how* likely. In fact, we will find an exact probability, using the familiar z score. That's right: If you know the z score for your result, you can use it to figure out the probability of getting that result by chance. Let's do that with the result from our dice experiment.

The formula to find a z score for a sample mean is:

$$Z = \frac{M - \mu}{\sigma_M}$$

Recall from above the standard error, σ_M, is equal to the standard deviation, σ, divided by the square root of N:

$$\sigma_M = \frac{\sigma}{\sqrt{N}}$$

First we find σ_M, then we plug that into the z score formula (which in this case we already found when we constructed our sketch: σ_M = 2.4 / √50 = 2.4/7.07 = **0.34**).

Our sample mean, M, was 7.52. Looking at the formula, you can see that just leaves μ, the mean of the null distribution, to be filled in. As discussed previously, the mean of the null distribution represents the result you'd expect to find if there is no effect. In this case, *no effect* means nothing (other than chance, of course) influenced the outcome of the dice rolls. μ is thus 7.

We can now calculate the z score for our sample. Look at each part of the equation below, noting where each value came from:

$$Z = \frac{M - \mu}{\sigma_M} = \frac{7.52 - 7}{0.34} = +1.53$$

* * *

Now that we know the z score for our sample is +1.53, we can use a statistical table, the z table, to find the probability of getting that result by chance. Let's do that now. A full z table is in the back of the book (Table 1), but the piece of it we need for the current problem is on the next page.

The numbers on the outside of the table, in bold, are z scores. The numbers inside are probabilities. Again, what we're trying to do here is determine the probability our result, which we've converted to a z score, was just chance. In this case, the z score for our sample is +1.53, so we need to find the probability associated with a z score of 1.53 (don't worry about the sign (+ or -) when using the z table, or any inferential statistical table we will use).

To look up the probability, always begin by putting your z score in the X.XX format. For example, if your z score is 1, write it as 1.00. If it's 2.1, write it as 2.10, if it's .5, write it as 0.50, and so on. Then, look at the first two digits. The first two digits of 1.53 can be found along the leftmost column of the table. That tells you the row you need. Next, look at the last digit: 1.53, and find it along the top row. That tells you the column you need.

Then all you need to do is find the cell where your row and column intersect. The number you find in that cell is, again, *the probability your result occurred by chance.* Remember, it doesn't matter whether the z score is positive or negative since the normal distribution is symmetrical: The left half (negative z scores) is a mirror image of the right half (positive z scores).

z	0	0.01	0.02	0.03	0.04	0.05	0.06	0.07	0.08	0.09
0.0	0.5000	0.4960	0.4920	0.4880	0.4840	0.4801	0.4761	0.4721	0.4681	0.4641
0.1	0.4602	0.4562	0.4522	0.4483	0.4443	0.4404	0.4364	0.4325	0.4286	0.4247
0.2	0.4207	0.4168	0.4129	0.4090	0.4052	0.4013	0.3974	0.3936	0.3897	0.3859
0.3	0.3821	0.3783	0.3745	0.3707	0.3669	0.3632	0.3594	0.3557	0.3520	0.3483
0.4	0.3446	0.3409	0.3372	0.3336	0.3300	0.3264	0.3228	0.3192	0.3156	0.3121
0.5	0.3085	0.3050	0.3015	0.2981	0.2946	0.2912	0.2877	0.2843	0.2810	0.2776
1.4	0.0808	0.0793	0.0778	0.0764	0.0749	0.0735	0.0721	0.0708	0.0694	0.0681
1.5	0.0668	0.0655	0.0643	0.0630	0.0618	0.0606	0.0594	0.0582	0.0571	0.0559
1.6	0.0548	0.0537	0.0526	0.0516	0.0505	0.0495	0.0485	0.0475	0.0465	0.0455
1.7	0.0446	0.0436	0.0427	0.0418	0.0409	0.0401	0.0392	0.0384	0.0375	0.0367

Here, that probability is 0.0630, meaning there is about a 6.30% probability our result occurred by chance.[70] You'll see next why, even though that seems like a pretty small number, we would conclude from it that our result (a sample mean of 7.52 with N = 50, which corresponds to a z score of 1.53), was indeed just due to chance—the 0.52 difference we found (7.52 vs. the expected 7) is likely to have been due to sampling error.[71]

We can now make an important addition to our sketch (in red):

---

[70] The table shows probabilities in the form of proportions. To convert those to a percentage (not necessary, but sometimes helpful), just multiply by 100. In the current example, 0.0630 x 100 = 6.30%.
[71] Remember, sampling error is the natural differences that you expect to exist whenever you take samples. Although the larger the sample, the less sampling error is expected, there is always *some* amount of sampling error. In this case, by deciding our result was due to chance, we're saying that the difference we found is likely within the range of sampling error we expect.

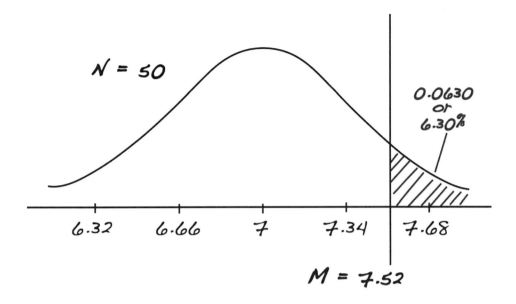

Now what? At what point do you go from concluding your result was due to chance, as we just did, to concluding your result was *not* just chance, and so it must be real? How far out into a tail does your result have to fall before you should conclude the result is real? Put differently, how low does that probability have to be?

Turns out there is no absolute rule, but there is a convention to choose either 0.05 (5%) or 0.01 (1%) as your criterion. Those are called *levels of significance*, or *alpha* (α) levels, and in actual research you choose one of them before you collect data.

> The **level of significance**, also called the **alpha level (α)**, conventionally 0.05 (5%) or 0.01 (1%), is chosen before data is collected. It forms the basis for what the researcher considers very unlikely to be chance.

You also choose whether you're looking for the result to fall in a particular tail of the null distribution (either the upper tail or the lower tail, called a *directional test*), or not specifying which tail you expect the result to fall in (a *non-directional test*).

> In a **directional**, or **one-tailed** test, the researcher is looking for the result to fall in a specific tail (upper or lower) of the null distribution. In a **non-directional**, or **two-tailed** test, the researcher is looking for the result to fall in either of the two tails of the null distribution.

This leaves four possible criteria to use for your decision.

1) α 0.05, one-tailed/directional test
2) α 0.05, two-tailed/non-directional test
3) α 0.01, one-tailed/directional test
4) α 0.01, two-tailed/non-directional test

Visually, those 4 options are:

1) alpha 0.05, one-tailed/directional test

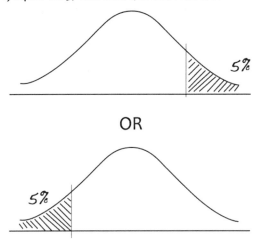

2) alpha 0.05, two-tailed/non-directional test

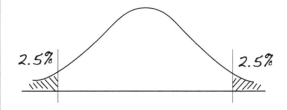

3) alpha 0.01, one-tailed/directional test

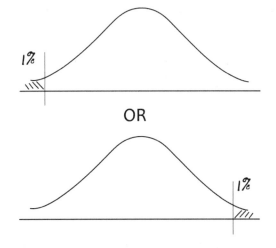

4) alpha 0.01, two-tailed/non-directional test

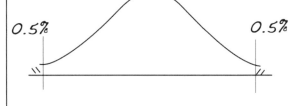

If your result falls in the shaded region, you define it as *very unlikely* to have occurred by chance (less than 0.05 or 0.01) and therefore you have an effect. If it does not fall in the shaded region, you define it as *likely* to have occurred by chance (greater than 0.05 or 0.01) and therefore you *do not* have an effect.

*   *   *

We will now look at another example, and you will apply what you've learned to decide whether a new pair dice are fixed.

Since we have no reason to suspect which direction the dice will be fixed, that is, whether they are biased toward lower than expected outcomes or higher than expected outcomes, we should do a non-directional (two-tailed) test. As for which alpha level to choose, 0.05 or 0.01, we just have to pick one... let's go with 0.05.[72] An alpha 0.05, non-directional test means our result will have to fall in an extreme 2.5% of the distribution for us to conclude the dice are fixed (see sketch #2 above to see where 2.5 % came from).

Here are the results:

9	11	4	12	5	9	8	10	8	12
5	4	7	7	8	8	4	4	10	9
8	11	6	9	9	11	7	8	9	6
9	5	9	12	9	7	9	5	10	4
7	5	11	10	6	5	4	12	5	10

The mean of the scores above is M = 7.84 (and N = 50). And we know from before that σ = 2.4. μ is still 7 since that is still what you'd expect from fair dice (i.e., that's the mean of the null distribution). We also know from earlier the standard error for N = 50 and σ = 2.4 is: σ_M = 2.4 / $\sqrt{50}$ = 2.4/7.07 = **0.34.**

Since we know the shape (normal), the mean (7) and the standard error (0.34) we can sketch the distribution and see where our sample mean of 7.84 falls within it (next page).

---

[72] In a later chapter, you'll learn the ramifications of the choice you make about which alpha level you choose. For now, we'll just pick one more or less randomly.

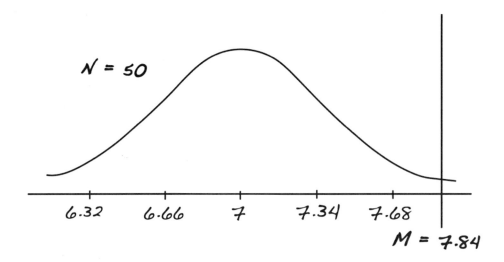

It's looking from the sketch like we will be concluding our result is *very unlikely* to have occurred just due to chance and therefore the dice must be fixed. But, we must calculate a z score and look up the exact probability to be sure that is the case. If you're going to be looking up probabilities you'll need a z score.

$$Z = \frac{M - \mu}{\sigma_M} = \frac{7.84 - 7}{0.34} = \mathbf{2.47}$$

Now, we need to see if that result ($z = +2.47$)[73] *meets our criteria*, that is, falls in the shaded region (very unlikely to have occurred by chance—see next sketch), or *does not meet our criteria*, that is, does *not* fall in the shaded region (likely to have occurred by chance). To do that, we need to find the probability of getting that z score, and see if it's less than 0.025. That requires the z table:

---

[73] Since a z score can be either positive (result is above the mean of the null distribution) or negative (below the mean), it is conventional to indicate this with a "+" or "-" in front of the z score.

z	0	0.01	0.02	0.03	0.04	0.05	0.06	0.07	0.08	0.09
0.0	0.5000	0.4960	0.4920	0.4880	0.4840	0.4801	0.4761	0.4721	0.4681	0.4641
0.1	0.4602	0.4562	0.4522	0.4483	0.4443	0.4404	0.4364	0.4325	0.4286	0.4247
0.2	0.4207	0.4168	0.4129	0.4090	0.4052	0.4013	0.3974	0.3936	0.3897	0.3859
0.3	0.3821	0.3783	0.3745	0.3707	0.3669	0.3632	0.3594	0.3557	0.3520	0.3483
0.4	0.3446	0.3409	0.3372	0.3336	0.3300	0.3264	0.3228	0.3192	0.3156	0.3121
2.3	0.0107	0.0104	0.0102	0.0099	0.0096	0.0094	0.0091	0.0089	0.0087	0.0084
2.4	0.0082	0.0080	0.0078	0.0075	0.0073	0.0071	0.0069	0.0068	0.0066	0.0064
2.5	0.0062	0.0060	0.0059	0.0057	0.0055	0.0054	0.0052	0.0051	0.0049	0.0048
2.6	0.0047	0.0045	0.0044	0.0043	0.0041	0.0040	0.0039	0.0038	0.0037	0.0036

As you can see, the probability of a z score of +2.47 is 0.0068. By our previously decided-upon criteria, that is defined as *very unlikely to have occurred by chance* because 0.0068(0.68%) is less than 0.025 (2.5%). Looking at a sketch should help you see:[74]

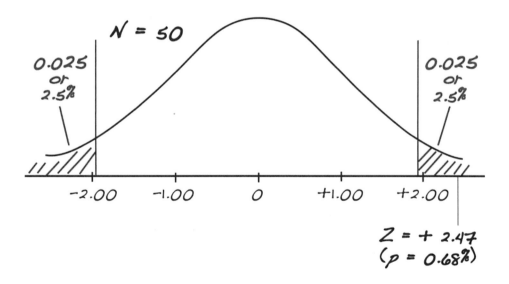

---

[74]Recall that probabilites get smaller and smaller as you go out into the tails (away from the center). You can see from the z table that a z score of 0.00—right in the center of the distribution—corresponds to 0.5000 (50%), and as you look at larger and larger z scores—move away from the center of the distribution—the probabilities get smaller and smaller. So, 0.68% is past our boundary line found at 2.5%.

So, in this current example, we would conclude the dice are fixed.[75] That's it. Don't overthink what goes into that decision. Draw the null distribution, marking and shading the tail (or tails), as shown. Then look up the probability of your result on the z-table, and mark where it falls. If it falls in the shaded region, you have an effect; if not, you don't. In this case, our result was in the shaded region, so we have an effect, that is, our dice are fixed. And don't worry about *exactly* where the result falls; what matters is simply whether or not it's past our boundary line.

Using the same logic and procedure we just used, let's now ask another question: Does darkening with a black magic marker all the dots on the "six" sides of a pair of dice (which would be invisible to the naked eye and would be relatively easy to do without anyone noticing) cause that pair of dice to produce smaller outcomes? In other words, would marked dice produce an average roll significantly less than fair dice (i.e., less than 7)?[76]

Let's do it—with 100 rolls this time (N = 100), and using a level of signficance (α) of 0.01. The rolls themselves were done for you already (though feel free to do it yourself and see what happens). The mean of the 100 rolls was **7.23**.

First, let's find standard error (σ_M):

$$\sigma_M = \frac{\sigma}{\sqrt{N}} = \frac{2.4}{\sqrt{100}} = \frac{2.4}{10} = \mathbf{0.24}$$

Now we can find the z score for our result (M = 7.23).

$$Z = \frac{M - \mu}{\sigma_M} = \frac{7.23 - 7}{0.24} = \mathbf{0.96}$$

We see from the z table that the probability that our result (z = +0.96) occurred by chance is 0.1685 (16.85%):

---

[75] And, sure enough, the dice used to get those results *were* fixed so that 2 and 3 could not come up. Also, in the main example from the last chapter (where the average of the 50 rolls was 7.52), the dice were indeed fair. How about that!

[76] If you're curious, the logic here is that coloring in the side of a die that has 6 dots would make that side slightly heavier and hence, possibly, slightly more likely to land down (and if the 6 side lands down, the 1 side would land up since 6 and 1 are on opposite sides).

z	0	0.01	0.02	0.03	0.04	0.05	0.06	0.07	0.08	0.09
0.0	0.5000	0.4960	0.4920	0.4880	0.4840	0.4801	0.4761	0.4721	0.4681	0.4641
0.1	0.4602	0.4562	0.4522	0.4483	0.4443	0.4404	0.4364	0.4325	0.4286	0.4247
0.2	0.4207	0.4168	0.4129	0.4090	0.4052	0.4013	0.3974	0.3936	0.3897	0.3859
0.9	0.1841	0.1814	0.1788	0.1762	0.1736	0.1711	0.1685	0.1660	0.1635	0.1611
1.0	0.1587	0.1562	0.1539	0.1515	0.1492	0.1469	0.1446	0.1423	0.1401	0.1379

When sketching the null distribution this time, let's put everything we need right in it from the start: the labels on the x-axis (z-scores), the shaded region representing our level of signficance of 0.01, the result from our 100 rolls (converted to a z-score), and the probability of that result occurring by chance. Notice there is only one shaded region, and it's in the right/positive end of the distribution. That's because we *specified* we were looking to see if altering the dice would produce an *increase* in the average performance of the dice. Remember, this is called a *directional* test.

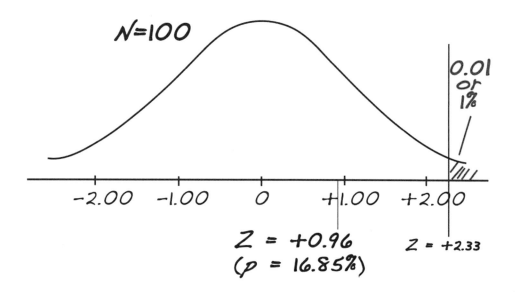

Notice the z score at which the shaded region begins (at the upper 1% of the distribution) is also marked. That little piece of information can actually be found by using the z table "backwards": You find the proportion/probability in your tail—well, as close as possible without going over, which happens to be 0.0099 in this case—then you see which z score that correponds to (see below).

z	0	0.01	0.02	0.03	0.04	0.05	0.06	0.07	0.08	0.09
0.0	0.5000	0.4960	0.4920	0.4880	0.4840	0.4801	0.4761	0.4721	0.4681	0.4641
0.1	0.4602	0.4562	0.4522	0.4483	0.4443	0.4404	0.4364	0.4325	0.4286	0.4247
0.2	0.4207	0.4168	0.4129	0.4090	0.4052	0.4013	0.3974	0.3936	0.3897	0.3859
2.3	0.0107	0.0104	0.0102	0.0099	0.0096	0.0094	0.0091	0.0089	0.0087	0.0084
2.4	0.0082	0.0080	0.0078	0.0075	0.0073	0.0071	0.0069	0.0068	0.0066	0.0064

We'd call 2.33 our *critical* z score. As an exercise, use the z table to find the critical z scores for the other 3 possibilities outlined earlier (α 0.05 one-tailed, α 0.05 two-tailed, and α 0.01 two-tailed), and compare it to the table below.

	Directional (one-tailed)	Non-directional (two-tailed)
α 0.05	1.65	1.96
α 0.01	2.33	2.58

By the way, the tables used for the other inferential statistics you'll be learning about are set up more like this one, where you're looking up a critical statistic to tell you whether the probability of your result occurring by chance is greater than alpha--not significant--or less than alpha—significant—as opposed to looking up an exact probability like you do with the z table. As you will see, all you need to do is compare the critical statistic you find on the table to the statistic you calculated based on the results you obtained (called the *obtained statistic*) to determine if you have a significant effect. That probably sound like quite a lot, but don't worry, you will be taken though all of it step-by-step.

In any case, looking at our last sketch, should we decide that marking dice in the manner described produces larger outcomes?

The answer is *no*, we shouldn't. The probability that our result occurred due to chance (i.e., not due to us marking up the dice but just due to sampling error) was 0.1685 (16.85%). That is higher than our alpha level of 0.01 (1%), and notice not past that critical boundary. We can also see all of this by observing that our result, $z = +0.96$, was not past that critical boundary of $z = +2.33$.[77]

In the next chapter, you will learn how to use a more versatile statistic, called the *t* test. You will also learn the more formal procedure for using inferential statistics, called *hypothesis testing*. That sounds like a lot for one chapter, but you have already learned much, if not most, of what you need in order to achieve those two goals.

---

[77] You may be wondering, if all we need to do is compare the obtained statistic to the critical statistic to determine if we have a signficant effect, why we bothered with all that probability stuff throughout this chapter. The answer is this: If we didn't, you would still be able to make the correct decision (because you can compare the obtained and critical statistic to each other quite easily), but you wouldn't understand what that comparison really means. By learning it the long way first, you see what's really happening.

Problems.

1) Will people bid more money for a product in an online auction if free shipping is offered? To test this, you get some information on a very common item sold in an online auction. The average opening bid on this product is $2.34 ($\sigma$ = $0.40). You go in and add "FREE SHIPPING!" to the item's description and record the opening bid on the next 16 sales of the item, and find the average opening bid in your sample is $2.55. Using a level of significance of 0.01, determine if adding "FREE SHIPPING!" increased the opening bid. (Notice a direction is specified: *Will people bid* more money ..., so you should do a one-tailed/directional test).

2) To test this same question again, you get some information on another very common item sold in an online auction. The average opening bid on this product is $52.95 ($\sigma$ = $1.84). You go in and add "FREE SHIPPING!" to the item's description and record the opening bid on the next 36 sales of the item, and find the average opening bid in your sample is $53.78. Using a level of significance of 0.01, determine if adding "FREE SHIPPING!" increased the opening bid.

3) The average score on a standardized test of happiness, worldwide, is 45 (σ = 10). You want to know if the happiness level of the citizens of a certain town differs from the average. You collect a sample of 25 citizens from this town, and give them the happiness test. Their average was 41. Using α 0.05, determine whether citizens in this town have a different happiness level than average. (Notice a direction is not specified.)

4) You repeat the last study, but with a different standardized test of happiness, which has a population mean of 86 (σ = 13). You again want to know if the happiness level of the citizens of that certain town differs from the average. You collect a sample of 9 citizens from this town, and give them the happiness test. Their average was 90. Using α 0.01, determine whether citizens in this town have a different happiness level than average.

Solutions to problems.

1) (sketch optional)

$\sigma_M = \sigma/\sqrt{N}$ = 0.40/$\sqrt{16}$ = 0.40/4 = 0.1

$z = (M - \mu)/\sigma_M$ = (2.55-2.34)/0.1 = 0.21/0.1 = +2.10

From table: $p(z = +2.10) = 0.0179$

0.0179 is *greater than* the alpha level specified of 0.01. Therefore, you should conclude the offer of free shipping does *not* increase the opening bid of a product in an online auction. The probability the result you got was just chance was not *very low*. 0.0179 (1.79%) may seem like a low probability, but, crucially, it is higher than the criterion of 1%.

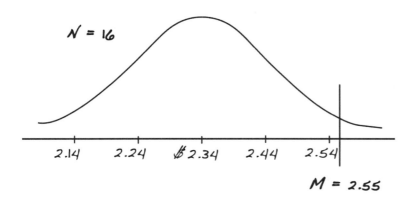

2) (sketch optional)

$\sigma_M = \sigma/\sqrt{N}$ = 1.84/$\sqrt{36}$ = 1.84/6 = 0.31

$z = (M - \mu)/\sigma_M$ = (53.78-52.95)/0.31 = 0.83/0.31 = +2.68

From table: $p(z = +2.68) = 0.0037$

0.0037 is less than the alpha level specified of 0.01. Therefore, you should conclude the offer of free shipping *does* increase the opening bid of a product in an online auction. The probability the result you got was just chance was *very low* (meaning the result was *very unlikely*).

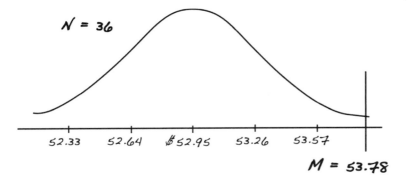

N = 36

52.33   52.64   52.95   53.26   53.57

M = 53.78

3) (sketch optional)

$\sigma_M = \sigma/\sqrt{N} = 10/\sqrt{25} = 10/5 = 2$

$z = (M - \mu)/\sigma_M = (41-45)/2 = -4/2 = -2.00$

From table: $p(z = -2.00) = 0.0228$

Remember, if you are doing a two-tailed test, you must split alpha (0.05/5% in this case) in half, because you're looking to see if the result falls in either of the two tails (that is, you're not specifying a direction).

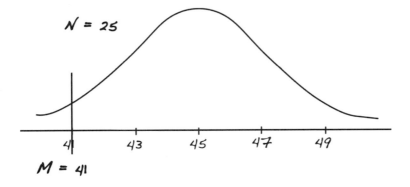

N = 25

41   43   45   47   49

M = 41

0.0028 (0.28%) is less than the alpha level specified of 0.025 (2.5%). Therefore, you should conclude citizens in that town are indeed less happy than average.

4) (sketch optional)

$\sigma_M = \sigma/\sqrt{N} = 13/\sqrt{9} = 13/3 = 4.33$

$z = (M - \mu)/\sigma_M = (90-86)/4.33 = 4/4.33 = +0.92$

From table: $p(z = +0.92) = 0.1788$

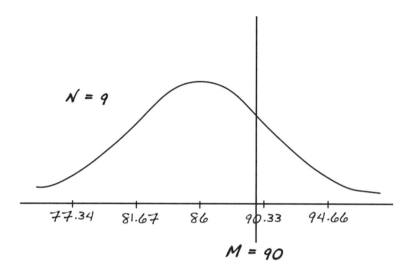

0.1788 (17.88%) is greater than the alpha level specified of 0.005 (0.5%, which is 1% cut in half since you're looking in both tails). Therefore, you should conclude citizens in that town do not differ from the average.

Chapter 10
Introduction to the *t* statistic

In this chapter, you will learn the formal process of testing a research hypothesis. You will also learn a new statistic, which you'll use in this hypothesis test. Fortunately, you've already learned most of what you need in order to accomplish these goals.

Although you learned in the last chapter how to use *z* as an inferential statistic, its use is very limited and therefore researchers in Psychology rarely use it that way. Instead, the first inferential statistic to be discussed in this portion of the book will be the *t* statistic, which is more flexible. To appreciate its flexibility, let's reflect on how inflexible the *z* statistic is.

Recall you computed *z* so you could find the probability of obtaining your result (sample mean) by chance. With this information, you could then make a decision about whether the result (the sample mean—but let's actually start thinking of the result as the *difference* between your sample mean and the population mean) was likely to be real. Also recall to do all that the population standard deviation and N also needed to be considered because, to find standard error, you need to divide the population standard deviation, σ, by the square root of N.

That was a lot, so here is a summary of the information you needed when dealing with a *z* score:

- The population mean
- The sample mean
- The population standard deviation
- The sample size

Remember, you need *all* that information in order to calculate the *z* score. If just one piece of that is missing, finding the *z* score is impossible. But what if you *don't* know it all?

To be sure, you'll *always* know information about your sample: its mean (M), how many participants are in it (N), and so on. But that is not always the case when it comes to the information about the *population*. Imagine, for example, rather than using an established test such as an IQ test or the SAT, or any other variable where the population information is known such as age or height (or dice rolls), you instead make up your *own* test. Or imagine we made up our own task for participants to perform, and timed them on how long it took them to complete it. Or say we designed our *own* IQ test. For any of these examples, ask yourself: *Who would I contact to get the population mean and standard deviation so I could find the z score for my sample?* The answer is simple: No one!

* * *

Thus, the z score does not work for every research situation. In fact, as mentioned before, in actual research it is quite common to not know some, or even *any*, of the population information. This all makes the z score often unusable.

That is where the t statistic comes in. The t statistic will work if only some or, as you'll see later, even if none of the population information is available.

Three types of t tests will be presented in this and the following chapters. Each was designed for a different situation, which will be explained as you go along. The three t tests are:

1. The **single sample** t statistic
2. The **independent samples** t statistic
3. The **related samples** t statistic

We will begin with the *single sample t statistic*.

First, some good news: The single sample t statistic works in almost the exact same way as the z statistic. The key difference is that the single sample t uses sample standard deviation instead of population standard deviation. Thus, the t will work when the population standard deviation is unknown. There are a couple consequences of this we'll have to deal with, but that is the key difference.

> The **single sample t statistic** is used when, although the population mean is known, the population standard deviation is unknown. It uses sample standard deviation instead.

You may wonder why you would know the population mean but not know the population standard deviation. Consider the following study.

Is a person's spending in a store affected by how scarce the items appear to be? In an attempt to answer this question, you set up two mock stores. One has many of each item available while the other has just one of every item. Will participants spend a different amount of money in the store where items appear to be scarce? You give each of your 25 participants $100 to spend, and measure the average amount they spend in the scarce store. You find the participants in the sample spent an average of $55 in the *scarce* store.[78] The sample standard

---

[78] If you're curious about why we don't compare the amount spent in the scarce store ($55) with the amount spent in the other store (which would have to be $45), it's because the amounts are *not* (footnote continued on next page)

deviation, s, is 8. Using α 0.01, decide whether the results suggest we are affected by the apparent scarcity of items.

The question, as always, is whether the result obtained represents a real difference or was just due to sampling error. In this case we're looking to see if we spend more money when items appear to be scarce. So, *do* the results suggest we spend more when items appear to be scarce?

As you can see from the situation describe above, we do not have any population information to go by. Therefore, the z statistic, which of course requires you know the population mean (μ) and population standard deviation (σ), is not an option. So what to do? Use the *t* statistic instead.

First, we actually do have *some* population data to go by in the example above because, even though the population mean is not provided for us, we can figure out what it is. How? Well, think about why we need the population mean in the first place. It's so we have something to compare our sample mean to, right? For example, in our first dice example, we had our result of M = 7.52, but we needed to have something to compare that to—namely, what we'd expect to find if the dice were fair, that is, the mean of the null distribution, $\mu = 7$.

So, what is the expected mean (the mean of the null distribution, μ) in the mock store example? In other words, if scarcity had *no effect* on our spending, how much would we spend in a store where items appear to be scarce (keeping in mind there are two stores, and we are given $100 to spend)?[79]

The mean of the *null distribution* would be $50, as in the sketch on the next page.

---

independent of one another: Every dollar spent in one store is a dollar that cannot be spent in the other. And think about it like this: If you can figure out participants spent $45 in the other store just by knowing how much they spent in the *scarce* store, then clearly the results from the two stores are not independent. So the approach we're taking here might seem a little strange, but let's just say it's *statistically necessary*.

[79] $50. If you did not get that, be sure to read over everything again and you see why the answer is $50 before continuing.

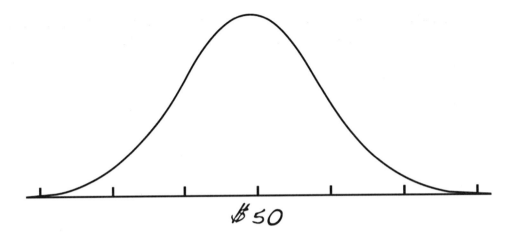

$50

Thus far, we have the following information:

- The population mean, μ. (50- about what we'd expect to find if there was no effect)
- The sample mean, M. (55- what we actually found)
- The sample size, N. (25—this will help us decide whether that difference is real)
- It is a non-directional, or two-tailed, test. This is because we are not specifying a direction. We're asking: *Is a person's spending in a store affected by how scarce the items appear to be? Affected* can mean scarcity will cause them to spend more or spend less.

Notice, though, we do not know something we knew before: the population standard deviation, σ. Notice instead the sample standard deviation, s, was given (from the problem: *The sample standard deviation, s, is 8...*). This is because there is no way for us to know the population standard deviation in this study, so we will estimate it by using the sample standard deviation, s, instead.

> *When the population standard deviation is not known, the sample standard deviation is used instead. The t test can accommodate this, while the z test cannot.*

We will tackle the research question about the scarce store by briefly going over the 4 steps of hypothesis testing, then formally going through them to get our answer.

* * *

The first thing you should always do in hypothesis testing is state your two hypotheses. The procedure is designed so you can choose one of the two in the end. The hypotheses are:

Null Hypothesis. Abbreviated H_0, the null hypothesis states that whatever effect or difference the researcher hopes to find *does not exist*. Think null = no difference or no effect. In this example, H_0 is *People spend the same amount of money in a store that contains apparently scarce items as one in which items do not appear scarce.*

Alternative Hypothesis. Abbreviated H_1, the alternative hypothesis states that the effect or difference the researcher hopes to find *does exist*. In this example, H_1 is *People spend a different amount of money in a store that contains apparently scarce items than one in which items do not appear scarce.*

Here's another way to word the hypotheses in the current example:

Null Hypothesis, H_0: People's spending is not affected by how scarce items in a store appear to be.

Alternative Hypothesis, H_1: People's spending is affected by how scarce items in a store appear to be.

Note there are many ways to word the two hypotheses. The key is that the alternative hypothesis is a statement of the effect you hope to find in the study, and the null hypothesis states the opposite—that there is no such effect. Note how the hypotheses above are consistent with this.

* * *

Next, you must figure out the value of the *critical statistic*. This was mentioned in the last chapter, but more explanation is now necessary. Think of the critical statistic as the score you have to 'beat' in order to conclude there is an effect. Recall from previous chapters what you do in inferential statistics to determine if there's an effect:

*Decide whether the probability the result you observed being due to chance is **a)** high enough to conclude your result was indeed just chance or, alternatively, **b)** low enough to conclude your result probably was not just chance and must therefore be real.*

Well, the way you make that determination with a t test is by comparing the *critical* statistic (which you find from the t table, Table 2 in the back of this book) with the *obtained* statistic you calculate based on the data.

NOTE: We could have actually done it that way with the z statistic earlier if we wanted to. That is, instead of looking up the probability of our z score and seeing if it's less than the alpha level we chose, we could have looked up the z score that corresponds with that alpha level, then compared that to the z score we calculated. Our old method just happens to demonstrate the underlying principles better.

* * *

Below is a sketch from the last chapter, but with some additions (in red). The sketch, along with the discussion below it, should help to clarify how the *result is chance* vs. *result is real* decision works.

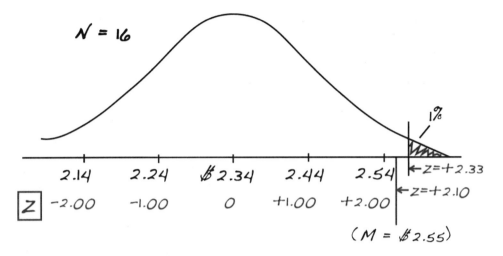

Notice the additions in red: First, z scores are labeled (remember, the z distribution always has a mean of 0 and a standard deviation of 1). Second, the z score that corresponds to 1% (the alpha level specified in the problem) is marked in the sketch (2.33). Finally, the z score based on our data, the *obtained z* score, is also marked (2.10). Note the z obtained score (2.10) didn't quite reach the shaded region, which began at z = 2.33.

Either of the methods presented—finding the probability associated with your z score and seeing if it's less than alpha, or finding the critical z score associated with alpha and seeing if your obtained z score is larger than it is— is fine. Both will lead you to the same conclusion. However, with a t test, we have no choice; we must use the latter method of finding the critical t score and then comparing it to the obtained t score.[80]

> The **critical statistic** is found on a table; it marks the border between a result you would conclude is chance and one you would conclude is real.

> The **obtained statistic** is calculated based on the data you collect. It is compared to the critical statistic to determine if your result is chance or real.

---

[80] This is not for any important reason, just that the t table is set up differently in order to save space. It would be many pages long if it was set up like the z table.

To find the critical t statistic (abbreviated t_{crit}), you need three pieces of information:

1. The level of significance, alpha (α).

    a. This is always given, as there is no way to read the problem and figure out what alpha should be.

2. Whether you are doing a directional test (also called a one-tailed test) or a non-directional test (also called a two-tailed test).

    a. The directionality of the test (whether it's a one- or two-tailed test) is usually not given in the exercises found in this book. Rather, you must read the question and figure out for yourself whether a direction is specified. In this case, no direction is specified because the question is: *Is a person's spending in a store affected by how scarce the items appear to be.* Notice a direction is not specified, since *affected* could refer to people spending more or less in a scarce store. This is therefore a two-tailed test.

3. The degrees of freedom (df). The degrees of freedom are simply the number of participants minus 1:

$$df = N - 1$$

To calculate the obtained t statistic (abbreviated t_{obt}), you need to use formulas. The formula for calculating t is:

$$t_{obt} = \frac{M - \mu}{S_M}$$

Notice from the formula you need to find S_M. S_M is the standard error, which you've seen before as σ_M. The difference is simply that, before, you had the population standard deviation, σ, and now you don't. So, you substitute the sample standard deviation, s. The formula for standard error when you know σ (and therefore would use z) is also below, for comparison.

$$S_M = \frac{s}{\sqrt{N}} \qquad\qquad \sigma_M = \frac{\sigma}{\sqrt{N}}$$

* * *

Finally, after determining t_{crit} and calculating t_{obt}, you simply compare the two, and apply the following rule:

> *If the obtained statistic is larger than the critical statistic, you reject the null hypothesis (conclude there is an effect). If not, you retain the null hypothesis (conclude there is no effect).*

You'll also state a more formal conclusion (not just *reject H_o* or *retain H_o*), and include an APA-formatted statistical report. You will learn how to do both, and indeed how to do a single sample *t* test from start to finish, right now.

*   *   *

Now that you have an idea of how the steps proceed, let's go through a hypothesis test, step-by-step, to answer the question about the stores. Here is the situation again for your reference:

> Is a person's spending in a store affected by how *scarce* the items appear to be? In an attempt to answer this question, you set up two mock stores. One has many of each item available while the other has just one of every item. Will participants spend a different amount of money in the store where items appear to be scarce? You give each of your 25 participants $100 to spend, and measure the average amount they spend in the scarce store. You find the participants in the sample spent an average of $55 in the *scarce* store. The sample standard deviation, s, is 8. Using α 0.01, decide whether the results suggest we are affected by the apparent scarcity of items.

Step 1. State the Hypotheses

Null Hypothesis, H_o: People spend the same amount of money in a store that contains apparently scarce items as one in which items appear to be abundant.

Alternative Hypothesis, H_1: People spend different amounts of money in a store that contains apparently scarce items as one in which items appear to be abundant.

Step 2. Set the criterion

The three pieces of information you need to find the critical *t* statistic (t_{crit}) are always given, or at least apparent, in the question. Here is the information you need for this particular problem:

- α 0.01. (*Using α 0.01, decide whether...*)

- two-tailed. (*Is a person's spending in a store affected by how scarce the items appear to be?*). No direction was specified.

- df = 24. (*You give **25 participants...***). Remember degrees of freedom, df, is equal to N minus 1.

Below is a small section of the *t* table so you can see how it works. The complete *t* table can be found at the end of the book, and you should make copies of it to have next to you as you work through exercises.

As discussed above, if the obtained statistic is larger than the critical statistic, you reject H_o (conclude there is an effect) and if it's not, you retain H_o (conclude there is no effect). Well, the *t* table provides you with that critical statistic; you need to look it up using those 3 pieces of information. The alpha (α) level and # of tails tells you which column to look in, and the degrees of freedom, df, tells you which row. The critical *t* statistic is in the cell where the column and row intersect.

See if you can find the critical *t* statistic for the mock store problem using the table below (or Table 2 in the back).

df	one tail, 0.05	two tails, 0.05	one tail, 0.01	two tails, 0.01
1	6.314	12.710	31.820	63.660
2	2.920	4.303	6.965	9.925
3	2.353	3.182	4.541	5.841
23	1.714	2.069	2.500	2.807
24	1.711	2.064	2.492	2.797
25	1.708	2.060	2.485	2.787
∞	1.645	1.960	2.326	2.576

Did you come up with 2.797? The level of significance (α) is 0.01 and we're doing a non-directional (two-tailed) test, so the critical statistic will be found somewhere in the right-most column. There are 25 participants, thus df = 24, which tells you it's in the row marked 24. The cell where that column and row intersect contains the value **2.797**. If you found a different value, make a note of what you did wrong (and don't make the same mistake again!). The trick to using the *t* table, and any statistical table, is to be careful.

t_{crit} = **2.797**

Step 3. Calculate the statistic.

This is where you apply the formulas to the data contained in the problem. Here are the formulas and the parts of the problem relevant for this step:

... You give each of your 25 participants $100 to spend, and measure the average amount they spend in the scarce store. You find the participants in the sample spent an average of $55 in the scarce store. The sample standard deviation, s, is 8...

$$t_{obt} = \frac{M - \mu}{S_M}$$

$$S_M = \frac{S}{\sqrt{N}}$$

If you look at the formulas, you can see what information is needed in order to calculate t_{obt}: s and N are needed to find S_M, and M and μ are needed to finally find t_{obt}. Look back to the problem and try to find these values. See if you come up with the following:

s = 8
N = 25
M = $55
μ = $50

Did you get the s, N and M, but don't know where that value of $50 for μ came from? If so, you're doing great, as that part is tricky (for this particular question, at least). Yes, μ is the *population mean*, but it's also *the value you would expect your sample mean to be* (well, be close to) *if there was no effect*. In this case, *if there was no effect of scarcity*, you'd expect participants to spend about $50 in the scarce store. Do you see why? Think about it: If participants were given $100 to spend in the 2 stores however they wanted, *and there was no effect of scarcity*, they'd spend about $50 in the scarce store, right? So the question we are trying to answer is: Is the $5 difference we found just a *chance* occurrence (due to sampling error), or does that difference represent a *real effect* of scarcity?

With the information provided, we can now start doing calculations. First find the standard error, s_M, then plug that into the formula for the obtained statistic, t_{obt}.

$$S_M = \frac{S}{\sqrt{N}} = \frac{8}{\sqrt{25}} = \frac{8}{5} = \mathbf{1.6}$$

$$t_{obt} = \frac{M - \mu}{S_M} = \frac{55 - 50}{1.6} = \frac{5}{1.6} = \mathbf{3.125}$$

Step 4. Make the statistical decision and state the conclusion.

Remember from above: If the obtained statistic is larger than the critical statistic, you reject H_o (conclude there is an effect) and if it's not, you retain H_o (conclude there is no effect).

Keeping this rule in mind, what should we do here?

t_{crit} = 2.797
t_{obt} = 3.125

Since t_{obt} is greater than t_{crit}, we reject H_o, meaning we *do* have a significant effect. In this example, that means people are indeed influenced by the apparent scarcity of the items in a store. In other words, that $5 difference we observed appears to have *not* just been a chance difference, but due to a *real effect* of scarcity; our finding is *statistically significant*.

You could also sketch it out, with the t_{crit} and t_{obt} marked. When we do that, notice our t_{obt} is past the t_{crit}, that is, far enough out into a tail for us to decide our result is *very unlikely* to have occurred by chance.

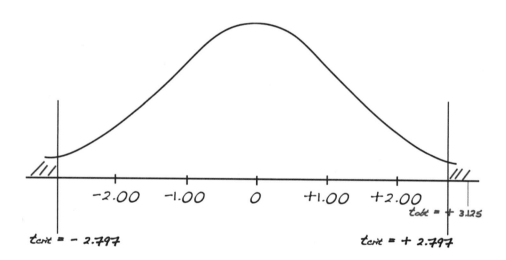

To formally state our conclusion, we write a sentence with some statistical information at the end of it. The exact way to do this is specified by the APA (who else?).

Following is the conclusion in APA format, followed by a diagram showing where each part came from.

> We found participants were influenced by the apparent scarcity of the items in a store, $t(24) = 3.125$, $p < 0.01$, two-tailed.

141

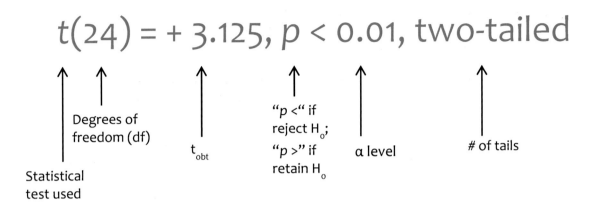

$$t(24) = + 3.125, p < 0.01, \text{two-tailed}$$

Degrees of freedom (df)

t_{obt}

"$p <$" if reject H_o;

"$p >$" if retain H_o

α level

# of tails

Statistical test used

You'll need to get used to the idea that *rejecting* the null hypothesis means you're going with the alternative hypothesis, which says *there is an effect.* On the other hand, if you *fail to reject* the null hypothesis (more simply known as *retaining* or *accepting* the null hypothesis), then you're saying *there's no effect.* Just remember that you're always testing the null hypothesis: You either *reject* it or you don't and, again, rejecting it means there *is* an effect.

People often ask why we test the null hypothesis rather than the seemingly more straightforward method of testing the alternative hypothesis. The answer goes back to the fact that you decide whether or not you have an effect based on the *probability* that your result is due to chance, and the *null* hypothesis is the one which says your result is due to chance (i.e., that there's no effect). And we can only know about the probability of things occuring by chance; we don't know the probability of something occuring if something more than just chance is at play (i.e., if there is an effect).

That is a little complicated, but it's easy to demonstrate with a couple questions. 1- What is the probability a coin will land on heads if the coin is fair, that is, if there is no 'effect' on the coin? 2- What is the probability a coin will land on heads if the coin *isn't* fair, that is, if there *is* some 'effect' (other than chance) on the coin? See how you can answer the first question (it's 50%, right?), but not the second? There you go! You can determine the probability of something occuring due to chance, but you cannot determine the probability of something occurring due to other influences.

To put that in terms of the hypotheses, you can determine the probability of the *null* hypothesis being true, but you cannot determine the probability of the *alternative* hypotheses being true. Again, if the probability of the null hypothesis being true is less than alpha, you say it's not true, meaning there is an effect (and vice versa).

In the coin example, you could compare your result--let's say your coin landed on heads 58% of the time--to 50% to see if the difference is significant. You can compare 58% to 50%, meaning you can determine the probability of getting 58% by seeing where it falls within the (null) distribution with a mean of 50%. You cannot compare 58% to nothing, that is, you cannot see where 58% falls within the (alternative) distribution because you don't know the mean of the alternative distribution.

As for the term *alternative* hypothesis: If we determine that the result was probably *not* due just to chance (reject the null), the *alternative* (the *only* alternative) is that there was an effect.

At the beginning of this chapter, you learned that the *t* test is more flexible than the *z* test because it works in situations where the population standard deviation, σ, is not known. Throughout this chapter you worked on a hypothesis test in which you were not given a population *mean*, μ, but you could figure it out because you know what mean to expect if your independent variable (scarcity) had no effect.

In the next two chapters you will learn about two more types of *t* tests which work when there is not only no population information *given*, but there is also no way to figure out what the population mean should be. The first is called the *t test for independent samples*, and the second is called the *t test for related samples*.

Problems.

1) Does receiving polite suggestions for improving ourselves make us angry? To help answer this question, you find a standardized test that measures anger. The test has been normalized so the average score is 0. Negative scores are *less angry* than average and positive scores are *more angry* (scores could be anywhere from -10 to +10). You select a group of 30 people and point out something about them they may consider improving. Afterwards, you ask them to take the anger test. You found the average score of the participants was + 0.5, with a standard deviation of 0.4. Using α 0.05, determine whether receiving polite suggestions for improving ourselves makes us angry.

2) You've noticed that you seem to sleep more after a day at the beach. To find out if the beach affecting sleep is a more general phenomenon, you bring a group of 20 people to the beach, and have them report back the next day how many hours they slept. Your sample of participants reported an average of 8.4 hours of sleep (s = 1.2). You know the population mean is 8 hours per night. Using α 0.01, determine whether going to the beach *affects* sleep duration.

3) You decide to repeat the beach study, but this time you do things a bit differently. For one, you decide to perform a directional test (read over question #2 to confirm which direction, if necessary). You also recruit 120 participants this time. This time around, the mean was about the same (8.3 hours), as was the standard deviation (1.3). Conduct a hypothesis test using a 1% level of significance.

4) It is widely accepted among the general public that children prefer colorful surroundings. You want to see if you can find evidence for this, so you design a room with two distinct sides to it. One side is very colorful and the other is much less colorful. You let kids play in this room for 40 minutes and measure how much time they spend in the colorful side. You find the average time spent on the colorful side in your sample of kids (N = 24) is 25 minutes. Standard deviation = 5.2 minutes. Does your finding suggest that, indeed, children prefer colorful surroundings? Use α 0.01. Remember: The mean of the null distribution, μ, is the result you'd expect if there was no effect. So begin by thinking about what mean you would expect (meaning how many minutes the kids would spend on the colorful side) if the kids were unaffected by the colorfulness of the room.

5) You repeat this study with some changes. First, even though your hypothesis is the same, you decide to measure how much time they spend in the less colorful side rather than on the more colorful side. More importantly, when you repeat the study you only had access to 9 kids. You again let the kids play in this room, but for <u>60</u> minutes this time, and measure how much time they spend in the less colorful side. You find the average time spent on the less colorful side in your sample of kids is 25 minutes (standard deviation = 5.9 minutes). Does your finding suggest that children prefer colorful surroundings? Use α 0.01.

Answers to problems.

1)

Step 1.

> Null Hypothesis, H_0: Receiving polite suggestions for improving ourselves does not make us angry.

> Alternative Hypothesis, H_1: Receiving polite suggestions for improving ourselves makes us angry.

Step 2.

α 0.05, one tailed, df = 29.

$t_{crit} = 1.699$

Step 3.

$M = 0.5$

$\mu = 0$
$S_M = 0.07$

$t_{obt} = 7.14$

Step 4.

$t_{obt} > t_{crit}$; Reject H_0.

We found that receiving polite suggestions for improving ourselves makes us angry, $t(29) = +7.14$, $p < 0.05$, one-tailed.

2)

Step 1.

Null Hypothesis, H_0: Going to the beach does not affect sleep duration.

Alternative Hypothesis, H_1: Going to the beach affects sleep duration.

Step 2.

α 0.01, two tailed, df = 19. (two tailed because the task was to ... *determine whether going to the beach* ***affects*** *sleep duration*).

t_{crit} = 2.861

Step 3.

M = 8.4

μ = 8
S_M = 0.27

t_{obt} = + 1.48

Step 4.

$t_{obt} < t_{crit}$; Retain H_0.

We found that going to the beach does not affect sleep duration, $t(19) = + 1.48$, $p > 0.01$, two-tailed.

3)

Step 1.

Null Hypothesis, H_0: Going to the beach does not increase sleep duration.

Alternative Hypothesis, H_1: Going to the beach increases sleep duration.

Step 2.

α 0.01, one tailed, df = 119.

$t_{crit} = 2.364$

Step 3.

M = 8.3

$\mu = 8$
$S_M = 0.12$

$t_{obt} = +2.50$

Step 4.

$t_{obt} > t_{crit}$; Reject H_0.

We found that going to the beach increases sleep duration, $t(119) = +2.50$, $p < 0.01$, one-tailed.

4)

Step 1.

Null Hypothesis, H_o: Children do not prefer colorful surroundings.

Alternative Hypothesis, H_1: Children prefer colorful surroundings.

Step 2.

α 0.01, one tailed, df = 23.

t_{crit} = 2.500

Step 3.

M = 25

μ = 20   Remember, the population mean is the result you'd expect if there was no effect/no difference. Here, if there was no effect of color, you'd expect the children to spend an average of **20** minutes on the more colorful side. After all, there were two sides to the room (a more colorful side and a less colorful side), and the children were in the room for 40 minutes. If the color had no effect then they'd spend, on average, 20 minutes on the more colorful side of the room (and 20 minutes on the less colorful side).

S_M = 1.06

t_{obt} = 4.72

Step 4.

$t_{obt} > t_{crit}$; Reject H_o.

We found that children prefer colorful surroundings, $t(23) = +4.72$, $p < 0.01$, one-tailed.

5)

Step 1.

Null Hypothesis, H_0: Children do not prefer colorful surroundings.

Alternative Hypothesis, H_1: Children prefer colorful surroundings.

Step 2.

α 0.01, one tailed, df = 8.

$t_{crit} = 2.896$

Step 3.

M = 25

μ = 30   This works the same as in the previous problem, except now since you let them play for 60 minutes, if there was no effect of color you'd expect the children to spend an average of **30** minutes on the less colorful side.

$S_M = 1.97$

$t_{obt} = -2.54$ Notice you have a *negative t* obtained score since you decided to measure time spent on the less colorful side this time (which was 25 min. on average—5 *less than* the expected 30 min.). Had you decided instead to measure the time spent on the more colorful side (which had to have been 35 min. on average—5 *more than* the expected 30 min.), you'd have ended up with $t_{obt} = +2.54$. Either way, the result was in the direction you expected (less time in less colorful time / more time in more colorful side). Now, whether the result was *significant*...

Step 4.

$t_{obt} < t_{crit}$; Accept H_0.

We found that children do not prefer colorful surroundings, $t(8) = -2.54$, $p > 0.01$, one-tailed.

Chapter 11
The *t* test for independent samples

The previous chapter introduced you to the single sample *t* test, which is used when you take one sample, and compare its mean to a population mean, which represents the finding that would indicate you have no effect (the *expected* finding). Believe it or not, often in research you do not even know the population *mean*, μ, and have no way to figure out what it should be. As a matter of fact, this type of situation is very common.

Do you see how not knowing the population mean presents a problem? Remember, the population mean is what you'd expect your sample mean to be if there is no effect. The population mean thus seems essential: You need it to compare your sample mean to so you can, ultimately, see if there is an effect. You may even recall that, even though we usually refer to the *sample mean* as our result, our result really is *how different the sample mean is from the population mean*. You can even see this all reflected in the numerator of the single sample *t* formula: M - μ.

So, if you *don't* know the population mean, μ, then what could you possibly compare the sample mean, M, to? The answer to this question is hinted at in the title of this chapter: *The t test for independent samples*; you take *two* samples, and compare the two sample means to each other[81]. Actually, the numerator of the formula for the independent samples *t* (the effect) is $M_1 - M_2$ (the mean of sample 1 minus the mean of sample 2), instead of M - μ.

> The effect in an independent samples t test is the difference between the two sample means: $M_1 - M_2$.

Importantly, the two samples have to be different in some way (otherwise, you don't have a *variable*). For example, if you were studying the effect of a summer reading program on student satisfaction, you'd have one group of students participate in the summer reading program (let's call the mean of this sample M_1) and another group not participate in it (let's call the mean of this sample M_2). The effect of the reading program could thus be measured as the *difference* in the mean level of satisfaction between the two groups: $M_1 - M_2$.

---

[81] There is another way to design a study that will also work when you don't have any population information. That will be discussed in the next chapter.

s is the case with any inferential statistical analysis, the effect cannot be examined in isolation; one must always take the *error* into account as well. The error, which is still called *standard error* but is now denoted $S_{M1\text{-}M2}$, is calculated from the variability across both samples (taking N into account, as usual). The formula for standard error when dealing with two independent samples is:

$$S_{M_1 - M_2} = \sqrt{\frac{S_p^2}{n_1} + \frac{S_p^2}{n_2}}$$

standard error

Notice a new symbol: Sp^2. That is the symbol for *pooled variance* (*pooled* meaning the variance across both samples). The formula for pooled variance is:

$$S_p^{\,2} = \frac{SS_1 + SS_2}{df_1 + df_2}$$

pooled variance

You have not seen SS for quite a while, but you may recall it is short for *sum of squares*, and it is the sum of the squared deviation scores. In short, SS is the total variability in a sample. SS_1 + SS_2 is thus the total variability across *both* samples. As can be seen in the formula, that total is then divided by the total degrees of freedom across both samples (df_1 + df_2) to give you the pooled variance, s_p^2.

Putting that all together, the formula for the independent samples *t* is:

$$t_{obt} = \frac{M_1 - M_2}{S_{M_1 - M_2}}$$

obtained t

* * *

We will now work through a situation where you would use an independent samples *t* test to evaluate your result:

> *Do students who participate in a summer reading program before beginning college have higher subsequent satisfaction with college than students who do not? You design*

a short questionnaire that measures satisfaction with college (on a 1 to 8 scale) and give it to two groups of students. One of the groups participated in the reading program and the other did not. Here are the results of your study:

Mean satisfaction level of the reading group = 7.3 (SS_1 = 121, N_1 = 21)
Mean satisfaction level of the non-reading group = 6.1 (SS_2 = 132, N_2 = 20)

Use a significance level of 0.05 to determine if the summer reading program increases satisfaction.

The steps are the same as before (and the same as they'll always be).

Step 1. State the Hypotheses

Null Hypothesis, H_o: Students who participate in a summer reading program do not have higher levels of satisfaction with college than students who do not.

Alternative Hypothesis, H_1: Students who participate in a summer reading program have higher levels of satisfaction with college than students who do not.

Step 2. Set the criterion

The same three pieces of information are needed in order to find the critical t statistic (t_{crit}): α, # of tails, and df.

- α 0.05. (*Use a significance level of **0.05** to...*)

- one-tailed. (*Do students who participate in summer reading program before beginning college have **higher** subsequent satisfaction...*) A direction was specified.

- df = 39. Degrees of freedom, df, is equal to N minus 1. If there are two samples, there are two df's. N in the reading group was 21, so df = 20; N in the non-reading group was 20, so df = 19; 20 + 19 = 39. In an independent samples t test, the formula for degrees of freedom is thus:

$$\star df = df_1 + df_2$$

With this information, find t_{crit}:

df	one tail, 0.05	two tails, 0.05	one tail, 0.01	two tails, 0.01
1	6.314	12.710	31.820	63.660
2	2.920	4.303	6.965	9.925
29	1.699	2.045	2.462	2.756
30	1.697	2.042	2.457	2.750
40	1.684	2.021	2.423	2.704

We hit a snag. Degrees of freedom is 39, but 39 is not on the table. The rule is: When the exact degrees of freedom is not on the table, choose the next *lower* df value. In this case you'd go with df of 30, even though it may be tempting to choose 40 since that's closer to 39 than 30 is. But don't. Always go with the *lower* df.

t_{crit} = **1.697**

Step 3. Calculate the statistic.

Several pieces of information, and several formulas, are relevant in Step 3. In each part of this step, the relevant information from the original setup of the problem is summarized for convenience, but you should always look back to the problem to see where the information came from. We will begin with the pooled variance, $S_p{}^2$.

Mean satisfaction level of the reading group = 7.3 (SS_1 = 121, N_1 = 21)
Mean satisfaction level of the non-reading group = 6.1 (SS_2 = 132, N_2 = 20)

SS_1 = 121
SS_2 = 132
df_1 = 20
df_2 = 19

If it was not specified which was group 1 and which was group 2, just assume the first one presented is group 1; it really doesn't matter how we label the groups, as long as we are consistent thoughout the hypothesis test.

$$S_p{}^2 = \frac{SS_1 + SS_2}{df_1 + df_2} = \frac{121 + 132}{20 + 19} = \frac{253}{39} = \textbf{6.49}$$

Now that we have S_p^2 we can calculate the standard error, S_{M1-M2}.

$S_p^2 = 6.49$

$N_1 = 21$
$N_2 = 20$

Note n is used in the standard error formula, but df is used in the pooled variance formula.

$$S_{M_1-M_2} = \sqrt{\frac{Sp^2}{n_1} + \frac{Sp^2}{n_2}} = \sqrt{\frac{6.49}{21} + \frac{6.49}{20}}$$

$$= \sqrt{0.31 + 0.32} = \sqrt{0.63} = \mathbf{0.79}$$

With standard error done, we can now finish calculating t_{obt}.

$M_1 = 7.3$
$M_2 = 6.1$
$S_{M1-M2} = 0.79$

$$t_{obt} = \frac{M_1 - M_2}{S_{M_1-M_2}} = \frac{7.3 - 6.1}{0.79} = \frac{1.2}{0.79} = \mathbf{1.52}$$

Step 4. Make the statistical decision and state the conclusion.

If the obtained statistic is larger than the critical statistic, you reject H_o (conclude there is an effect) and if it's not, you retain H_o (conclude there is no effect). In this study, we found the following t_{crit} and t_{obt} (and see sketch on next page).

$t_{crit} = 1.697$
$t_{obt} = 1.52$

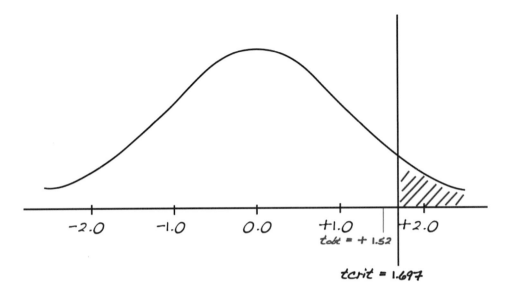

Since t_{obt} is not greater than t_{crit}, we *retain* H_o, meaning we do *not* have a significant effect. In this example, that means students who participate in the summer reading program do not have higher satisfaction with college as compared with students who do not participate. In other words, that 1.2 point difference we observed appears to have just been a chance difference, that is, due to sampling error, not due to a *real effect* of the reading program. Our finding is thus *not statistically significant*.

The APA statement follows the same format as it did with the single sample *t* statistic:

$$t(39) = + 1.52, p > 0.05, \text{one-tailed}$$

Statistical test used

Degrees of freedom (df)

t_{obt}

"*p <*" if reject H_o; "*p >*" if retain H_o

α level

# of tails

Thus, our conclusion for this study is as follows:

> We found students who participated in the summer reading program did not have higher levels of satisfaction with college than students who did not participate, $t(39)$ = 1.52, $p > 0.05$, one-tailed.

Note here we specified $p >$ (greater than) 0.05. Why greater than ($>$)?[82]

Next we will deal with a research study where we have one group of participants, tested under both of the conditions. Such a situation requires yet a different type of t test: the related samples t test.

---

[82] Remember the rule: If you reject the null hypothesis (find an effect), you put "$p < [\alpha]$"; if you retain the null hypothesis, you put "$p > [\alpha]$". In this case, we retained H_o, so we put "$p > [\alpha]$". We're saying that the probability of our result occurring due to chance/sampling error is *greater than* 5%.

Problems.

1) Does mood affect verbal fluency? To address this question, a researcher gives good news to one group (the *good mood* group) and bad news to another (the *bad mood* group). She then gives both groups a test of verbal fluency by asking participants to list as many words as they can in 60 seconds that begin with the letter T. The average number of words provided by the 10 participants in the good mood group was 23 (SS = 190) while the average number of words provided by the 8 participants in the bad mood group was 21 (SS = 175).
Using α 0.05, determine whether mood affects verbal fluency.

2) Does *hunger* affect verbal fluency? To address this question, a researcher gives food to one group (the *full* group) before the experiment, but does not give food to another group (the *hungry* group). She then gives both groups a test of verbal fluency by asking participants to list as many words that begin with the letter M in 60 seconds. The average number of words provided by the 50 participants in the full group was 24 (SS = 180) while the average number of words provided by the 50 participants in the hungry group was 22 (SS = 165). Using α 0.01, determine whether hunger affects verbal fluency.

3) Do we trust a person more if they look similar to ourselves than if they look different? An experimenter generated faces with a computer program; some of these faces were made to contain features of each individual participant (familiar faces) and others were not (unfamiliar faces). Participants were asked to rate (on a 1 to 100 scale) how much they felt they would trust the person. Familiar faces were shown to a group of 21 participants. Those participants' average rating was 71 (SS = 990). Unfamiliar faces were shown to a group of 20 participants. Those participants' average rating was 61 (SS = 1200). Using α 0.01, decide whether we trust a person more if they look similar to ourself.

4) Do jurors sentence violent offenders who were abused as children differently than violent offenders who were not abused? A researcher sets up a mock trial, where evidence is presented and subjects taking the role of jurors are instructed to impose a prison sentence for a defendant previously found guilty of a crime. One group of 28 subjects is told the defendant was abused as a child. They imposed an average of a 13 year prison sentence (SS = 1800). Another group of 26 subjects is told the defendant was not abused as a child. They imposed an average of 19 years (SS = 1650). Using α 0.05, decide whether the prison sentence imposed is affected by whether or not a defendant was abused as a child.

5) Do jurors sentence female violent offenders less severely than male violent offenders? A researcher presents the same evidence to two groups of subjects. For one of the groups, the offender is female and for the other the offender is male. In both cases, the subjects were told the offender was already found guilty, and their task is to impose a prison sentence. The group with the female offender imposed an average sentence of 14 years (SS = 550) and the group with the male offender imposed an average sentence of 23 years (SS = 500). For each of the two groups, n = 12. Using α 0.05, decide whether the prison sentence imposed is less severe for a female offender than for a male offender.

Solutions to problems.

1)

<u>Step 1.</u>

> <u>Null Hypothesis, H_o</u>: Mood does not affect verbal fluency.

> <u>Alternative Hypothesis, H_1</u>: Mood affects verbal fluency.

<u>Step 2.</u>

α 0.05, two tails, df = 16.

t_{crit} = 2.120

<u>Step 3.</u>

SS_1 = 190
SS_2 = 175
N_1 = 10
N_2 = 8
df_1 = 9
df_2 = 7
M_1 = 23
M_2 = 21
S_p^2 = 22.81
S_{M1-M2} = 2.26

t_{obt} = 0.88

<u>Step 4.</u>

$t_{obt} < t_{crit}$; Retain H_o.

We found mood does not affect verbal fluency, $t(16)$ = 0.88, $p > 0.05$, two-tailed.

2)

<u>Step 1.</u>

 <u>Null Hypothesis, H_0:</u> Hunger does not affect verbal fluency.

 <u>Alternative Hypothesis, H_1:</u> Hunger affects verbal fluency.

<u>Step 2.</u>

α 0.01, two tails, df = 98.

t_{crit} = 2.639

<u>Step 3.</u>

SS_1 = 180
SS_2 = 165
N_1 = 50
N_2 = 50
df_1 = 49
df_2 = 49
M_1 = 24
M_2 = 22
S_p^2 = 3.52
S_{M1-M2} = 0.37

t_{obt} = 5.41

<u>Step 4.</u>

$t_{obt} > t_{crit}$; Reject H_0.

We found hunger affects verbal fluency, $t(98) = 5.41$, $p < 0.01$, two-tailed.

3)

<u>Step 1.</u>

Null Hypothesis, H_0: We do not trust a person more if they look similar to ourselves.

Alternative Hypothesis, H_1: We trust a person more if they look similar to ourselves.

<u>Step 2.</u>

α 0.01, one tailed, df = 39.

$t_{crit} = 2.457$

<u>Step 3.</u>

$SS_1 = 990$
$SS_2 = 1200$
$N_1 = 21$
$N_2 = 20$
$df_1 = 20$
$df_2 = 19$
$M_1 = 71$
$M_2 = 61$
$S_p^2 = 56.15$
$S_{M1-M2} = 2.34$

$t_{obt} = 4.27$

<u>Step 4.</u>

$t_{obt} > t_{crit}$; Reject H_0.

We found that we trust a person more if they look similar to ourselves, $t(39) = 4.27$, $p < 0.01$, one-tailed.

4)

<u>Step 1.</u>

        <u>Null Hypothesis, H_0</u>: The prison sentence imposed on a guilty defendant is not affected by whether or not that defendant was abused as a child.

        <u>Alternative Hypothesis, H_1</u>: The prison sentence imposed on a guilty defendant is affected by whether or not that defendant was abused as a child.

<u>Step 2.</u>

α 0.05, two tailed, df = 52.

t_{crit} = 2.009

<u>Step 3.</u>

SS_1 = 1800
SS_2 = 1650
N_1 = 28
N_2 = 26
df_1 = 27
df_2 = 25
M_1 = 13
M_2 = 19
S_p^2 = 66.35
$S_{M1\text{-}M2}$ = 2.22

t_{obt} = - 2.70

<u>Step 4.</u>

$t_{obt} > t_{crit}$; Reject H_0.

We found the prison sentence imposed on a guilty defendant is affected by whether or not that defendant was abused as a child, $t(52) = -2.70, p < 0.05$, two-tailed.

5)

<u>Step 1.</u>

Null Hypothesis, H_0: The prison sentence imposed is not less severe for a female offender than for a male offender.

Alternative Hypothesis, H_1: The prison sentence imposed is less severe for a female offender than for a male offender.

<u>Step 2.</u>

α 0.05, one-tailed, df = 22.

t_{crit} = 1.717

<u>Step 3.</u>

SS_1 = 550
SS_2 = 500
N_1 = 12
N_2 = 12
df_1 = 11
df_2 = 11
M_1 = 14
M_2 = 23
S_p^2 = 47.73
S_{M1-M2} = 2.82

t_{obt} = - 3.19

<u>Step 4.</u>

$t_{obt} > t_{crit}$; Reject H_0.

We found the prison sentence imposed is less severe for a female offender than for a male offender, $t(22) = -3.19$, $p < 0.05$, one-tailed.

Chapter 12
The *t* test for related samples

In the previous chapter, you learned about the *t* test for independent samples. Naturally, it is the test you would use if you had two *independent* samples. The samples are independent because they are made up of separate sets of participants; one group of participants is tested under one condition, and a separate group of participants is tested under the other condition. That is called a between-subjects design.

But studies are not always conducted that way. Sometimes, your two samples are made up of the same participants. That is, instead of putting one group of participants in one condition and another group of participants in another condition, you test *one* group of participants under *both* conditions. This is referred to as a *within-subjects design*.

> In a **between-subjects** design, separate groups of participants are tested under the various conditions. In a **within-subjects** design, the same group of participants is tested under all conditions.

The rule about which test to use for which type of design is as follows: If you have a between-subjects design, you use the independent samples *t* test, and if you have a within-subjects design, you use the related samples *t* test.[83]

> A between-subjects design uses the **independent samples t test** to analyze the data. A within-subjects design uses a **related samples t test**.

You will again go through the four steps of hypothesis testing you did in the previous chapter. However, the effect in a related samples *t* test works in a slightly different way as compared to the independent samples *t* test, and the error in the two tests are fundamentally different. Those differences will be discussed now, and then you'll go through a formal hypothesis test using the related samples *t*.

* * *

---

[83] There are certain types of between-subjects studies that would actually use the related-samples t, but those are the exception. Therefore, we will always stick with the rule that a between-subjects design uses an independent samples *t* test and a within-subjects design uses a related samples t test.

The Effect

Recall in the independent samples t test, the effect is the difference between the two sample means ($M_1 - M_2$). But in the related samples t test, another approach is taken which involves calculating a difference score (called a d score) for each participant. To get a d score, you subtract a participant's score in one condition from their score in the other condition ($X_2 - X_1$). You do that for all participants, and then you compute the average of the resulting d scores.

For example, say Participant A scored $X = 10$ in Condition #1 and $X = 5$ in Condition #2, and Participant B scored $X = 15$ in Condition #1 and $X = 11$ in Condition #2. Participant A's d score would be $5 - 10 = -5$, and Participant B's d score would be $11 - 15 = -4$. The average d score, denoted M_D, would be: $-5 + -4 = -9/2 = -4.5$. M_D—the average difference score, is the effect (numerator in the t formula) in a related samples t test.

The Error

There is a fundamental difference between the independent samples t test and the related samples t test when it comes to how error is calculated. While the error in the independent samples t test is calculated from the scores in the two samples (the X scores), the error in the related samples t test is calculated from the difference scores (the d scores). To illustrate why that is such an important distinction, we will compare two sets of hypothetical research results that are the same, except one is from a between subjects study, where error is based on X scores, and the other is from a within subjects study, where error is based on d scores.

Below are the results from two such hypothetical experiments. In both, participants were asked to play a word game against another person. That other person was either *known* or *unknown* to the participant. Of course, in the *between* subjects study one group of participants played against someone they knew and a *separate group* of participants played against someone they didn't, while in the *within* subjects study, one group of participants played against both someone they knew and, at another time, against someone they didn't. The dependent variable was the participants' scores.

Here are the results from the **between subjects** study:

Opponent unknown	Opponent known
75	85
175	190
236	250
379	390
483	500
M = 269.6	M = 283

Take a look at how much variability/variance there is among the scores within each of the two conditions. This large variability in scores will result in a relatively large standard error, since standard error depends, in part, on the variability of the scores within the sample (or samples). Note the effect, $M_1 - M_2$, for the above data is 13.4 (283 – 269.6) and the error (standard error, S_{M1-M2}) is 72.6.[84]

Here are the results from the **within subjects** study:

Participant	Opponent unknown	Opponent known
A	75	85
B	175	190
C	236	250
D	379	390
E	483	500

Notice the scores are the same, but there is now a column labeled *Participant*, which we haven't had before. This column is included because both scores in each row are from the same participant. For example, Participant B scored 175 when his opponent was unknown to him and 190 when his opponent was known to him. This is what makes it possible to find a difference, or *d*, score, for that participant (and we will do the same for the rest of the participants). Remember, in a related samples *t* test, the error is calculated from the *d* scores. For this reason, once we calculate the *d* scores, we can disregard the original (*X*) scores. Let's take a look at that now:

Participant	Opponent unknown	Opponent known	**d score**
A	75	85	10
B	175	190	15
C	236	250	14
D	379	390	11
E	483	500	17

Take a look at how there is much more variability in the *X* scores than in the *d* scores. But why is that? Begin by asking yourself why there should be differences among the (*X*) scores of participants in the same condition in the first place. Why, for example, would Participants A and B differ so much in their scores on the word game when their opponent was unknown

---

[84] If you're curious, that standard error was calculated with the formulas from the last chapter.

to them (Participant A scored 75 while Participant B scored 175)? After all, they played the same game, under the same condition!

Think of some reasons you think Participant A's score on the word game was so much lower than Participant B's.

There are hundreds of things you could have come to mind, since there are hundreds of things that could potentially affect someone's score in a word game. But the bottom line is that none of them have anything to do with *whether the opponent is known or unknown* (in other words, the independent variable). How could we know that? Easy: Because all participants in that condition played against an opponent who was *unknown* to them! The same goes for the scores in the *known* condition: They're all over the place, despite the fact that the participants played the same game under the same condition (against a player known to them).

*   *   *

The variability that occurs *within* conditions is thus due to influences *other than* what you're studying. Think about it: The variability in the scores within the conditions is a) not due to the independent variable (whether the opponent was known or unknown) and b) *is* due to many factors we can't even identify with any confidence, and even if we could, we'd have no way to figure out *how much* they are influencing scores. It is therefore fair to call the variance of the scores within conditions due, at least in part, to *individual differences*.

The rest of the variance of the scores within conditions is due to *unknown error*. Note there is still some of that unknown error left in the *d* scores; as you can easily see, there is still variability in the *d* scores. But there's not as much as in the *X* scores, because the *X* scores contain variability due to individual differences *and* unknown variability/error, while the *d* scores contain only unknown variability (the variability due to individual differences has been eliminated).

> *The variance in scores within the conditions, the X scores, is due to 1)* **individual differences** *among the participants and 2) other,* **unknown error.**
>
> *The variance in the difference scores within the conditions, the d scores, is due only to* **unknown error**—*the variance due to individual differences is eliminated when the d scores are calculated.*

To summarize, in a within-subjects design, you eliminate the variability due to individual differences. This leaves only unknown variability. All else being equal, this results in less error (a smaller denominator in the t formula), and thus a larger obtained statistic.

To further clarify, and demonstrate, just how that variability ends up being eliminated (this is a vital concept), take another look at the X scores and the d scores. To simplify, we will continue by focusing just on Participants A and B:

Participant	Opponent unknown	Opponent known	d score
A	75	85	10
B	175	190	15

Go ahead and cover up the two middle columns, which contain the X scores (the columns labeled *Opponent unknown* and *Opponent known*). All you see now is that Participant A's d score is 10 and Participant B's d score is 15. The variability created by the fact that Participant B's X scores were higher overall gets eliminated when you calculate those d scores.

Simply put, the d scores, the differences between scores in the two conditions, are the important thing; the actual scores themselves don't matter. Participant A's d score of 10 means he scored 10 points higher in one condition, relative to the other. Similarly, Participant B's d score of 15 means he scored 15 points higher in one condition, relative to the other.[85] The X scores themselves can be ignored after you use them to find the d scores.

*　*　*

Let's work through an example when the related samples t test would be used.

> Which is a more unpleasant sound: fingernails on a blackboard or a baby screaming? To answer this question, you get a group of 25 of your classmates, play the sound of fingernails scraping across a blackboard over loudspeakers, and have them rate it from 1 (very unpleasant) to 50 (very pleasant). You do the same with the sound of a baby screaming. You find that, on average, participants rated the baby screaming as 6 points higher (more pleasant) than the fingernails (standard deviation = 4.5). Using α 0.01, determine whether there is a difference in pleasantness between the two sounds.

---

[85] The way you do the subtraction (scores in *opponent known* minus scores in *opponent unknown* vs. scores in *opponent unknown* minus scores in *opponent known*, that is, $X_2 - X_1$ vs. $X_1 - X_2$) doesn't matter, just as long as you do it the same way for all the participants.

Step 1. State the Hypotheses

Null Hypothesis, H_0: There is no difference in the unpleasantness of the sounds of fingernails on a blackboard and a baby screaming.

Alternative Hypothesis, H_1: There is a difference in the unpleasantness of the sounds of fingernails on a blackboard and a baby screaming.

Step 2. Set the criterion

The same three pieces of information are needed in order to find the critical t statistic (t_{crit}): α, # of tails, and df.

- α 0.01. (Using α **0.01**, determine …)
- two-tailed. (… determine whether there is a difference …) A direction was not specified.
- df = 24. Degress of freedom, df, is equal to N minus 1. In a related samples t test, N is the number of d scores, which is also the number of participants (… you get a group of 25 of your classmates…)

df	one tail, 0.05	two tails, 0.05	one tail, 0.01	two tails, 0.01
1	6.314	12.710	31.820	63.660
2	2.920	4.303	6.965	9.925
3	2.353	3.182	4.541	5.841
23	1.714	2.069	2.500	2.807
24	1.711	2.064	2.492	2.797
25	1.708	2.060	2.485	2.787
∞	1.645	1.960	2.326	2.576

t_{crit} = 2.797

Step 3. Calculate the statistic.

The parts of the problem relevant to this step (calculating t_{obt}) are in bold below.

Which is a more unpleasant sound: fingernails on a blackboard or a baby screaming? To answer this question, **you get a group of 25 of your classmates** and play them the sound *of fingernails scraping across a blackboard over loudspeakers and have them rate it from 1 (very unpleasant) to 50 (very pleasant). You do the same with the sound of a baby screaming. You find that, on average, **participants rated the baby crying as 6 points higher (more pleasant) than the fingernails (standard deviation = 4.5).** Using α 0.01, determine whether there is a difference in pleasantness ratings between the two sounds.*

The formulas for the related samples *t* test are very similar to the formulas for a single sample *t* test. You can think of it like this: In a single sample *t* test, you're determining whether the mean of your sample of *X* scores (M) is significantly different from the population mean (μ), and in a related samples *t* test you're determining whether the mean of your sample of *d* scores (M$_D$) is significantly different from zero. Standard error is denoted s$_{MD}$ in a related sample *t* test. The formulas are below.

$$\text{Standard Error} \quad S_{MD} = \frac{S}{\sqrt{N}}$$

$$t_{obt} = \frac{M_D}{S_{MD}}$$

Notice that, just like the *independent samples t test*, the *related samples t test* does not need any population information.

Plugging in the values given in the problem, the standard error is:

$$S_{MD} = \frac{S}{\sqrt{N}} = \frac{4.5}{\sqrt{25}} = \frac{4.5}{5} = \mathbf{0.9}$$

And t$_{obt}$ is:

$$t_{obt} = \frac{M_D}{S_{MD}} = \frac{6}{0.9} = \mathbf{6.67}$$

Step 4. Make the statistical decision and state the conclusion.

As always, if the obtained statistic is larger than the critical statistic, you reject H_o (conclude there is an effect) and if it's not, you retain H_o (conclude there is no effect).

t_{crit} = 2.797
t_{obt} = 6.67

Since t_{obt} is greater than t_{crit} we *reject* H_o, meaning we have a significant effect. In this example, that means there is indeed a difference in how pleasant we find the sounds of fingernails on a blackboard and a baby screaming. In other words, that 6 point mean difference score we observed (which means, of course, that participants, on average, rated the two sounds 6 points different from each other) appears to have not just been a chance difference, so instead probably reflects a *real difference*.

The APA statement works the same here as before:

We found there was a significant difference in how pleasant participants found the two sounds, $t(24)$ = 6.67, $p < 0.01$, two-tailed.

* * *

You have now learned all 3 types of t tests. Below are two tables that summarize how the effect and the error, and thus t_{obt}, are calculated in the three tests. The first table describes the effect and the error in words, and the second specifies the statistical notation used.

	Single sample t	Independent samples t	Related samples t
Effect	Difference between the sample mean and the population mean	Difference between the two sample means	The mean difference score
Error	Standard error, calculated from the (X) scores in the sample (and N)	Standard error, calculated from the (X) scores in the two samples (and Ns)	Standard error, calculated from the difference (d) scores (and N)

	Single sample t	Independent samples t	Related samples t
Effect	$M - \mu$	$M_1 - M_2$	M_D
Error	S_M	S_{M1-M2}	S_{MD}

Notice the descriptions (and symbols) for the effect in all 3 t tests. See how they all come down to a subtraction, in other words, a *difference* between two numbers? In the single sample t test, the effect is the *difference* between the sample mean (M) and the population mean (μ). In the independent samples t test, the effect is the *difference* between one of the sample means (M_1) and the other sample mean (M_2). Finally, in the related samples t test, the effect is the average *difference* between participants' scores in one of the conditions and their scores in the other condition.

You are now done with learning about t tests, but before moving on to the next inferential test, you need to understand something very important when you're conducting research: *Your statistical decision may be wrong.* You are making an *inference*, after all. The next chapter is all about the errors you may make every time you use an inferential test.

Problems.

1) Does how polite someone is influence how powerul they are percieved to be by others? To test this, you have a group of 42 participants exposed to two different experimenters: one who is rude and another who is polite. Participants are given a questionnaire about the experimenters which assesses their perception of how powerful the experimenter is. You found ratings for the rude experimenter were 4.1 points higher, on average (it was a 50 point scale), than for the polite experimenter (s = 3). Using α 0.05, determine whether how polite someone is affects their perceived level of power.

2) We've all heard that visualizing success helps us to be more successful. To test this when it comes to test taking, you have a group of 25 participants take a test twice: once after they visualize themselves doing well and once when they don't do so. You found that, on this 20-item test, subjects performed an average of 0.35 points higher when they visualized themselves being successful (s = 1.1). Using α 0.01, determine whether visualizing success increases test performance.

3) Are people willing to pay more for something if they choose it among many alternatives? To find out, an experimenter tested a group of participants (N = 10) under two conditions. In one, participants choose their favorite chocolate bar among 3 choices. In the other, they choose their favorite among 10 choices. In both conditions participants were asked, after they made their choice, how much they'd be willing to pay for it. It was found the average mean difference score between the two conditions was $0.45 (participants offered to pay an average of $0.45 more when there were 10 choices relative to when there were only 3), with a standard deviation of $0.19. Should we conclude from these findings that, indeed, people are willing to pay more for something if they choose it among many alternatives? Use α 0.01.

4) You ask the same research question (*Are people willing to pay more for something if they choose it among many alternatives?*), but this time you use non-food items. So, you test a group of participants (N = 20) under two conditions. In one, participants choose their favorite pair of gloves among 4 choices. In the other, they choose their favorite among 12 choices. Again, in both conditions participants were asked, after they made their choice, how much they'd be willing to pay for it. It was found the average mean difference score between the two conditions was $4.25 (participants offered to pay an average of $4.25 more when there were 12 choices relative to when there were only 4), with a standard deviation of $2.54. Should we conclude from these findings that, indeed, people are willing to pay more for something if they choose it among many alternatives? Use α 0.05.

Solutions to problems.

1)

Step 1.

    Null Hypothesis, H_o: How polite someone is does not affect their perceived level of power.

    Alternative Hypothesis, H_1: How polite someone is affects their perceived level of power.

Step 2.

α 0.05, two tails, df = 41.

$t_{crit} = 2.021$

Step 3.

$M_D = 4.1$

$S_{MD} = 0.46$

$t_{obt} = + 8.91$

Step 4.

$t_{obt} > t_{crit}$; Reject H_o.

We found how polite someone is affects their perceived level of power, $t(41) = + 8.91, p < 0.05$, two-tailed.

2)

<u>Step 1.</u>

<u>Null Hypothesis, H_0</u>: Visualizing success does not increase test performance.

<u>Alternative Hypothesis, H_1</u>: Visualizing success increases test performance.

<u>Step 2.</u>

α 0.01, one tailed, df = 24.

t_{crit} = 2.492

<u>Step 3.</u>

M_D = 0.35

S_{MD} = 0.22

t_{obt} = + 1.59

<u>Step 4.</u>

$t_{obt} < t_{crit}$; Retain H_0.

We found visualizing success does not increase test performance, $t(24) = +1.59$, $p > 0.01$, one-tailed.

3)

Step 1.

Null Hypothesis, H_o: People are not willing to pay more for something if they chose it among many alternatives.

Alternative Hypothesis, H_1: People are willing to pay more for something if they chose it among many alternatives.

Step 2.

α 0.01, one tailed, df = 9.

$t_{crit} = 2.821$

Step 3.

$M_D = 0.45$

$S_{MD} = 0.14$

$t_{obt} = + 3.21$

Step 4.

$t_{obt} > t_{crit}$; Reject H_o.

We found people are willing to pay more for something if they choose it among many alternatives, $t(9) = + 3.21$, $p < 0.01$, one-tailed.

4)

<u>Step 1.</u>

       <u>Null Hypothesis, H_0</u>: People are not willing to pay more for something if they choose it among many alternatives.

       <u>Alternative Hypothesis, H_1</u>: People are willing to pay more for something if they choose it among many alternatives.

<u>Step 2.</u>

α 0.05, one tailed, df = 19.

t_{crit} = 1.729

<u>Step 3.</u>

M_D = 4.25

S_{MD} = 0.57

t_{obt} = + 7.46

<u>Step 4.</u>

$t_{obt} > t_{crit}$; Reject H_0.

We found people are willing to pay more for something if they choose it among many alternatives, $t(19) = +7.46$, $p < 0.05$, one-tailed.

Chapter 13
Errors in hypothesis testing

Before moving on to the next inferential statistical test, let's discuss an unfortunate but unavoidable possibility when conducting research in Psychology, or any other discipline. This possibility is present no matter what type of research you are conducting or what type of statistical test you are employing.[86]

The issue is this: When you make the statistical decision to either reject or accept the Null Hypothesis (H_o) *you may be wrong*, that is, you may have made an *error*. Importantly, *error* refers not to a mistake made by the researcher, but to an error that can occur *any* time you make an inference about a population based on a sample. This kind of inference, like any inference, could be wrong, even when you've done everything the way you should.

But if you could be wrong, that means you could also be correct-- in fact, inferential statistical procedures (i.e., hypothesis tests) are set up to maximize your chances of being correct. Put simply: You may make the wrong decision, but if you follow the procedures correctly, you will probably make the right one. And remember, when we refer to *the decision*, we mean the decision to either reject H_o (decide an effect is present) or accept H_o (decide an effect is not present).

Although it is impossible to know for certain whether the decision you made is correct, you *can* know:

- the *type* of error you might have made
- the approximate *probability* you have made that error
- the *consequences* of the particular error you might have made

We will now take each of these in turn

Types of errors

The types of possible errors in hypothesis testing can be visualized easily with a 2 x 2 table. Why 2 x 2? Because you have *two* options when making your decision (1- reject H_o; 2- accept H_o) and there are *two* possible realities (1- H_o is false; 2- H_o is true). Though we don't usually ever know the reality, we do know exactly two are possible (either 1- H_o is false, or 2- H_o is true). This all results in 4 possible outcomes to an experiment, where two of the four are errors and the other two are correct decisions:

---

[86] So, the concepts presented here apply to both the tests you've learned and the ones you have yet to learn.

Actual reality:

	H_o is false (effect exists)	H_o is true (no effect exists)
Your decision: reject H_o (effect exists)	1	2
accept H_o (no effect exists)	3	4

Let's examine each of the four possibilities (numbered 1 through 4 above):

1. *Rejecting H_o when H_o is indeed false*[87]

   This is a correct decision; you have concluded there is an effect (rejected H_o), and indeed there *is* one (H_o is false).

   > This is the best outcome. You decided based on your statistical analysis that there is a relationship between the variables you were studying (e.g., between *age* and *memory ability*)—that is, that there was an effect. And, in reality, there is one.

2. *Rejecting H_o when H_o is actually true*

   An error has been made. Namely, you have concluded there is an effect (rejected H_o), but there is not one (H_o is true).

   > This is called a **Type I Error**, and it is the worst outcome of a study (an explanation of why it's so bad is coming soon).

3. *Accepting H_o when H_o is actually false*

   An error has been made here as well; you have concluded there is no effect / difference / relationship, but in fact there *is* one.

   > This is called a **Type II Error**. It is not a desirable outcome (it is an *error*, after all), but it's not as bad as a Type I Error.

4. *Accepting H_o when H_o is indeed true*

---

[87] Remember, if H_o (the null hypothesis) is false, that means there is an effect. That is because H_o says there's no effect, so if that's false, then there *is* an effect (double negative = positive).

This is a correct decision; you have concluded there is no effect / difference / relationship, and indeed there isn't one.

This is not the greatest outcome, but it's better than making an error.

A **Type I Error** occurs when a researcher concludes that an effect exists (rejects H_o) but in fact an effect does not exist (H_o is true).

A **Type II Error** occurs when a researcher concludes that an effect does not exist (accepts H_o) but in fact an effect does exist (H_o is false).

* * *

Those are the four possible outcomes of an experiment. So before you begin a research study, you know in the end one of those four will occur.

However, once you make your statistical decision, which of course you always will, two of the possibilities are eliminated. Look:

If you *reject* H_o, then you either made the correct decision or you made a Type I Error:

Actual reality:

	H_o is false	H_o is true
reject H_o	**Correct decision**	**Type I Error**
accept Ho	Type II Error	Correct Decision

Your decision:

If you *accept* H_o, then you either made the correct decision or you made a Type II Error:

Actual reality:

	H_o is false	H_o is true
reject H_o	Correct decision	Type I Error
accept H_o	**Type II Error**	**Correct Decision**

Your decision:

Remember, however, you never know for *certain* whether you've made the correct decision or made an error. Referring to the table above, you know the *row* you're in once you've made your decision, but you can never know the *column*. Think about it: If you knew the actual reality, that is, whether H_o is false or true (whether an effect exists or doesn't exist), then why would you have done the study in the first place?

Fortunately, as stated earlier, although we can never know for sure whether we've made an error, we *can* know the approximate *probability* of making errors.

Probability of Type I and II errors occurring

Type I: If you *reject* H_o, the probability you made a Type I error is equal to your level of significance, α. If you reject H_o using α 0.05, the probability you've made a Type I error is 0.05 or 5%. If you reject H_o using α 0.01, the probability you've made a Type I error is 0.01 or 1%.

Type II: If you *accept* H_o, the probability you made a Type II error is equal to β (beta). Calculating β is well beyond the scope of this book. Just know β is a probability, but also know it is only an estimate; you can never know the exact value of β.

The following table summarizes the probabilities of the various possible outcomes:

| | | Actual reality: | |
		H_o is false	H_o is true
	reject H_o	(correct dec.) $p = 1 - \beta$	Type I Error ($p = \alpha$)
Your decision:			
	accept H_o	Type II Error ($p = \beta$)	(correct dec.) $p = 1 - \alpha$

Finally, we also know the *consequences* of making the two types of errors.

Consequences of Type I and II errors

To understand the consequences of errors, consider the following two scenarios.

> Scenario 1. You found people who were in your *high fear* condition—told they'd soon be receiving electric shocks—did not talk to each other any more during a break than participants in your *low fear* condition (subjects told they'd soon be receiving ice cream). In other words, you found no effect of fear on how much participants talked with one another.

Did you make the correct decision, or did you make a Type II Error? That's hard to say, right? Well, what if during the 2 years after you conducted your experiment, 15 *other* experiments were conducted using the same variables as yours, and 14 of those 15 found that high fear participants *did* talk to each other more than low fear participants? It's starting to look like you probably made a Type II Error. People who are afraid of something do seem to want to talk to other people more than people who are not afraid, and for some reason you failed to detect this effect in your experiment.[88]

> Scenario 2. You hypothesized that people who wear hats are more shy than people who do not. Therefore, you walked around campus and found the first 20 people you could find who were wearing a hat and gave them a test of shyness. You did the same with the first 20 people you could find who were not wearing a hat. You found the average score of the 20 people wearing hats was significantly higher, indicating more shyness, than the 20 people not wearing hats. In other words, you rejected H_0.

So far, so good—you found the effect you were looking for. However, after publishing your findings, ten other researchers performed very similar studies, and none of them found a significant relationship between hat wearing and shyness like you did. Again, although we can never know for sure, it is beginning to look like you've made a Type I Error: claiming there is an effect / difference / relationship, when really there is not one.

Given these two scenarios, which do you think is the worse type of error, I or II, and why? Think about the consequences of your decisions in both cases, assuming they were the wrong ones.

Answer: A Type I error, in psychological research at least, is almost always worse. Why? Because if you find an effect, you typically publish and/or publicly present your findings. But then if your finding turns out to be wrong, you can't go back in time. Your incorrect finding is out there, in published journals, both in print and online, forever! On the other hand, if you conclude there is *no* effect you do *not* typically publish the results. So your error (assuming you've made an error—Type II in this case) is *not* out there; you have time to start over or move on to something else.

Importantly, the fact that the consequences of a Type I error are so much worse than those of a Type II error is the reason the level of significance, α, is so small (only 0.05 or 0.01). After all, you want there to be only a small chance of making a Type I Error. Recall the probability of making a Type I error when you reject the null hypothesis is equal to alpha.

---

[88] One possible culprit in why you didn't find an effect when one seems to exist (based on all that subsequent research which found an effect) is that your sample size was too small. But other possibilities exist, as will be discussed in the next chapter.

Now, using such a small value makes it more difficult to find an effect (reject H_o), but if you *do* reject H_o with an alpha of 0.05 or 0.01, you're pretty confident you haven't made an error. If you used a large alpha level, say 0.30 (30%), you'd be making it easier to find an effect but then if you find that effect (reject H_o), you're not feeling so good because you know there's a 30% chance (as opposed to a 5% or 1% chance) you've made a Type I error.[89]

A quick question before moving on: What is the probability you've made a Type I error if you accept H_o?[90]

*　*　*

It is important you realize that Type I and II errors are not particular to hypothesis testing. The same principle can be found in many disciplines and applications. In fact, almost any time you make a *dichotomous*, or *binary*, decision (that is, a decision in which there are only *two* options) you may be correct or you may have made an error (either Type I or II, depending on your decision).

Example: **Is the climate changing as a result of human activity?**

| | | Actual reality: | |
		It is	It is not
Your decision:	Yes, it is	Correct Decision	Type I Error
	No, it is not	Type II Error	Correct Decision

Different terminology is sometimes used, but the concept is exactly the same. Take a look at the following table, and note the use of the terms *true* and *false* (which refer to whether you made the *correct* or *incorrect* decision, respectively) and of the terms *positive* and *negative* (which refer to whether you decided there *was* or *was not* an effect, respectively):

---

[89] This is a very important concept and will be reiterated and expanded upon in the next chapter.
[90] Zero. If you accept H_o, you've either made the correct decision or you've made a Type II error. You could not have made a Type I Error. If you don't see that, look back at any of the tables presented in this chapter.

Actual reality:

	It is	It is not
Yes, it is	True Positive	False Positive
No, it is not	False Negative	True Negative

(Your decision: — rows labeled "Yes, it is" / "No, it is not")

Or, to use the terminology of an area of Psychology called *Signal Detection Theory* (and which may help you conceptualize the four possible outcomes):

Actual reality:

	It is	It is not
Yes, it is	Hit	False Alarm
No, it is not	Miss	Correct Rejection

(Your decision: — rows labeled "Yes, it is" / "No, it is not")

Something to keep in mind which the above illustrates: A Type I Error is not *always* the worst outcome. Take the example just presented. Is concluding that climate change is due to human activity when actually it is not (a Type I Error) worse than concluding climate change is *not* due to human activity when actually it *is* (a Type II Error)? What are the ramifications of a Type I Error in this scenario? A Type II Error? It is not as straightforward in this example as in a typical research study.

The climate change example also illustrates that you do not always know the probabilities, or even the approximate probabilities, of making errors. α and β only apply with inferential statistics. It's probably safe to say that, when it comes to the question of climate change, we have no idea what the chances of Type I and II errors are.

The next chapter presents a concept any researcher needs to understand: *statistical power*—more commonly just called *power*. You will no doubt notice that power is relevant to the ongoing discussion on errors (and avoiding them). The chapter on power should also serve as a review of several key concepts you've learned about.

Questions.

1- You performed a hypothesis test and decided an effect was present. You may have made what type of error?

2- Researcher X rejected his null hypothesis. What type of error may he have made?

3- What is the *probability* that Researcher X from question #2 made an error? What about the probability that you made an error in the hypothesis test referenced in question #1?

4- You performed a hypothesis test and decided in the end that there was not an effect. You may have made a _____ (Type I / Type II) error, and the probability that you've done so is _____.

5- The doctor examines you and thinks you have a cold. She subscribes cold medication. However, it doesn't work because you didn't have a cold after all. The doctor's diagnosis sounds like a (circle all that apply):

      Type II Error
      Hit
      Correct Rejection
      Type I Error
      Miss
      False positive

Answers to questions.

1) You may have made a Type I error. But you definitely did not make a Type II error.
2) He may have made a Type I error. See how this is the same question as #1, but asked differently?
3) In both cases, the probability that a (Type I) error was made was whatever the alpha/α level was (either 5% or 1%, probably). Notice in both cases the probability of a Type II error is *zero*.
4) *Type II error* (note you could not have possibly made a Type I error); *unknown*. Note that, although the probability is unknown, we give that probability a label anyway: β (beta).
5) Type I Error; False Positive

Chapter 14
Statistical Power

You learned in the last chapter that, even though inferential statistical tests are designed to differentiate the significant/real differences from those caused by chance, they cannot do so perfectly. Since an *inference* is being made (never forget you're always trying to learn about populations but can only make inferences about them based on samples), errors—making the wrong decision despite doing everything the way you're supposed to—are always possible.

You also learned about the *probabilities* of making errors. Specifically, if you decide you have an effect, the chance you made a (Type I) error is equal to your alpha level, and if you decide you do *not* have an effect, the chance you made a Type II error is equal to a probability called beta (β).

Take another look at the table from the last chapter that lays out the possible outcomes and how we represent their respective probabilities of occurring.

	Actual reality:	
	H_0 is false	H_0 is true
reject H_0	*(correct dec.)* $p = 1 - \beta$ = **power**	Type I Error ($p = \alpha$)
accept H_0	Type II Error ($p = \beta$)	*(correct dec.)* $p = 1 - \alpha$

Your decision:

In this chapter, we will focus on the upper left cell of the table. As indicated on the table, the probability (p) of that outcome—rejecting H_0 when H_0 false (deciding an effect exists when, in fact, one does)—is 1 minus β. As discussed previously, however, we don't actually know the value of β (and therefore don't know what $1 - \beta$ is). Though it would be nice if we did know that—that is, the probability of deciding an effect exists when, in fact, one does—what's actually more important is knowing *how to maximize our chances of that outcome.*[91]

Why is that important? Remember that the researcher *wants* to find an effect, but *only* if there really is one. He doesn't want to find an effect if there actually isn't one. Think of it this way: The most desirable outcome is the upper left of the table (*correctly* deciding there's an effect), and the least desirable outcome is the upper right of the table (*incorrectly* deciding there's an effect).

---

[91] Which is more important: knowing the probability that you'll find a good job, or knowing how to maximize your probability of getting one?

A study's probability of finding an effect, if there is one to be found, is referred to as the study's *statistical power* (or just *power*).

> The **statistical power** of a study is a study's ability of finding an effect if there is one, or how likely it is a study will find an effect if there is one.

It may help to consider why *power* is the term used to describe a study's ability to find an effect (to reject the null hypothesis). First, think about where else this term is used in science, as with the power of a microscope or telescope. These instruments are designed to see things that are small and/or far away and thus need to be (relatively) powerful. And, the more powerful the one you're using, the more likely it is you will find what you're looking for. Well, a research study is not a physical device but it is most certainly an instrument—one designed to "see" relationships between variables (i.e., effects). Thus, the more powerful your study, the more likely it is you will find what you're looking for (which is an effect, of course!).

The term *sensitivity* may also come to mind. For example, if a microphone is very sensitive, then it is more likely to pick up sounds—and more able to detect softer sounds than a less sensitive microphone. Studies work the same way. As a matter of fact, sometimes the term *sensitivity* is used rather than *power*. Just like power, a study's sensitivity is its probability of finding an effect if there is one.

*   *   *

Now that you have a general idea of what power is, let's discuss what the researcher should do to increase it, that is, to increase her chances of rejecting H_o (of finding an effect).

First, think about what has to happen for you to reject H_o. No doubt you recall the rule for determining if you should reject H_o: *If the obtained statistic is larger than the critical statistic, you reject H_o (conclude there is an effect) and if it's not, you retain H_o (conclude there is no effect).* But let's briefly review exactly what that means—*why* it's the rule.

When inferential statistics was first presented, you learned that it works in two steps (at least conceptually):

Step 1) Determine the probability that your result was due to chance/sampling error.

Step 2) Decide whether that probability is **a)** high enough to conclude your result was indeed just chance or, alternatively, **b)** low enough to conclude your result probably was *not* just chance and must therefore be real.

As things went along, though, we were able to short-cut things a little. Rather than first finding a probability as stipulated in Step 1 (remember looking up probabilities/proportions on the z table?), then deciding if that probability is less than or greater than alpha, you could simply jump right to Step 2. That is, if the obtained statistic is larger than the critical statistic, that tells you the probability that your result was due to chance/sampling error is low enough (less than alpha) to conclude your result probably was *not* just chance and must therefore be real—no need to know the exact probability.

* * *

So, how do you increase your chance of finding an effect if there is one, that is, increase power? To answer that simply, we increase power primarily by doing things that will *increase the size of your obtained statistic*. Doing this makes it more likely that your obtained statistic will be greater than your critical statistic. Thus, the way you increase power is by doing things you expect will increase the magnitude of your obtained statistic[92]. Importantly, doing this will only increase the size of your obtained statistic if there is actually an effect; it will not increase your chance of finding an effect if there isn't one (i.e., of making a Type I error).

Several factors affect power, which the researcher has varying levels of control over. They apply to virtually any kind of study researchers in Psychology use, but when it is necessary to use concrete examples, we will focus on single sample studies that use single-sample t tests to analyze the data.

Each of the factors to be discussed influences power in one of two ways: by influencing either the effect or the error. Remember, the obtained statistic is a *ratio* of effect to error; the effect is found in the numerator of the formula (for example, in a single sample t test the numerator is M - μ), and the error is found in the denominator (e.g., S_M, standard error). Thus, there are two ways a given factor can increase the overall value of the obtained statistic and thus increase power: 1-reduce the denominator or 2-increase the numerator. Note any given factor could also reduce power by doing the opposite: 1-increasing the denominator or 2-decreasing the numerator.

The factors affecting power that will be discussed in this chapter are: the variability in the scores, sample size (N), and the size of the treatment effect. You'll notice that each influences either the effect or the error.

Variability in the scores

As discussed in earlier chapters, variability in the scores within a given group or condition is considered error because it's variability that occurs due not to one of the variables being

---

[92] Keep in mind that *magnitude* is the distance a value is from zero—the sign doesn't matter. For example, -10 has a greater magnitude (or size) than 8.

studied but instead due to unknown causes. Intuitively, it seems that less error in the scores—less variability occurring for unknown reasons—is a good thing. And it is! We can look more closely at why that's the case by examining almost any formula used to calculate an obtained statistic, but again we'll go with a single sample t situation.

Below is the formula used to find the single sample t score (t_{obt}). Notice the denominator is S_M, which as you know is called standard error. Well, if the denominator were smaller (less error), then the overall t_{obt} would be larger. And remember that's exactly what we need to do in order to increase power: *increase the size of the obtained statistic.*

$$t_{obt} = \frac{M - \mu}{S_M} \qquad \text{And recall: } S_M = \frac{s}{\sqrt{N}}$$

Let's demonstrate how this can happen by calculating t_{obt} for two sets of results (Study A and Study B) which are identical except for the variability in the scores, s.

Study A: M = 900; μ = 1000; N = 25; s = 400

$$S_M = \frac{s}{\sqrt{N}} = \frac{400}{\sqrt{25}} = 80 \quad t_{obt} = \frac{M - \mu}{S_M} = \frac{900 - 1000}{80} = -1.25$$

Study B: M = 900; μ = 1000; N = 25; s = 300

$$S_M = \frac{s}{\sqrt{N}} = \frac{300}{\sqrt{25}} = 60 \quad t_{obt} = \frac{M - \mu}{S_M} = \frac{900 - 1000}{60} = -1.67$$

To summarize, when we decreased the variability in the scores (but kept everything else the same to isolate the influence of doing so), the magnitude of the obtained statistic increased, and therefore power increased. Note that increasing s would have the opposite effect on power.

> *Less variability in scores increases power by decreasing the error, while more variability in scores decreases power.*

It may help to read over some other ways to summarize the effect of decreasing the variability in scores:

Less variability in scores » *smaller standard error* » *larger obtained statistic, or;*

Smaller s » *smaller S_M* » *larger t_{obt}, or;*

Smaller numerator of S_M formula » *smaller denominator of t_{obt} formula* » *larger t_{obt}*

Finally, let's briefly consider how you might actually go about trying to reduce the variability in the scores. Well, you can't do it directly—unlike with sample data made up for a demonstration, you cannot mess around with *real* data! But you could make decisions as you design your study that you expect would *probably* end up reducing the variability in scores.

For example, if your dependent variable were reaction time in a widely used task with an established population mean reaction time (say, $\mu = 1000$ milliseconds), and you wanted to see if people have a faster reaction time after consuming a 12 ounce caffeinated beverage, but you knew that reaction time varies with age, you could reduce the variability of age in your study, say by only studying participants between the ages of 18 and 20, and thus probably reduce the variability in scores (reaction times).

On the other hand, you may *not* want to restrict the age range of your participants like this since doing so makes your results less generalizable; if you only study a small age range, your results may only apply to that small age range. Or maybe you don't care—it all depends on your particular situation.

Another way to decrease variability in the scores is by using a within-subjects design (as opposed to a between-subjects design). This was discussed in considerable depth in Chapter 12 when contrasting the independent samples *t* test, used when you have a between-subjects design, to the related samples *t* test, used when you have a within-subjects design.

To very briefly review that discussion: By using a within-subjects study, you are able to calculate difference scores, which are simply each participant's score in one condition minus their score in the other condition. Crucially, these difference scores do not contain variability due to pre-existing individual differences among the participants, and are therefore usually less variable than the original X scores, which *do* contain variability due to pre-existing individual differences among participants.

You should know from the *current* discussion how reduced sample variability, whether by using a within-subjects design or by some other means such as restricting the ages of your participants, translates into a larger obtained statistic. And you are also now learning how these things increase something called *power*.

You cannot always use a within-subjects design, so this is not always a viable option, but luckily other factors affect power as well. The next to be discussed is *sample size (N)* which is, by the way, almost always a viable option. After all, there is usually nothing stopping you from going out and finding more participants.

Sample size (N)

Another option for increasing power is to increase the sample size, N. Just as with variability, the effect N has on power may be intuitive for you. Your intuition may be telling you that the larger the sample, the more powerful the study. If so, your intuition is once again correct! But let's again discuss *why* that's the case by examining the formulas and by using two example results from the caffeine/reaction time study describe previously. But this time we'll vary N:

Study A: M = 900; μ = 1000; N = 25; s = 400

$$S_M = \frac{s}{\sqrt{N}} = \frac{400}{\sqrt{25}} = \mathbf{80} \quad t_{obt} = \frac{M-\mu}{S_M} = \frac{900-1000}{80} = \mathbf{-1.25}$$

Study C: M = 900; μ = 1000; N = 49; s = 400

$$S_M = \frac{s}{\sqrt{N}} = \frac{400}{\sqrt{49}} = \mathbf{57.14} \quad t_{obt} = \frac{M-\mu}{S_M} = \frac{900-1000}{57.14} = \mathbf{-1.75}$$

To summarize, when we increased N but kept everything else the same (to isolate the influence of increasing N), the magnitude of the obtained statistic increased, and therefore power increased. Note decreasing N would have the opposite effect on power.

> *A larger N increases power by decreasing the error, while a smaller N decreases power.*

It may help to read over some other ways to summarize the effect of increasing sample size:

Larger sample size » smaller standard error » larger obtained statistic, or;

Larger N » smaller S_M » larger t_{obt}, or;

Larger denominator of S_M formula » smaller denominator of t_{obt} formula » larger t_{obt}

Note that increasing N, in addition to increasing the magnitude of the obtained statistic as just demonstrated, also *reduces* the magnitude of the critical statistic.[93] If you look at the t table, you will see the critical t for Study A (n = 25) is 1.711 and for Study C (N = 49) the critical t is 1.684.[94] The next factor that influences power to be discussed is the *size of the treatment effect*.

Size of the treatment effect

Another way to increase power is to manipulate your independent variable in a way that you expect will produce a relatively large effect. In the caffeine study described earlier, we said you gave your participants a 12 oz caffeinated beverage to see if it sped up (reduced) reaction time. Well, if caffeine does in fact affect reaction time, it's likely that more caffeine will affect reaction time even more, that is, will produce a larger treatment effect. Makes sense, right? But let's once more examine *how* this influences the obtained statistic by comparing two studies which are identical except for one factor, in this case, the size of the treatment effect. We have tried to increase the size/magnitude of the treatment effect by giving participants a 24 oz caffeinated beverage instead of 12 oz beverage as in our original Study A.

Study A: M = 900; μ = 1000; N = 25; s = 400

$$S_M = \frac{s}{\sqrt{N}} = \frac{400}{\sqrt{25}} = \textbf{80} \quad t_{obt} = \frac{M-\mu}{S_M} = \frac{900-1000}{80} = \mathbf{-1.25}$$

Study D: M = 800; μ = 1000; N = 25; s = 400

$$S_M = \frac{s}{\sqrt{N}} = \frac{400}{\sqrt{25}} = \textbf{80} \quad t_{obt} = \frac{M-\mu}{S_M} = \frac{800-1000}{80} = \mathbf{-2.5}$$

In this case, a larger obtained statistic resulted not because there was less error as was the case when variability in scores is smaller or when N is larger, but because there's a greater effect. Or, in terms of the formulas, the larger obtained statistic resulted not because the

---

[93] Don't lose track of the fact that the factors being discussed affect power because they influence the size of the obtained statistic, which needs to be larger than the critical statistic in order to reject H_o. Well, another way to make it more likely that your obtained statistic will be larger than your critical statistic is to have a smaller critical statistic. Increasing N both increases the size of your obtained statistic *and* decreases the size of your critical statistic.

[94] Assuming alpha 0.05, one-tailed. But notice the critical t is always smaller with larger N's regardless of the alpha and # of tails.

denominator was smaller as was the case when variability in scores is smaller or when N is larger, but because the numerator was larger.

In any case, the rule at hand is:

> *A larger treatment effect increases power by increasing the effect, while a smaller treatment effect decreases power.*

You may not be able to manipulate your independent variable more strongly as we did here, or you may not have any control over an independent variable at all. But again this is one option among several which can increase power.

*   *   *

It was pointed out in the last chapter that, to increase your chance of finding an effect (having an obtained value larger than the critical value), you *could* simply increase your alpha level higher than those conventionally used (e.g., to 30%). After all, doing so would reduce the size of the critical statistic (remember, higher alpha level = smaller critical statisic). However, this is highly undesirable, and would likely even render your study unpublishable, because doing so would simultaneously increase your chance of a Type I error. As a matter of fact, most statistical tables, including the one at the end of this book, do not even list critical statistics corresponding to alpha levels higher than 5%. But, if they did, you know they'd be smaller and would hence make it easier to find an effect.

Conversely, going the other way and using an alpha level smaller than 1% makes you more confident you haven't made a Type I error if you find an effect. But, it makes it more difficult to find an effect in the first place. Therefore, choosing a smaller alpha level reduces power. So you can think of the conventional 5% and 1% alpha levels as representing a balance between the need to have significant confidence that you haven't made a Type I error when you reject H_0 (which is why alpha levels are so low), and the necessity of being able to reject H_0 in the first place if it's warranted (which is why conventional alpha levels aren't *too* tiny).

Thus, all the methods discussed in this chapter truly do increase power, meaning they increase the chance (probability) of finding an effect if there is one *without simultaneously increasing the chance of finding an effect if there isn't one* (i.e., of making a Type I error).

*   *   *

Power Analysis

Although a detailed discussion is beyond the scope of this book, you should have an awareness and very basic knowledge of something called *power analysis*.

Technically, you could peform a power analysis on an existing study to get an estimate of how powerful it is. However, it's probably more practical, and it's more common, to perform a power analysis *before* conducting your study.

What you usually do is calculate how many participants you'd need in order to be relatively certain (you choose the certainty) that, if an effect exists, you'd be able to detect it (reject H_0). This would depend mainly on how large of a treatment effect you expect (again, if there even *is* a treatment effect). Think of it like this: You're "asking" the power analysis formula "If I want to be 90% certain of finding an effect, assuming that if there *is* an effect it would be about 10 points, and if I plan to use an alpha level of 5%, how many participants do I need?" You may be picking up an important thing to know about power analysis: It's just an *estimate* to help the researcher get an idea of how many participants he may need.

Again, a detailed discussion is not warranted here. But even if you don't know how to perform a power analysis, know this: If you suspect the possible treatment you're investigating is pretty small, you know you'll need a relatively powerful study to find that (possible) effect.[95] Therefore, you need to do what you can to maximize power. And that you should now know *plenty* about!

*   *   *

It's now time to move on to the next type of inferential statistical test you need to know about. And remember, everything from this chapter applies to it, too.

But why do you need to learn all about another test? Well, you may have noticed that in all the studies presented so far, there have been only one or two groups (or conditions). You need to know what to do if you have *more than two* groups, because many studies have just that. Say, for example, we wanted to see if there were differences in pleasantness ratings among *three* sounds, or we wanted to compare the effectiveness of *three* summer programs? A different approach must be taken in such cases since *t* tests can only handle 2 groups/conditions. That approach is called Analysis of Variance, abbreviated *ANOVA*.

---

[95] The smaller the effect, the more powerful the study needs to be in order to detect it (remember the microscope analogy?).

Questions.

1. A more powerful study would have a higher probability of _____ (rejecting H_o / accepting H_o) if _____ (H_o is true / H_o is false). In other words, studies with more power are more likely to _____ (not find an effect / find an effect) if there _____ (is one / isn't one).

2. Assuing an effect was found, it is _____ (more / less / equally) likely that a Type I error was committed in a more powerful study relative to in a less powerful study.

3. Which of the following would tend to <u>increase</u> power?

  a) Increasing the variability in the scores
  b) Decreasing alpha (e.g., from 5% to 1%)
  c) Increasing N
  d) Increasing the size of the treatment effect
  e) Decreasing N
  f) Use a survey with fewer items
  g) Using a within-subjects design

4. What from the list above would tend to <u>decrease</u> power?

5. Assuming everything else is equal, a within-subjects study would usually have _____ (more / less) power than a between-subjects study due to a difference in the amount of _____ (effect / error) you'd expect to have.

6. One study has more power than another. As such, the more powerful one probably has a _____ (larger / smaller) ratio of effect to error. The obtained statistic formula in the <u>less</u> powerful one would probably have a _____ (larger / smaller) denominator and/or a _____ (larger / smaller) numerator.

7. Increasing N affects power in two ways. What are those two ways?

8. In a scenario presented in an earlier chapter, we wanted to find out if marking up a pair of dice with a magic marker in a certain way would affect the behavior of the dice. In this situation, we had reason to believe that the effect of marking the dice, if there is one at all, would likely be very small.

  a. Would you say we need a very powerful study to adequately test our hypothesis, or would a relatively non-powerful study suffice? Explain your answer.
  b. Regardless of whether or not we *need* to increase power in this study, what is the most likely strategy we would take to if we were to try to increase it?

9. What is the most likely reason a researcher would perform a power analysis before conducting her study?

Answers to questions.

1. rejecting H_0; H_0 is false; find an effect; is one

2. equally

3. Increasing N (c), Increasing the size of the treatment effect (d), Using a within-subjects design (g)

4. Increasing the variability in the scores (a), Decreasing alpha (b), Decreasing N (e)

5. more; error

6. larger; larger; smaller

7. N tends to reduce the amount of error (tends to reduce the size of the denominator of the formula for the obtained statistic), and thus tends to *increase the size of the obtained statistic*. N also *reduces the size of the critical statistic*, since for any given criterion a higher N/df corresponds to a lower critical statistic (which you can verify by examining any statistical table).

8a. We would need a relatively powerful study here since we think the (possible) effect would be very small. To put it in terms of the formula for the obtained statistic, we expect a small numerator (small effect), so we had better do what we can to end up with a *very* small denominator (*very* small error) if we want any chance of detecting this (possible) effect.

8b. The most sensible and practical strategy to increase power in this study would be to increase N. In other words, we'd roll the dice a large number of times (e.g., N = 1,000 or more). Decreasing the variability of the outcomes of your indvidual dice rolls isn't possible (right?). We could *try* to increase the size of the treatment effect by marking up the dice as much as possible, but we really wanted to determine if there was an effect caused by marking them up *in a particular way* (which could be done quickly and stealthily), so that's probably not an option, either. To summarize: decrease variability-No; increase N-Yes; increase treatment effect; possibly.

9. Most likely, a researcher would conduct a power analysis in order to get an estimate of how many participants she was likely to need in order to find an effect, if there is one. Note: To get this estimate of N she would need to specify, among other things, how large she expects the possible treatment effect to be (based on similar research and such).

Chapter 15
Analysis of variance (ANOVA)

You may have noticed that all the research studies we've dealt with so far have had only *two* levels of the independent variable (IV). Below is a list of the IVs, and the two levels of them, for several of those research studies from previous chapters.

- IV-*scarcity*: Participants shopped in a store where items were either 1) scarce or 2) not scarce.
- IV-*gender*: Participants were either 1) male or 2) female.
- IV-*summer reading program*: Students either 1) participated in it or 2) didn't.
- IV-*whether opponent is known*: Opponents were either 1) known to participants or 2) unknown to participants.

However, many research studies have an independent variable with *more than* two levels. Many even have more than two independent variables. For example, a study may have 4 independent variables, where some or all of them have more than 2 levels. There could even be multiple *dependent* variables.[96]

This chapter will explain the statistical test used when you have one independent variable with more than two levels. Since there is one independent variable, the test used is called a *One-way* Analysis of Variance.

*   *   *

Consider the following:

> An experimenter sought to find out whether or not children become more able to delay gratification as they got older. The experimenter had access to children of ages 6, 8, and 10. He placed a chocolate bar in front of the kids one at a time, and told them that the longer they waited before eating the chocolate bar, the more of a reward they would receive afterwards.

List the independent variable and its levels, and the dependent variable.[97]

---

[96] The statistical procedures used to analyze the results of this type of study are called *multivariate statistics*.

[97] IV is *age*; levels of IV are 6 years old, 8 years old, and 10 years old. DV is the time elapsed before kids ate the chocolate bar.

Notice there are *three* levels of the independent variable—in this case, three groups of children. But before this chapter, we have always had only two conditions, and so we used a *z* test or a *t* test.

That's because, in a *z* or *t* test, the effect is always the difference between *two* things. You can see that clearly when you review how the effect is measured in those tests. You may recognize the effects listed below as the numerators of the respective formulas:

- *z* test: effect = **M - μ**
- Single sample *t* test: effect = **M - μ**
- Independent samples *t* test: effect = **M₁ - M₂**
- Related samples *t* test: effect = **M_D** [98]

For all of those tests, the effect was based on a subtraction between two things, which makes perfect sense when you have two conditions. But it doesn't make any sense if you have more than two. Therefore, for studies with more than two conditions, you take a different approach. That is where Analysis of Variance, ANOVA [pronounced ANN-OH-VUH], comes in.

> *One-way analysis of variance (ANOVA)* is used when you have one independent variable with more than two conditions.

Since subtracting three or more means from each other to measure the effect won't give you anything meaningful,[99] ANOVA instead measures the effect by measuring how much variability (variance) there is between the means.

> The **effect** in an Analysis of Variance (ANOVA) is the variance **between** the means of the conditions.

* * *

Let's clarify what is meant by *variance between the means*. First, recall that variance is a measure of variability. Variance is actually just the standard deviation squared, so you can think of variance as a measure of variability similar to standard deviation. To quantify the

---

[98] Recall M_D was based on *difference* scores (scores in one condition *subtracted* from scores in the other condition).

[99] Imagine, for example, the mean time the 6 year olds waited was 1 minute, the 8 year olds waited 3 minutes, and the 10 year olds waited 5 minutes. If you calculated the effect by subtracting the means from the youngest group to the oldest group (1 minus 3 minus 5), you'd get -7 for your effect. Or, if you subtracted the other way (5 minus 3 minus 1—which makes just as much sense), you'd get 1 for your effect. See the problem?

effect in an ANOVA, you're finding the variability of *means*—specifically, the variance between means.

To demonstrate how measuring the variance between means provides a good measure of the effect, consider the following studies:

Study 1: Does *lighting* affect the comprehension of a story? You give three groups of participants a two-page story to read, then afterwards give them a 60-question test designed to measure their comprehension of what they read. One of the groups reads the story in a brightly lit room, another reads it in a room with a medium amount of light, and a third group reads it in dim light. You found the following means for the three conditions:

Bright room	Medium room	Dim room
M = 26	M = 25	M = 23

Study 2: Does the *amount of action* that takes place in a story affect the comprehension of the story? You give three groups of participants three different stories to read, then afterwards give them a 60-question test designed to measure their comprehension of the story. One of the stories contains a lot of action in it, another contains some action, and another contains only a little bit of action. You found the following means for the three conditions:

High action	Medium action	Low action
M = 25	M = 17	M = 6

Look up at the results from the two studies. Which independent variable appears to affect reading comprehension scores more: *lighting* (Study 1) or *amount of action* (Study 2)?

You probably answered *amount of action.* But why? Is it because the differences between the means (25, 17, 6) were greater for that variable, as compared with the lighting study (26, 25, 23)? If so, you've got the idea. Another way to express the same thing is to say there is more *variability* in 25, 17, and 6 (i.e., more variance between those means) than there is in 26, 25, and 23.

All in all, then, it looks like measuring the *variance* that exists between the conditions (means) is a good way to measure the effect when you have more than two conditions.

* * *

Now that we've discussed how to measure the *effect* in an ANOVA, at least in general terms, let's turn to the other part of any inferential statistical statistic: the *error*.

Previously, when we had just two means, we couldn't make a statistical decision by looking only at the difference between them (i.e., the effect). We had to compare that effect to the amount of error present. We did that by dividing the effect by the error, which gives us the *ratio of effect to error*.

Well, it's the same here with ANOVA. We can't look only at the effect. We must compare the effect to the error by, again, dividing the effect by the error, which gives us the ratio of effect to error.

The error in an ANOVA is the *variance within* the conditions. That term is meant to capture the fact that the error is the variance among the individual scores within each of the conditions.

> The **error** in an Analysis of Variance (ANOVA) is the variance of the scores **within** each of the conditions.

To clarify what *variance within* is, and why it is the appropriate measure of error, let's look back at the two studies just presented. But this time we will look at the scores themselves rather than just the means:

Study 1

Bright room	Medium room	Dim room
27	24	21
26	26	25
25	25	23
25	24	24
27	26	22

Study 2

High action	Medium action	Low action
2	43	17
35	12	2
13	5	7
22	9	3
53	16	1

Don't pay attention to differences in scores across conditions—after all, that's *variance between*. Instead, take a close look at the variability of scores within each of the conditions. Do that for both studies. Do you see any difference between Study 1 and Study 2?

The trend is that scores within the conditions in Study 1 are much less variable than the scores within the conditions in Study 2. What may not be as clear is why this variability within the conditions (called *variance within*) should be our measure of error. So, why *should* we consider variance within to be error? And why must this variance be taken into account when we decide whether the differences (variance) between the means we observed are real or just reflect sampling error?

To begin to answer this, think about why there would be differences in scores within a condition in the first place. For example, scores within the *high action* condition were 2, 35, 13, 22, and 53. Someone in that condition scored 2 and another scored 53! But *why* is there such variability?

Name three reasons such variability among the scores in a given condition may occur, keeping in mind the dependent variable was *score on a reading comprehension test*. To ask the question differently: Why might one participant's score differ from another participant's score, when they are tested under the same condition, on a reading comprehension test?[100]

There are hundreds of things you could have come up with there, since there are hundreds of things that could potentially affect someone's score on a test. But the bottom line is that none of them have anything to do with *the amount of action* (the independent variable) that's in the story. How could we know that? Easy: Because all participants in that condition read a story with the *same amount of action in it*. We could say the same about scores within the other conditions as well.

The variance that occurs within conditions is thus due to influences *other than* what you're studying. Think about it: The variability in the scores within the conditions is not due to the independent variable (the amount of action that takes place in the story) but rather is due to many factors we can't even identify with confidence. And even if we could identify some of these factors, we'd have no way to figure out *how much* they are influencing things. It is therefore fair to call the variance of the scores within conditions *error variability*.[101]

* * *

---

[100] Some examples of things you may have thought of: One participant tried harder than the other; one is simply a better reader; one wasn't paying as much attention as the other; one was more in the mood to read a story than the other; one forgot their glasses that day; one just received some terrible news right before the experiment.

[101] This is the same concept discussed in the related samples *t* test chapter.

Understanding exactly what *variance between* and *variance within* measure is a very important step in understanding how ANOVA works. And now that you understand it, we will move on to specify exactly how you go about making your statistical decision, that is, determining whether the results you observed occurred simply due to chance/sampling error, or are real.

That means using formulas to compute a statistic on the data collected, and seeing if that statistic is significant. Sound familiar? It should—it's the same thing the researcher always does!

To determine whether we have statistical significance in an ANOVA situation, we perform what is called an F test. Guess what: We calculate an obtained F score (F_{obt}) based on the data, then compare that with a critical F (F_{crit}) that we find on a statistical table (the F table, naturally—Table 3 in the back of this book).

Let's begin with the formula for F, which takes the effect and divides it by the error, just like the z and t tests. As previously explained, the effect is the variance between the conditions and the error is the variance within the conditions. That makes the formula for F, at least conceptually:

$$F_{obt} = \frac{effect}{error} = \frac{variance\ between\ conditions}{variance\ within\ conditions}$$

The variance between conditions is abbreviated MS_{BT}, and the variance within conditions is abbreviated MS_{WI}. MS stands for *mean squares*, which is just another term for variance, so:

$$F_{obt} = \frac{MS_{BT}}{MS_{WI}}$$

The formula for mean squares will look familiar; it is the same formula for variance you encountered in the variability chapter earlier. It's also, effectively, the same formula you used for standard deviation, except you don't find the square root at the end. And fortunately, instead of starting from the beginning with the raw scores, we will now start with SS already known (but note SS = $\Sigma(X-M)^2$). The generic formula for MS is thus:

$$MS = \frac{SS}{df}$$

That makes the formulas for MS_{BT} and MS_{WI} :

$$MS_{BT} = \frac{SS_{BT}}{df_{BT}}$$

$$MS_{WI} = \frac{SS_{WI}}{df_{WI}}$$

In practice problems, you will always be provided with SS and therefore will not have to actually calculate it from the raw data[102]. However, it is important that you know what SS *is*. You've seen SS before, so some of the following may be review.

SS is short for *Sum of Squares*. It is the *total* amount, as opposed to the *average* amount, of variability present. SS_{BT} is the total amount of variability *between* the conditions; typically this means the variability between means, as we've been discussing here. SS_{WI} is the total amount of variability of scores *within* the conditions. In each case, you divide SS by the respective degrees of freedom (df) to find MS_{BT} (the effect, numerator of the F_{obt} formula) and MS_{WI} (the error, denominator of the F_{obt} formula).

The formulas for degrees of freedom are:

$$df_{BT} = k - 1 \qquad df_{WI} = N - k$$

k = the number of groups/conditions
N = the total number of participants in the study (sum of n's from all conditions)

For example, if there are 4 conditions, each with 10 subjects,

$$df_{BT} = 4 - 1 = 3 \qquad df_{WI} = 40 - 4 = 36$$

---

[102] Learning the formulas for SS_{BT} and SS_{WI} doesn't help most people to understand ANOVA.

Another way to find df_{WI} is to add up the df's $(n - 1)$ from all conditions. So if we had 4 conditions, each with 10 subjects, each condition has df = 9, and 9+9+9+9 = 36.

*   *   *

Let's continue discussing how ANOVA works by considering some hypothetical data. You can see below there are some scores listed for participants in 3 different groups/conditions.[103] Below that are the means for each group, and below that is the total variability, SS, of the scores in each group.

	Group 1	Group 2	Group 3
	10	15	21
	10	16	21
	11	17	20
	10	15	20
	11	16	21
Mean	10.4	15.8	20.6
SS	1.2	2.8	1.2

SS_{BT} = 260.4; SS_{WI} = 5.2. Remember, SS_{BT}, the total variance between the conditions, and SS_{WI}, the total variance within the conditions, will always be given, so don't worry about how those were calculated; just know what they *mean*!

As explained above, we need to find the variance between the conditions, MS_{BT}, and divide it by the variance in the scores within each condition, MS_{WI}, to find our obtained statistic, F_{obt}. Let's start by plugging the information from the current example into the formula for MS_{BT}. Remember, SS_{BT} was given and df_{BT} = k -1, and therefore:

$$MS_{BT} = \frac{SS_{BT}}{df_{BT}} = \frac{260.4}{2} = 130.20$$

---

[103] In this chapter we will only consider studies that use a between-subjects design (different groups of subjects in each condition). Since each group is tested under a different condition, we can use the terms *group* and *condition* interchangeably (Group 1 was tested under Condition 1, Group 2 was tested under Condition 2, and so on.).

Now MS_{WI}. SS_{WI} was given, and $df_{WI} = N - k$:

$$MS_{WI} = \frac{SS_{WI}}{df_{WI}} = \frac{5.2}{12} = 0.43$$

Now we're ready to calculate F_{obt}:

$$F_{obt} = \frac{MS_{BT}}{MS_{WI}} = \frac{130.20}{0.43} = 302.79$$

That is a very large *F* value. *Why* is it so large? The answer lies in how little variability there is in the scores within each condition...

      10,10,11,10,11 (very little variability)
      15,16,17,15,16 (very little variability)
      21,21,20,20,21 (very little variability)

... as compared to the variability in the scores *between* the conditions, which we can see by comparing the respective means:

      10.4, 15.8, 20.6 (quite variable by comparison)

Or we could phrase it the other way: There is a lot of variability in the scores *between* the conditions (means are 10.4, 15.8, 20.6) as compared with the variability within each condition individually (10,10,11,10,11;   15,16,17,15,16;   21,21,20,20,21).

No matter how you frame it, you can see that the relatively little variability within the conditions is producing a very small value for MS_{WI} (0.43). This makes sense since MS_{WI} is the variance within the conditions. Conversely, you can also see the large amount of variability *between* the conditions is producing a relatively large value for MS_{BT} (130.20). This makes sense since MS_{BT} is the variance between the conditions.

We then figure out by dividing 130.20 by 0.43 that the former (remember, the effect) is 302.79 times bigger than the latter (the error). Again, just like all the statistics you've seen, the F score represents a ratio of effect to error.[104] As such, 302.79 is a huge value; it means the effect is about 300 times as large as the error. Such a value is sure to be significant, but of course you would have to make sure by comparing that F_{obt} to the F_{crit} you find in the F table.

To find the critical F value, F_{crit}, on the F table (at the end of the book), you need to know 3 things:

> 1) The level of signficance, α
> 2) The degrees of freedom between, df_{BT}
> 3) The degrees of freedom within, df_{WI}

Notice you do not need to know whether it is a one- or two-tailed test. This is because ANOVA, an F test, is always one-tailed. This is due to the fact that both the numerator and denominator of the F ratio are variance, a measure of variability, and variability cannot be negative. The least amount of variability/variance you can have is *none* (variance = 0).

Just as with all statistical tables, the F table consists of rows and columns. In the case of the F table, degrees of freedom *between* determine the column and degrees of freedom *within* determine the row. As always, you must find the cell at the intersection of the appropriate row and column. On the F table, you will notice there are two F_{crit}s in the cell you locate. One will always be larger than the other. If your level of significance, α, is 0.01, the larger of the two is your F_{crit}; if α is 0.05, the smaller of the two is your F_{crit}.

In the current example, as you saw when the df formulas were introduced, df_{BT} = 2 and df_{WI} = 12. Find F_{crit} in the section of the F table on the next page.

---

[104] As a matter of fact, it is often called the *F*-ratio.

df within (denominator)	df between (numerator)					
	1	**2**	**3**	**4**	**5**	**6**
2	18.51	19.00	19.16	19.25	19.30	19.33
	98.50	99.00	99.16	99.25	99.30	99.33
3	10.13	9.55	9.28	9.12	9.01	8.94
	34.12	30.82	29.46	28.71	28.24	27.91
11	4.84	3.98	3.59	3.36	3.20	3.09
	9.65	7.21	6.22	5.67	5.32	5.07
12	4.75	3.89	3.49	3.26	3.11	3.00
	9.33	6.93	5.95	5.41	5.06	4.82

In this case the critical F would be 3.89 for α 0.05 or 6.93 for α 0.01. Of course the alpha level would need to be specified to do an actual hypothesis test so you'd know which of the two to go with.

*   *   *

But before getting to that, let's illustrate a very important point by seeing what happens if we go back and make the scores within each condition more variable, but keep the means the same:

	Group 1	Group 2	Group 3
	15	9	18
	12	20	30
	4	12	5
	16	17	26
	5	21	24
Mean	10.4	15.8	20.6
SS	125.2	106.8	379.2

Notice the means are still 10.4, 15.8, and 20.6, but there is now more variability in the scores within each condition. What effect do you think this change will have on MS_{BT}? What about on MS_{WI}? On F_{obt}?[105]

Let's do the calculations to confirm the answers above (and just for practice).

First, MS_{BT}:

$$MS_{BT} = \frac{SS_{BT}}{df_{BT}} = \frac{260.4}{2} = \mathbf{130.20}$$

Remember not to worry about exactly how SS_{BT} was calculated—but you should understand why it's the same now as it was before.

Now MS_{WI}:

$$MS_{WI} = \frac{SS_{WI}}{df_{WI}} = \frac{611.2}{12} = \mathbf{50.93}$$

Same with SS_{WI}—just trust it's 611.2, and instead focus on understanding why it's larger now than it was before

And F_{obt}:

$$F_{obt} = \frac{MS_{BT}}{MS_{WI}} = \frac{130.20}{50.93} = \mathbf{2.56}$$

Look above carefully, and confirm our predictions:

---

[105] MS_{BT} will stay the same because the variability (variance) between the means is still the same. MS_{WI} will increase because there is now more variability in the scores within each condition. F_{obt} will decrease because now the ratio of *variance between* to *variance within* is smaller (the numerator is the same as before, but the denominator is larger).

- ☐ MS_{BT} remained the same, since the means are the same (and thus the variance between them is the same)
- ☐ MS_{WI} increased because there is more variability in the scores within the conditions than in the previous example.
- ☐ F_{obt} is smaller now because a larger error (denominator) with the same effect (numerator) produces a smaller ratio of effect to error.

The opposite would happen if we changed the scores so the variance between the means increased but the variance of the scores within each condition stayed the same. This would increase MS_{BT} (but not affect MS_{WI}) and thus increase F_{obt}.

*   *   *

We will now use ANOVA to analyze the results of a hypothetical study. In other words, we will perform an *F* test. Here is the situation:

> A researcher wants to know whether the price paid for something affects consumers' subsequent judgment regarding the quality of the product they bought. She arranges with a store to sell the same item at different prices throughout the day. Each time someone buys the product, another researcher interviews them outside the store, asking them to rate the quality of the product on a 1 to 15 scale.

Here is what she found:

	$10 price	$20 price	$30 price
	8	4	12
	5	12	8
	11	8	9
	5	8	11
	6	7	9
	4	9	15
Mean	6.5	8.0	10.7
SS	33.5	34	33.33

Using α 0.05, we will determine whether the price of a product affects its perceived level of quality. We will also include in our conclusion the APA-formatted statistical report.

NOTE: SS_{BT} = 53.44   ; SS_{WI} = 100.83.

We could do a full hypothesis test, with the 4 steps you're used to, but it isn't necessary at this point. Instead, we will do only what we need to in order to ultimately come to a conclusion and write our APA statistical report. That is, we will find our critical statistic, F_{crit}, calculate our obtained statistic, F_{obt}, then based on those two values decide whether or not the price of a product affects its perceived level of quality.

*   *   *

First, F_{crit}:

As you know, we need df_{BT}, df_{WI}, and α.

$df_{BT} = k - 1 = 3 - 1 = $ **2**

$df_{WI} = N - K = 18 - 3 = $ **15**

$\alpha = $ **0.05**

df_{within} (denominator)	df between (numerator)					
	1	**2**	**3**	**4**	**5**	**6**
2	18.51	19.00	19.16	19.25	19.30	19.33
	98.50	99.00	99.16	99.25	99.30	99.33
14	4.60	3.74	3.34	3.11	2.96	2.85
	8.86	6.51	5.56	5.04	4.69	4.46
15	4.54	**3.68**	3.29	3.06	2.90	2.79
	8.68	6.36	5.42	4.89	4.56	4.32
16	4.49	3.63	3.24	3.01	2.85	2.74
	8.53	6.23	5.29	4.77	4.44	4.20

$F_{crit} = $ **3.68.** Recall we're using α 0.05, so we choose the smaller (less strict) F_{crit} in the cell we located.

Next, F_{obt}:

As specified earlier, this requires finding the variance between conditions, MS_{BT}, the variance within conditions, MS_{WI}, and then dividing the former by the latter:

$$MS_{BT} = \frac{SS_{BT}}{df_{BT}} = \frac{53.44}{2} = \textbf{26.72}$$

$$MS_{WI} = \frac{SS_{WI}}{df_{WI}} = \frac{100.83}{15} = \mathbf{8.4}$$

$$F_{obt} = \frac{MS_{BT}}{MS_{WI}} = \frac{26.72}{8.4} = \mathbf{3.18}$$

Since our F_{obt} (3.18) is smaller than our F_{crit} (3.68) we must decide that we do not have a significant effect, making our conclusion:

> We found that the price of a product does not affect its perceived quality, $F(2,15) = 3.18, p > 0.05$.

Note that APA statistical report follows the same formatting as with other statistical tests, but is tailored to the ANOVA. Specifically, *two degrees of freedom are listed* since there is a df_{BT} and a df_{WI} in an ANOVA (and they are always listed in that order and separated by a comma). And the number of tails is not specified since an ANOVA is always one-tailed. Similarly, you do not specify whether the obtained statistic is positive or negative (note "3.18" is indicated, not "+ 3.18") since it's *always* positive.

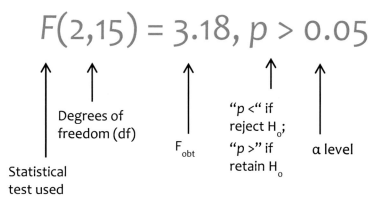

So, we concluded that price does not matter when it comes to a product's perceived level of quality. This is despite the fact that the differences between the means (i.e., *variance between*) seemed pretty big. Specifically, when the product cost $10, the average perceived quality was 6.5, when the product cost $20, the average perceived quality was 8.0, and when the product cost $30, the average perceived quality was 10.7 (see next page).

	$10	$20	$30
Mean	6.5	8.0	10.7

Seems like a lot of variance between means, so what happened? Well, remember when it comes to deciding on statistical significance, that is, whether a result is real or not, it's all about the *ratio* of effect to error. Here, we had what appeared to be large differences between our means—lots of variance between conditions—but there were also large differences among the scores within the conditions:

$10	$20	$30
8	4	12
5	12	8
11	8	9
5	8	11
6	7	9
4	9	15

The ratio of the variance between conditions to the variance within conditions was only 3.18 to 1. It needed to be 3.68 to 1 for us to conclude that variance between means was real.

Now, don't let the focus on the ratio of effect to error here mislead you: We could also say the reason we had to conclude there was no effect is that the probability the differences between our means occurred due to chance/sampling error was greater than our chosen level of significance, 0.05/5% (as we've been saying). Both explanations are true, and are perfectly acceptable ways to describe things.

* * *

One final point needs to be made before moving on to the next chapter. Recall from above that in all the example research studies in this chapter, we used a between-subjects design, meaning different groups of participants were tested under the different conditions. Another option is, as you know, a within-subjects design, where a single group of participants is tested under all the conditions. ANOVA works basically the same way with that type of design, but with one major difference.

As it turns out, the major difference is the same as you saw when we transitioned from the independent samples t test, used for a between-subjects design, to the related samples t test, used for a within-subjects design. Namely, all else being equal, there is less *error* in the ANOVA from a within-subjects design. This occurs for the exact same reason as before: The error variability due to pre-existing individual differences can be identified, and hence subtracted out, when analyzing data from a within-subjects design (called a repeated-measures ANOVA). You can do this because, when you test subjects under all the conditions, you can see how the subjects differ from each other *overall*, that is, regardless of the condition they are in. You can't do this if you only test them under one condition each, as you do in a between-subjects design.

We don't need to look at the actual formulas, but taking a quick look at some sample data may clarify the concept. Consider a study where we measure participants' ratings of happiness on a 1 to 20 scale as they mimicked three facial expressions: a smile, a neutral expression, and a frown. We found the following:

	Smile	Neutral	Frown	Average
Jim	19	16	13	16.0
Michael	4	3	1	2.7
Nashi	12	9	6	9.0
Erika	9	6	2	5.7
Justin	13	9	6	9.3
Mean	11.4	8.6	5.6	

This is the same setup as you've seen throughout the current chapter, but with an important exception: the addition of the Average column at the end, which shows the average score for each participant. You could never do that if the scores in the 3 conditions came from different subjects—what would averaging together, say, Frank's happiness rating when he smiled, Sharon's happiness rating when she had a neutral expression, and John's happiness rating when he frowned, tell you? Exactly—nothing.

By contrast, averaging together Jim's happiness ratings when he smiled, frowned, and made a neutral expression tells you something very important: Jim's *overall* (or *general*) happiness, regardless of what expression he was making. See for example in that last column how much higher Jim's scores were overall (16.0) relative to Michael's (2.7). By calculating averages for *all* participants, you can examine the variance of those averages. This tells you how much variance there is across those individuals overall. Take another look at that last column and note how variable the participants are in how they generally (meaning regardless of the facial expressions they make) rate their happiness.

Once you have a measure of this variance, due to what we call *individual differences*, you can subtract it from the error variance (which is, as you know, the variance of the scores within the conditions). This makes the error variance smaller (or at worst, the same[106]). With less error variance and, presumably, the same size effect, do you think being able to eliminate

---

[106] Error variance would be the same if none of it was due to overall individual differences between the participants. After all, you're subtracting out this variance, so if there was none of it, you'd be subtracting nothing (e.g., 25 – 0 = 25). Note however, especially with humans who tend to have tons of individual differences, this would rarely occur.

variability due to individual differences in this way *increases* or *decreases* statistical power?[107] You cannot do any of that in a between-subjects design; whatever the variance of the scores within the conditions is, *that's* the error you're stuck with.

The next inferential statistical test you'll learn is used when you don't have groups or conditions, but rather you *measure* participants on the two variables.

---

[107] Reducing error variability always *increases* power.

Problems.

1) In order to assess whether there is an effect of providing written feedback on papers to students, a professor performs an experiment. She randomly divides a class into 3 groups: Students in one of the groups get feedback on their papers *immediately*, a second group gets feedback a *week later*, and a third group gets *no feedback* on their papers. She then records all the students' grades on the next paper to see whether the feedback affected grades.

Here is what she found:

	Immediate feedback	Delayed feedback	No feedback
	75	78	80
	82	59	90
	62	91	58
	89	83	80
	80	80	76
Mean	77.6	78.2	76.8
SS	405.2	558.8	548.8

Using α 0.01, determine whether feedback has a significant effect on subsequent paper grades. Include in your conclusion the APA-formatted statistical report.

NOTE: $SS_{BT} = 4.93$; $SS_{WI} = 1512.8$.

2) In order to assess whether there is an effect of providing **verbal** feedback on papers to students, the professor performs the experiment again (but with verbal feedback). She again randomly divides a class into 3 groups: Students in one of the groups get feedback on their papers *immediately*, a second group gets feedback a *week later*, and a third group gets *no feedback* on their papers. She then records all the students' grades on the next paper to see whether the feedback affected grades.

Here is what she found:

	Immediate feedback	Delayed feedback	No feedback
	83	77	68
	82	58	75
	75	91	58
	89	82	70
	82	71	65
Mean	82.2	75.8	67.2
SS	98.8	610.8	158.8

Using α 0.05, determine whether feedback has a significant effect on subsequent paper grades. Include in your conclusion the APA-formatted statistical report.

NOTE: SS_{BT} = 566.53; SS_{WI} = 868.4.

3) Is *age* associated with our ability to mentally rotate 2-dimensional objects? You want to find out, so you sample 4 groups of participants of different ages and give them a test which measures their ability to mentally rotate objects on a 1 to 10 scale. Here is what you found:

	5-8 yrs old	9-12 yrs old	13-16 yrs old	17-20 yrs old
	5	5	6	7
	4	3	6	8
	4	6	4	8
	5	5	7	5
	4	4	4	6
Mean	4.4	4.6	5.4	6.8
SS	1.2	5.2	7.2	6.8

Using α 0.05, determine whether age is associated with a change in the ability to mentally rotate objects. Include in your conclusion the APA-formatted statistical report.

NOTE: SS_{BT} = 17.8; SS_{WI} = 20.4.

4) Is *age* associated with our ability to mentally rotate **3**-dimensional objects? You want to find out, so you sample 4 groups of participants of different ages and give them a test which measures their ability to mentally rotate 3-D objects on a 1 - 10 scale. Here is what you found:

	5-8 yrs old	9-12 yrs old	13-16 yrs old	17-20 yrs old
	3	5	4	7
	4	3	3	4
	5	2	1	8
	2	5	7	6
	2	4	7	7
Mean	3.2	3.8	4.4	6.4
SS	6.8	6.8	27.2	9.2

Using α 0.01, determine whether age is associated with a change in the ability to mentally rotate objects. Include in your conclusion the APA-formatted statistical report.

NOTE: SS_{BT} = 28.95; SS_{WI} = 50.

Solutions to problems.

1)

$df_{BT} = 2$, $df_{WI} = 12$

$MS_{BT} = 4.93/2 = 2.47$

$MS_{WI} = 1512.8/12 = 126.07$

$F_{obt} = 2.47/126.07 = 0.02$

F_{crit} ($df_{BT} = 2$, $df_{WI} = 12$, α 0.01): 6.93

Conclusion: $F_{obt} < F_{crit}$. It was found that written feedback on papers did not affect students' grades, $F(2,12) = 0.02$, $p > 0.01$.

2)

$df_{BT} = 2$, $df_{WI} = 12$

$MS_{BT} = 566.53/2 = 283.27$

$MS_{WI} = 868.4/12 = 72.37$

$F_{obt} = 283.27/72.37 = 3.91$

F_{crit} ($df_{BT} = 2$, $df_{WI} = 12$, α 0.05): 3.89

Conclusion: $F_{obt} > F_{crit}$. It was found that verbal feedback on papers affects students' grades, $F(2,12) = 3.91$, $p < 0.05$.

3)

$df_{BT} = 3$, $df_{WI} = 16$

$MS_{BT} = 17.8/3 = 5.93$

$MS_{WI} = 20.4/16 = 1.28$

$F_{obt} = 5.93/1.28 = 4.63$

F_{crit} ($df_{BT} = 3$, $df_{WI} = 16$, α 0.05): 3.24

Conclusion: $F_{obt} > F_{crit}$. We found that aging was associated with a change in the ability to mentally rotate 2-dimensional objects, $F(3,16) = 4.63$, $p < 0.05$.

4)

$df_{BT} = 3$, $df_{WI} = 16$

$MS_{BT} = 28.95/3 = 9.65$

$MS_{WI} = 50/16 = 3.13$

$F_{obt} = 9.65/3.13 = 3.08$

F_{crit} ($df_{BT} = 3$, $df_{WI} = 16$, α 0.01): 5.29

Conclusion: $F_{obt} < F_{crit}$. We found that aging was not associated with a change in the ability to mentally rotate 3-dimensional objects, $F(3,16) = 3.08$, $p > 0.01$.

Chapter 16
Correlation

It is time to point out something all the studies presented so far have in common. Namely, they all had an independent variable which was used to define groups or conditions, for example the *brightness of a room*, the type of *sound subjects heard*, and *whether subjects participated in a summer reading program*, along with a dependent variable which was measured, for example the comprehension of a paragraph, ratings of pleasantness, and levels of satisfaction.

However, many studies are not set up that way, where one variable defines groups or conditions and the other is measured. In this type of study, there are no groups or conditions—the researcher instead measures two variables. Of course the primary interest of the researcher is still to discover if there is a relationship between the variables, except in this case, both variables are measured, and the relationship being investigated is called a *correlation.*

Imagine we measured two variables in a class of 10 statistics students. The two variables are:

1) How often each student has lucid dreams per month. Lucid dreams are those in which we realize we are dreaming. We measured this variable with a survey.

2) How creative each student is. We measured this variable by giving students a Torrance Test of Creative Thinking (TTCT).

Here is what we found:

Student	Lucid dreams per year	Score on TTCT
1	11	51
2	10	73
3	18	51
4	8	60
5	15	82
6	19	80
7	20	90
8	1	40
9	3	32
10	18	85

You'll notice it is difficult to assess the correlation by looking only at the table. Therefore, a *scatterplot* is created from that data, where each subject is plotted according to their score on the X variable (this is plotted on the X axis) and their score on the Y variable (plotted on the Y axis).

So you can see how the scatterplot is created, we will consider just two of the students for now: Student 1 and Student 5. As shown in the table above, Student 1 reported **11** lucid dreams per year and scored **51** on the creative thinking test, and Student 5 reported **15** lucid dreams per year and scored **82** on the creative thinking test. If we put them on a scatterplot, we get:

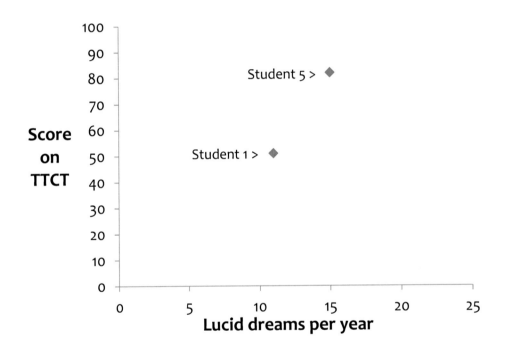

And now a scatterplot with all the data:

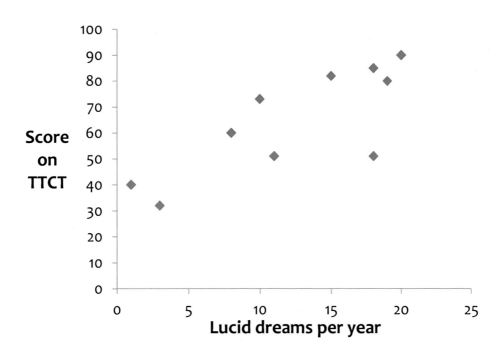

Now you can see a trend in the data, can't you? Try describing it.

As is usually the case, there are several ways to describe a result. In this case, some correct ways to explain the trend are:

- The more lucid dreaming students do, the higher they score on the creativity test.
- The higher students score on the creativity test, the more lucid dreaming they do.
- The less lucid dreaming students do, the lower they score on the creativity test.
- The lower students score on the creativity test, the less lucid dreaming they do.
- High levels of lucid dreaming are associated with high scores on the creativity test, and vice versa.

*　　*　　*

Variables can be correlated any number of ways, but we will focus only on the type shown above: The *linear* correlation. You have a linear correlation when the relationship between the variables resembles a straight line. You can see in our results a straight line can be drawn which follows the trend of the data points in the scatterplot below. That line is called the *regression line*, and you'll be learning more about it in the next chapter.

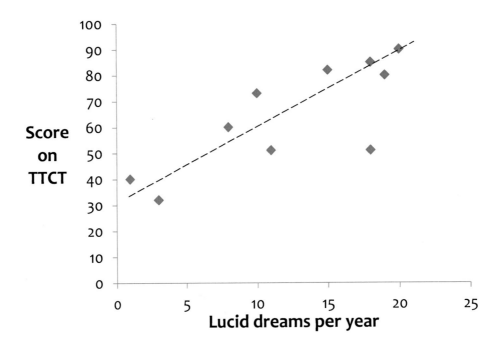

Scatterplots are very useful because they give us a visual picture of the data, allowing us to see patterns we otherwise would not be able to see. However, they do not provide us with a *precise measure* of how strongly our variables are correlated.

That is where the *correlation coefficient, r,* comes in.

> The **correlation coefficient, r,** is computed from all the X and Y scores. It gives us a measure of 1) the strength and 2) the direction of the correlation.

The correlation coefficient can range from 0.00 (no correlation) to 1.00 (a perfect correlation). As the definition above suggests, since it mentions *direction*, it can also be positive or negative. That makes the total range of the correlation coefficient -1.00 to + 1.00.

Here are some examples of scatterplots, along with the correlation coefficients[108]:

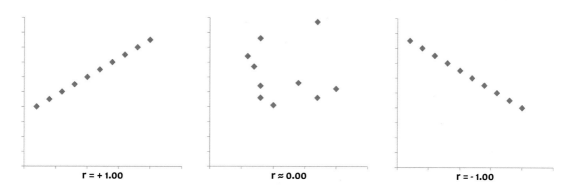

The scatterplots on the left and right of the previous figure depict a *perfect* linear correlation since the data points form a perfectly straight line. The difference between the two is that the one on the left depicts a perfect *positive* correlation (notice r = + 1.00), and the one on the right depicts a perfect *negative* correlation (r = - 1.00).

A *positive* correlation is when high scores on one variable are associated with high scores on the other (and thus low scores on one variable are associated with low scores on the other). In other words, participants who scored high on one variable tended to score high on the other, and vice versa. You saw this with the correlation between lucid dreaming and scores on the TTCT.

A *negative* correlation is when high scores on one variable are associated with low scores on the other (and thus low scores on one variable are associated with high scores on the other). In other words, participants who scored high on one variable tended to score low on the other, and vice versa.[109]

> In a **positive correlation,** *high scores on one variable are associated with high scores on the other variable (and vice versa), while in a **negative correlation,** high scores on one variable are associated with low scores on the other variable (and vice versa).*

---

[108] By the way, the correlation coefficient of the data above (lucid dreaming and TTCT scores) is r = + 0.79.

[109] Note *participants* (i.e., people) don't really even need to be involved. You could say, for example, that *iced latte sales* and *temperature* are positively correlated (higher temps associated with higher sales, etc.), and that *hot latte sales* and *temperature* are negatively correlated (higher temps associated with lower sales, etc.).

Note the direction of the correlation (i.e., whether it's positive or negative) is completely independent of its strength: *Strength* and *direction* are separate things. For example, r = - 0.85 represents a stronger correlation than r = + 0.65. The following diagram may help you keep this straight:

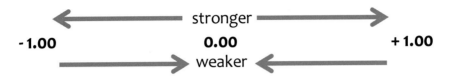

The sign of the correlation coefficient (+ or -) tells you the direction of the relationship (for example, - 0.85 is a negative correlation, while + 0.65 is a positive one), and the value itself tells you the strength. As the diagram shows, the closer r is to 0.00, the weaker the correlation, and the further it is from 0.00, the stronger the correlation.

Now focus on the middle scatterplot, labeled r ≈ 0.00. That scatterplot shows quite the opposite of the other two: almost no correlation. Note the use of the term *almost*, and also the use of the symbol ≈ rather than = in the middle scatterplot. This is because you never have absolutely zero correlation. Even if you were to create two sets of random numbers, the two sets of numbers would actually show *some* sort of correlation.

That seems odd. Since the numbers are random, there shouldn't be any correlation between them. But remember an important fact from previous chapters: There is always *some* difference in scores between your conditions, even if there is no actual effect/relationship. Well, the same general principle is at play here. The word *difference* doesn't fit anymore, but in both cases, what seems like something which may be a real finding is actually just the result of *sampling error*.

So how can we tell what only *seems* to be an effect but is really just sampling error from an actual, real effect? Same way as always— we employ an inferential statistical test.

And how do we do that? Also, the same way as always: A statistic is calculated from the data and compared to a *critical* statistic found on a statistical table. If the calculated statistic is larger than the critical statistic, we conclude the effect/relationship is real. Otherwise, we conclude it isn't, that is, that the *apparent* effect/relationship is just due to sampling error.

*   *   *

So when it comes to a correlation, a correlation coefficient (called r) is calculated and then compared to a *critical* correlation coefficient obtained from the r table (Table 4 in the back of this book). If the calculated r (r_{obt}) is larger than the critical r (r_{crit}), we conclude the correlation is real. Otherwise, we conclude there is no correlation, that is, that the *apparent* correlation is just due to sampling error.

Before going through an example, let's take a look at how to calculate the correlation coefficient, r. First, the formula itself:

$$r_{obt} = \frac{SP}{\sqrt{SS_X SS_Y}}$$

The numerator, SP (*sum of products*, if you're curious) is a measure of how much X and Y specifically vary *together*—to what extent increases in X coincide with increases (or decreases) in Y, and vice versa. This is also referred to as the variability that is *accounted for*: the variability in X that is accounted for by variability in Y, and vice versa. This value can be found with the following formula:

$$SP = \Sigma(X - M_X)(Y - M_Y)$$

The denominator, $\sqrt{SS_X SS_Y}$, is a measure of the *total* amount of variability in the data. This is variability due to the variability created by X and Y varying together just discussed *and* by X and Y varying separately. The latter is also referred to as the variability that is *not accounted for (unexplained)*,--the variability in X that is *not* accounted for by variability in Y, and vice versa. This total variability comes from the variability in X, measured by SS_X, and the variability in Y, SS_Y. You should be familiar with SS (Sum of Squares) from previous chapters as the total amount of variability in the data. In the examples you do in this chapter, SS_X and SS_Y will always be given.

Though these formulas may look a little different than what you've become accustomed to, the r formula still provides us with something very much like a *ratio of effect to error*, like inferential statistics almost always do. In this case, however, the largest that ratio can be is **1.00.** A ratio of 1.00 would mean that the *total variability* is the same as the *variability due to X and Y varying together*; the ratio is 1 to 1. In other words, *all* of the variability present in the data comes from X and Y varying together (or all of the variability in Y is *explained* by the variability in X). By contrast, a ratio of 0.00 (remember, this is the smallest r can be) would mean *none* of the variability present in the data is due to X and Y varying together; the ratio is 0 to 1.

* * *

Now an example.

Is there a correlation between *how much music* people listen to and *how outgoing* they are? To address this, you hand out a survey to 5 fellow students which contains 1) a number of items designed to measure how outgoing they are (their *extroversion score*), and 2) a question that asks them how many hours per week, on average, they listen to music. You found the following:

Classmate	hours of music/wk (X)	extroversion score (Y)
A	14	43
B	4	39
C	12	28
D	8	23
E	3	40

Determine whether there is a correlation between how much music people listen to and how outgoing they are (use α 0.05). NOTE: $SS_X = 92.8$ and $SS_Y = 297.2$.

Step 1. State the Hypotheses

Null Hypothesis, H_0: There is no correlation between how much music people listen to and how outgoing they are.

Alternative Hypothesis, H_1: There is a correlation between how much music people listen to and how outgoing they are.

Step 2. Set the criterion

The three pieces of information you need to find the critical r statistic (r_{crit}) are always given, or apparent, in the question. Here is the information you need for this particular problem:

- α 0.05. (... (*use α 0.05*).)

- two-tailed. (*Determine whether there is a correlation...*). No direction was specified, so we're looking for either a positive or a negative correlation, rather than just one or the other (which would have been a one-tailed test).

- df = 3. Degrees of freedom, df, in a correlation, is the number of participants minus 2.

$$df = n - 2$$

To find the critical r, we use a statistical table. Below is the section of it we need for this problem.

	One Tailed Probabilities			
	0.05	0.025	0.01	0.005
	Two-Tailed Probabilities			
df	0.10	0.05	0.02	0.01
2	0.900	0.950	0.980	0.990
3	0.805	0.878	0.934	0.959
4	0.729	0.811	0.882	0.917
5	0.669	0.754	0.833	0.875

In this example, we are using a level of significance, α, 0.05, and we're doing a non-directional (two-tailed) test. We have 5 participants, so df = 3. With this information we can see from the table that the critical statistic, r_{crit}, is **0.878**. Since we did not predict a direction (either a positive correlation or a negative one), we don't have to worry about the sign of r_{crit}.

<u>Step 3. Calculate the statistic.</u>

Now that we have established our criterion for deciding if there is an effect—an r_{crit}—we now have to see if we reached that criterion. That means calculating a correlation coefficient, r, from the data we obtained using the formulas you saw earlier. Let's start with the numerator:

$$SP = \Sigma(X - M_X)(Y - M_Y)$$

As you can see, we need to 1) find $(X - M_X)$ for all the X values and $(Y - M_Y)$ for all the Y values, 2) multiply them, then 3) add up the resulting values. We will need to create a table to keep things organized. Carefully follow 3 steps:

1) Find $(X - M_X)$ for all the X values. To do that, first find the mean of the X values (here, that's 8.2) and subtract that mean from each of the X scores—see column labeled **X -** **M_X** in the table that follows. Next, find the mean of the Y values (34.6) and subtract that mean from each of the Y scores—see column labeled **Y - M_Y**.

Classmate	hours of music/wk (X)	$X - M_X$	extroversion score (Y)	$Y - M_Y$
A	14	14 - 8.2 = 5.8	43	43 - 34.6 = 8.4
B	4	4 - 8.2 = -4.2	39	39 - 34.6 = 4.4
C	12	12 - 8.2 = 3.8	28	28 - 34.6 = -6.6
D	8	8 - 8.2 = -0.2	23	23 - 34.6 = -11.6
E	3	3 - 8.2 = -5.2	40	40 - 34.6 = 5.4
	$M_X = 8.2$		$M_Y = 34.6$	

2) Multiply each of those values—see column labeled $(X - M_X)(Y - M_Y)$ below:

Classmate	hours of music/wk (X)	$X - M_X$	extroversion score (Y)	$Y - M_Y$	$(X - M_X)(Y - M_Y)$
A	14	5.8	43	8.4	5.8 * 8.4 = 48.72
B	4	-4.2	39	4.4	-4.2 * 4.4 = -18.48
C	12	3.8	28	-6.6	3.8 * -6.6 = -25.08
D	8	-0.2	23	-11.6	-0.2 * -11.6 = 2.32
E	3	-5.2	40	5.4	-5.2 * 5.4 = -28.08
	$M_X = 8.2$		$M_Y = 34.6$		

3) Sum those values

Classmate	hours of music/wk (X)	$X - M_X$	extroversion score (Y)	$Y - M_Y$	$(X - M_X)(Y - M_Y)$
A	14	5.8	43	8.4	48.72
B	4	-4.2	39	4.4	-18.48
C	12	3.8	28	-6.6	-25.08
D	8	-0.2	23	-11.6	2.32
E	3	-5.2	40	5.4	-28.08
	$M_X = 8.2$		$M_Y = 34.6$		-20.6

We now have SP. Remember, this is a measurement of the degree to which X and Y vary together—the *effect*. Now we need to know the *total* amount of variability—the *error*. The error (denominator of the formula) is much simpler to find since we already know the variability of X and Y independent of each other (i.e., SS_X and SS_Y). All we need to do now is multiply them and get the square root of the result (recall the denominator is $\sqrt{SS_X SS_Y}$).

The Sums of Squares were given: $SS_X = 92.8$ and $SS_Y = 297.2$. So, $92.8 * 297.2 = 27580.2$, and the square root of that number is 166.07.

The numerator is -20.6 (effect) and the denominator is 166.07 (error).

$$r_{obt} = \frac{-20.6}{166.07} = -0.12$$

Step 4. Make the statistical decision and state the conclusion.

Our usual rule applies: If the obtained statistic is larger than the critical statistic, you reject H_o (conclude there is an effect) and if it's not, you retain H_o (conclude there is no effect). In this study:

r_{crit} = +/- 0.878
r_{obt} = - 0.12

Since r_{obt} is not greater than r_{crit}, we *retain* H_o, meaning we do *not* have a significant correlation (for this decision, focus on the *values* of r; don't let the signs distract you). In this example, that means there is not a correlation between how much music people listen to and how outgoing they are. In other words, the correlation coefficient of $r = -0.12$ appears to have not been due to a real correlation between the variables, but due to sampling error.

The APA statement follows the usual format:

> We found that there was not a significant correlation between how much music people listen to and how outgoing they are, $r(3) = -0.12$, $p > 0.05$, two-tailed.[110]

*   *   *

There are several types of correlation coefficients, but the one presented here, called the Pearson correlation, is the most widely used. Others include the Spearman correlation (used if one of your variables is ordinal, for example the correlation between GPA and how you ranked relative to your classmates on a presentation- 1st, 2nd, 3rd, etc.) and the Point-biserial

---

[110] Note the APA report: Positive/negative is specified in the obtained value reported, and the number of tails is indicated (since an r test can be one-tailed, where you specify whether you're looking for a positive or for a negative correlation, or two-tailed, where you don't specify).

correlation (used if one of your variables can take on only two values, for example *pass or fail*).

The next chapter will present a statistical procedure called *regression*. In Regression, you use the fact that two variables are correlated to make predictions—when you know someone's score on just one of the variables, you can use that information to predict their score on the other variable. You can even then figure out how accurate your predictions are, overall.

Problems.

1) You want to find out if there is a correlation between how much horses eat and how much they sleep. So, you studied four horses. You measured how much each ate in an average day, and how much each slept over an average night. You found the following:

Horse	amount of food eaten (X)	time spent sleeping (Y)
A	45	8.1
B	39	7.3
C	31	9.8
D	53	6.4
	M_X = 42 lbs	M_Y = 7.9 hrs

Using α 0.01, determine whether there is a correlation between how much horses eat and how much they sleep. NOTE: SS_X = 260 and SS_Y = 6.26

2) Is more time spent at the library associated with higher GPAs? To address this question, a researcher measured two variables on a group of 5 students: how many nights per month they spent at the library, and their GPA. The following results were obtained:

Student	GPA (X)	nights/mo. spent at library (Y)
Jim	2.10	3
Terrance	2.60	11
Jasmine	2.50	10
Michael	3.30	11
Stephanie	3.50	14
	M_X = 2.80	M_Y = 9.8 hrs

Using α 0.05, determine whether there is a positive correlation between the number of nights per month spent at the library and GPA. Notice a direction is being specified.

NOTE: SS_X = 1.36 and SS_Y = 66.8

3) Some people think we are less happy when it's colder. To find out if this is true, you investigate the correlation between these two variables. For 6 months, you track the average temperature, and the average score on a mood test online (hundreds of people take the test every day). You found the following

Month	Temperature (X)	Average mood test score (Y)
Jan	38	61
Feb	39	58
Mar	47	67
Apr	56	69
May	62	67
Jun	70	71
	$M_X = 52$	$M_Y = 65.5$

Using α 0.05, determine whether there is a positive correlation between temperature and mood. NOTE: $SS_X = 830$ and $SS_Y = 123.5$

Solutions to problems.

1)

Step 1:

H_0: There is no correlation between how much horses eat and how much they sleep.

H_1: There is a correlation between how much horses eat and how much they sleep.

Step 2:

$r_{crit} = 0.990$ (α 0.01, two-tailed, df = 2)

Step 3:

Horse	amount of food eaten (X)	X - M_X	time spent sleeping (Y)	Y - M_Y	(X - M_X)(Y - M_Y)
A	45	45 - 42 = **3**	8.1	8.1 - 7.9 = **0.2**	0.6
B	39	39 - 42 = **-3**	7.3	7.3 - 7.9 = **-0.6**	1.8
C	31	31 - 42 = **-11**	9.8	9.8 - 7.9 = **1.9**	-20.9
D	53	53 - 42 = **11**	6.4	6.4 - 7.9 = **-1.5**	-16.5
	M_X = 42 lbs		M_Y = 7.9 hrs		-35
					Σ(X - M_X)(Y - M_Y)

SP = -35

SS_X = 260 and SS_Y = 6.26. 260 * 6.26 = 1627.6. The square root of that number is 40.34.

r_{obt} = -35 / 40.34 = **-0.867**

Step 4:

Decision & Conclusion:

r_{obt} (-0.867) < r_{crit} (0.990) Accept H_0

We did not find a correlation between how much horses eat and how much they sleep, r(2) = -0.867, p > 0.01, two-tailed.

2)

Step 1:

H_0: There is not a positive correlation between GPA and the number of hours per month spent at the library.

H_1: There is a positive correlation between GPA and the number of hours per month spent at the library.

Step 2:

r_{crit} = **0.805** (α 0.05, one-tailed, df = 3)

Step 3:

Student	GPA (X)	X - M_X	nights/mo. spent at library (Y)	Y - M_Y	(X - M_X)(Y - M_Y)
Jim	2.10	2.10 - 2.80 = **-0.7**	3	3 - 9.8 = **-6.8**	4.76
Terrance	2.60	2.60 - 2.80 = **-0.2**	11	11 - 9.8 = **1.2**	-0.24
Jasmine	2.50	2.50 - 2.80 = **-0.3**	10	10 - 9.8 = **0.2**	-0.06
Michael	3.30	3.30 - 2.80 = **0.5**	11	11 - 9.8 = **1.2**	0.6
Stephanie	3.50	3.50 - 2.80 = **0.7**	14	14 - 9.8 = **4.2**	2.94
	M_X = 2.80		M_Y = 9.8 hrs		8
					Σ(X - M_X)(Y - M_Y)

SP = 8

SS_X = 1.36 and SS_Y = 66.8. 1.36 * 66.8 = 90.85. The square root of that number is 9.53.

r_{obt} = 8 / 9.53 = **+0.839**

Step 4:

Decision & Conclusion:

r_{obt} (**+0.839**) > r_{crit} (**0.805**) **Reject H_0**

We found a positive correlation between GPA and nights spent at the library, $r(3)$ = +0.839, $p < 0.05$, one-tailed.

3)

<u>Step 1:</u>

H_0: There is not a positive correlation between temperature and mood.

H_1: There is a positive correlation between temperature and mood.

<u>Step 2:</u>

r_{crit} = **0.729** (α 0.05, one-tailed, df = 4)

<u>Step 3:</u>

Month	Temperature (X)	$X - M_X$	Average mood test score (Y)	$Y - M_Y$	$(X - M_X)(Y - M_Y)$
Jan	38	-14	61	-4.5	63
Feb	39	-13	58	-7.5	97.5
Mar	47	-5	67	1.5	-7.5
Apr	56	4	69	3.5	14
May	62	10	67	1.5	15
Jun	70	18	71	5.5	99
	$M_X = 52$		$M_Y = 65.5$		281

$$\Sigma(X - M_X)(Y - M_Y)$$

SP = 281

SS_X = 830 and SS_Y = 123.5. 830 * 123.5 = 102,505. The square root of that number is 320.16.

r_{obt} = 281 / 320.16 = **+0.877**

<u>Step 4:</u>

Decision & Conclusion:

r_{obt} **(+0.877) > r_{crit} (0.729) Reject H_0**

> We found a positive correlation between temperature and mood, $r(4)$ = +0.877, $p <$ 0.05, one-tailed.

Chapter 17
Regression

Regression is the process used to make predictions when you have two variables that you've shown to be significantly correlated in a hypothesis test (like the ones you've been conducting). For example, if the variables *SAT score* and *college GPA* are correlated, then knowing a person's SAT score would help you predict what their college GPA will be.

You can probably see right away that you could not predict any student's college GPA *perfectly*. For one thing, there is a degree of random fluctuation when it comes to college GPA—it varies from student to student (even students with the exact same SAT score), for unknown reasons[111]. But more generally, so many variables correlate with college GPA that knowing about just one of them (their SAT score) couldn't possibly allow you to predict college GPA perfectly.

Nevertheless, as long as SAT score and college GPA are correlated, you could predict students' college GPAs more accurately if you knew their SAT scores than if you did not know their SAT scores. The reverse is true as well: If you knew someone's college GPA, you could predict their SAT score *more accurately than if you did not know their college GPA.*

In this chapter, you will learn about the process used to make predictions about participants' scores on one variable, when you know their score on another variable. This process is called *regression*.

Many types of regression procedures exist. You will be learning about the one called *simple linear regression*. The word *simple* is used because you are using information about *just one* variable to make predictions about another.[112] *Linear* means *line*. We will be dealing with variables whose correlation resembles a straight line when plotted on a scatterplot.

> Simple linear **regression** is the process of using information about one variable to make predictions about another variable, when those two variables are linearly correlated.

* * *

---

[111] The word *error* may be coming to mind.

[112] Another type of regression is called *multiple regression*, where you use information about more than one variable (*multiple* variables) to make predictions about another. For example, if we not only knew a person's SAT score, but also had their high school GPA, we could use both those variables together to predict, usually more accurately than if we only knew one, that person's college GPA.

Let's consider an example. Say you discover that, for people living in the northern hemisphere, the variables *latitude* and *neuroticism* are correlated. Specifically, you found the lower the latitude you live in (the further south, toward the equator), the lower you score on a test of neuroticism (and vice versa, by definition). Here is a scatterplot of the data you collected from 8 participants:

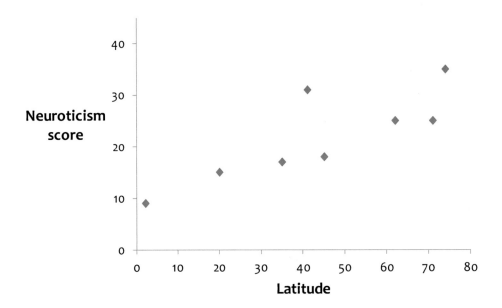

You can see the points do not form a perfectly straight line, but as a general trend they go up as you look from left to right. And you are well-versed enough in statistics at this point to know that means you have a positive correlation. You also know that talking about two variables being correlated must mean a hypothesis test was done, and the correlation coefficient was found to be statistically significant. Actually, the correlation coefficient calculated from the data above is $r_{obt} = +0.82$, which is statisically significant at the 0.05 level.[113]

Whenever two variables are correlated, we can use our knowledge of one of them to make predictions about the other. In this case, since we previously established that latitude and

---

[113] Note the correlation between those particular variables would never actually be that high. We needed a high hypothetical correlation here because it has to be significant; if it weren't, we would not use it make predictions in the first place.

neuroticism are correlated, we can make predictions about an unknown person's neuroticism if we know the latitude they reside in.[114]

Since we are going to use a person's latitude of residence to make predictions, that is called the *predictor variable*. Just remember it's the predictor because it's the one *doing* the predicting. The variable we are trying to predict, in this case neuroticism, is called the *outcome variable*.

> The variable used to make predictions is called the **predictor variable**; the variable you are trying to predict is called the **outcome variable**.

As stated earlier, we will never be able to make perfect predictions. In this case there are obviously many factors that influence a person's level of neuroticism, so knowing only their latitude would not be enough to perfectly predict how neurotic they are. However, as you may have guessed, the higher the correlation, the more accurate our predictions will be.

> The higher the correlation between two variables, the more accurately you can predict one when you know the other.

The basic process for making predictions—performing regression—is:

1. Create an equation, called the *regression equation*, based on the correlational data collected. The regression equation can also be thought of as a mathematical description of the *regression line-* a straight line drawn through the data points.
2. Given a score on one of the variables, for example a person's *latitude* of residence, make a prediction about their score on the other variable, for example their *level of neuroticism*.

> The **regression equation** is used to make predictions. You plug in the score you know (the X score) for a participant, and the formula provides you with the predicted Y score, Y', for that participant.

What you're doing in regression is using the data of the people in your study to make predictions about people in the future, who were not in your study. You will see, however, we also make predictions about the people in our study, but only as a way to measure the accuracy of our predictions.

---

[114] We could do the opposite just as easily: Make a prediction of where they live based on the level of neuroticism. Often, however, one type of prediction makes more intuitive sense, so we will focus on predicting neuroticism based on latitude of residence, rather than the other way around.

To create the *regression equation*, which is what makes predictions possible, we need correlational data. This type of data should look familiar to you; it's the same type of data you encountered in the previous chapter. As before, each subject gets two scores: a score on the *X* variable, *latitude* in this case, and a score on the *Y* variable, *neuroticism*.

Resident	Latitude (deg.) (X)	Neuroticism score (Y)
1	74	35
2	71	25
3	62	25
4	20	15
5	45	18
6	41	31
7	35	17
8	2	9

The regression equation is:

$$Y' = a + bX$$

Remember, our goal here is to take someone who you only have an *X* score for (you know where they live), and use that to predict their score on *Y* variable (how neurotic they are). So it makes sense that two parts of the regression equation are as follows:

- **X** is the participant's score on the predictor variable. This is the one you know when you're making predictions, such as someone's latitude of residence.
- **Y'** (pronounced *Y-PRIME*) is that person's *predicted* score on the outcome variable.

For example, if we had a person who lived at latitude 30 degrees (*X*) and you wanted to predict their neuroticism score (*Y'*), we'd plug 30 into the formula:

$$Y' = a + b(30)$$

To solve the equation, that is, to make a prediction about this person's neuroticism score (*Y'*), we clearly need to also find **a** and **b**.

- **b** is the *slope* of the regression line. The slope is just what it sounds like—how steep the line is. But slope also indicates whether the regression line goes up or down on the scatterplot (when looking left to right). The slope can thus be *positive* (+), sloping up from left to right, or *negative* (-) sloping down from left to right. Below is the formula for finding **b**, the slope of the regression line.

$$b = r\frac{s_Y}{s_X}$$

  - **r** is the correlation coefficient, s_Y is the standard deviation of the Y scores, and s_X is the standard deviation of the X scores.

- **a** is the *y-intercept* of the line. That's a somewhat strange term, but, like the slope, the y-intercept is just what it sounds like—it's where the line intercepts (crosses) the y-axis. Below is the formula for finding the y-intercept, **a**, of the regression line.

$$a = M_Y - b(M_X)$$

  - **M**$_Y$ is the mean of the Y scores and **M**$_X$ is the mean of the X scores (and recall **b** is the slope).

*   *   *

Now that you have a general idea about what regression is, and have the formulas you will need, let's work through a problem. Here is a typical regression situation:

> You found that *latitude* of residence and *neuroticism* score are significantly correlated based on a sample of people you collected (r_{obt} = + 0.82). Now, you want to be able to predict neuroticism scores in new people, when you only know the latitude they live in.

> Create a regression equation using the information provided, and then predict the neuroticism score for a person who lives at a latitude of 39 degrees. NOTE: s_X = 25.02 and s_Y = 8.68. The results are on the next page.

Resident	Latitude (X)	Neuroticism (Y)
1	74	35
2	71	25
3	62	25
4	20	15
5	45	18
6	41	31
7	35	17
8	2	9
	$M_X = 43.75$	$M_Y = 21.88$
	$s_X = 25.02$	$s_Y = 8.68$

We know we will ultimately need to plug an X score of 39 into the regression equation...

$$Y' = a + b(39)$$

... but to make a prediction about a neuroticism score, that is, to find Y', we'll need to find the slope, **b**, and the y-intercept, **a**. Always start with the slope.[115] In this case, we know $r_{obt} = +0.82$, $s_X = 25.02$, and $s_Y = 8.68$, so all we need to do is plug those numbers into the formula for the slope, **b**:

$$b = r\frac{s_Y}{s_X} = +0.82 * \frac{8.68}{25.02}$$
$$= +0.82 * 0.35 = \mathbf{0.29}$$

Note a positive correlation will always mean a positive slope, and a negative correlation will always mean a negative slope.

Next, we find the y-intercept, **a**. To find the y-intercept, you need the slope, **b**, the mean of the Y scores, M_Y, and the mean of the X scores, M_X. Looking at the table of data provided, you will see the mean of the X scores (latitude) is 43.75 and the mean of the Y scores (neuroticism) is 21.88.

---

[115] because the formula for the y-intercept requires that you know the slope first

Thus:

$$a = M_Y - b(M_X)$$
$$= 21.88 - 0.29(43.75)$$
$$= 21.88 - 12.69 = \mathbf{9.19}$$

The completed regression equation is therefore:

$$Y' = 9.19 + 0.29(X)$$

We could now plug in any X value we want, and the formula will give us a predicted score on the Y variable (Y'). But we are being asked to plug in X = 39, so let's do that:

$$Y' = 9.19 + 0.29(\mathbf{39}) = 9.19 + 11.31 = \mathbf{20.50}$$

We now have our answer, but don't lose track of what the question was. Remember, what this means is, based on the data previously collected, you predict someone from latitude 39 would have a neuroticism score of 20.50.

For the sake of getting some practice with the regression equation, predict neuroticism scores for the residents below. [116]

Resident	Latitude (deg.)
A	70
B	45
C	17

Now take a look at the scatterplot on the next page. You may recall from the last chapter that a line was drawn through the data points in one of the scatterplots. In that case, the line was just sketched in as a way to more easily see the general trend in the data. But such a line,

---

[116] Resident A: Y' = 9.19 + 0.29(70) = 29.49. Resident B: Y' = 9.19 + 0.29(45) = 22.24. Resident C: Y' = 9.19 + 0.29(17) = 14.12.

when carefully placed as to *best fit* the data points, can also be used to make approximate predictions. We're talking about the *regression line*, of course.

The regression line can be easily plotted by making two (or more) predictions, like you just did above. You make the predictions, put points on the scatterplot where those predictions fall, then draw a straight line through those points. When we do that with the 3 predictions you just made (X = 70 → Y' = 29.49; X = 45 → Y' = 22.24; X = 17 → Y' = 14.12), we get:

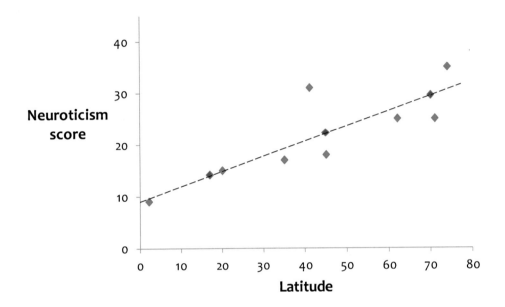

The regression line is probably in *about* the same place it would be if you simply drew it as best you could through the data points. But by doing it properly, we know our regression line fits the data points as best as it possibly could. As a matter of fact, another name for the regression line is *the line of best fit*.

Remember the prediction we made earlier, using the regression equation, for that person who lives at latitude 39? We predicted their neuroticism score would be 20.50. We could have used the regression line instead to *estimate* their neuroticism score:

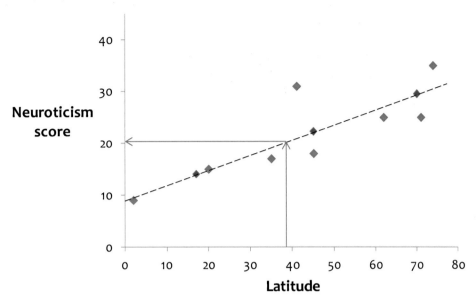

Once carefully drawn, the regression line can be used for quick predictions. See how fast you can eyeball a prediction on Y for an X (latitude) of, say 52? 65? 8?

*   *   *

Now to point out something important: Earlier, you predicted a neuroticism score of 22.24 for someone living at latitude 45, but you actually had someone in your study who lives at latitude 45, but whose level of neuroticism was *not* 22.24.

Actually, that person's neuroticism score was 18, several points away from the prediction. On the other hand, look at Resident #4, who lives at latitude 20. You would predict that someone at latitude 20 would have a neuroticism score of 14.99...

$$Y' = 9.19 + 0.29(20) = \mathbf{14.99}$$

... which is very close to the actual score of Resident #4, whose neuroticism level is 15.

One thing to take from this is that the accuracy of your predictions varies. But to get a basic feel for how accurate your predictions are *overall*, you have two options. One is to look back and simply see how far off the data points are from the regression line. But to get a precise measure of the accuracy of your predictions, you should calculate something called the *standard error of the estimate*. This statistic is calculated in a very straightforward manner: by comparing the *actual scores* of participants on the outcome variable with the *predictions you would have made* on those participants on the outcome variable.

Doing this for all the participants tells you how far off, on average, your predictions are.

> The **standard error of the estimate** *is how far off, on average, your* *predictions of the outcome variable are from the* actual scores on the *outcome variable.*

Since the standard error of the estimate is how far off, on average, actual scores are from predicted scores, it should make sense to you that the formula for the standard error of the estimate (σ_{est}) looks a lot like the formula for standard deviation. After all, both standard deviation and standard error of the estimate are measures of how far, on average, one thing is from another. Standard deviation is the average distance scores are from the mean, while, again, standard error of the estimate is the average distance predicted scores are from actual scores.

Below is the formula for the standard error of the estimate, σ_{est}. Note its similarity with the formula for standard deviation (on the right).

$$\sigma_{est} = \sqrt{\frac{\Sigma(Y - Y')^2}{N}} \qquad S = \sqrt{\frac{\Sigma(X - M)^2}{N - 1}}$$

Y in the formula refers to the actual *Y* scores of participants studied, and *Y'* refers to the *Y* scores you *predicted* for those subjects. Now, that may seem a little odd. After all, why would you care what *Y* score you would have predicted for a partcipant if you know that participant's *actual Y* score?

The answer is simple: When you know how accurate your predictions are (which you could only do if you knew *both* of the participants' actual scores), you can then have an idea of how accurate your predictions are for new participants, whose *Y* scores you do *not* know. And that's really when you would want to make a *prediction*, right?

* * *

Let's now continue the example from above, where we used correlational data we collected to make predictions about how neurotic people are based on the latitude they live in.

The first thing we need to do before we can figure out how far off our predictions are, on average, is to make the predictions. We would make these predictions based on the regression equation, of course.

So, if we apply the regression equation to each of the participants, we get the following:

Resident	Latitude (deg.) X	Neuroticism score Y	(regression equation)	Y'
1	74	35	Y' = 9.19 + 0.29(74) =	30.65
2	71	25	Y' = 9.19 + 0.29(71) =	29.78
3	62	25	Y' = 9.19 + 0.29(62) =	27.17
4	20	15	Y' = 9.19 + 0.29(20) =	14.99
5	45	18	Y' = 9.19 + 0.29(45) =	22.24
6	41	31	Y' = 9.19 + 0.29(41) =	21.08
7	35	17	Y' = 9.19 + 0.29(35) =	19.34
8	2	9	Y' = 9.19 + 0.29(2) =	9.77

Note we now have predicted Y scores, (Y'), for all participants. And we already had their actual Y scores. Now all we need to do is apply the standard error of the estimate formula to find, well, the standard error of our estimates (predictions):

$$\sigma_{est} = \sqrt{\frac{\Sigma(Y - Y')^2}{N}}$$

As the formula specifies, we need to first find the difference between the actual score and the predicted score for each participant (Y – Y'). Then we need to square those values. Let's start with that:

Resident	Neuroticism score Y	Y'	Y - Y'	(Y - Y')^2
1	35	30.65	4.35	18.92
2	25	29.78	-4.78	22.85
3	25	27.17	-2.17	4.71
4	15	14.99	0.01	0.00
5	18	22.24	-4.24	17.98
6	31	21.08	9.92	98.41
7	17	19.34	-2.34	5.48
8	9	9.77	-0.77	0.59

Next, again as specified by the formula, we add up all those values (18.92 + 22.85 +...+ 0.59), which gives us 168.94. The formula says we then divide that by N, which is 8 in this example: 168.94/8 = 21.12. Finally, we take the square root of that number: $\sqrt{21.12}$ = **4.60**.

Thus, in our latitude/neuroticism example, σ_{est} = **4.60**, meaning when we make predictions about individuals' neuroticism based on the latitude they live in, we can expect our predictions to be off, *on average*, by about 4.60 points.[117]

＊ ＊ ＊

This ends the section regarding correlation. In the correlation chapter, you learned how to find out whether or not two variables are correlated. In the current chapter, you learned how to then (if a correlation did exist) use that information to make predictions, and also to have an idea about how accurate you could expect your predictions to be.

The next chapter will cover another inferential statistical test. The test to be presented is used in studies where subjects are not *measured* on any variable, as has always been the case to this point in the book, but instead are simply put into categories (e.g., *came on time* vs. *came late*, or *chose a History course* as an elective vs. *chose a Sociology course* as an elective vs. *chose a Political Science course* as an elective). That test is called the *chi square goodness-of-fit test.*

---

[117] Note we don't know how far off we are for any *one individual's* prediction (i.e., future participants, for whom we only know latitude and are trying to predict their neuroticism scores). We could be closer than 4.60, or further than that, on any given future prediction. But, over a relatively large number of predictions, we expect to be off by about 4.60, *on average.*

Questions and problems.

1. Why would it not make any sense to perform regression analysis on variables which were found to not be significantly correlated?

2. You have found that two variables, X and Y, are signifcantly correlated, based on a study involving 25 participants. Now, you come across Sophie, and you want to predict how she'll do on the Y variable. What do you need to know in order to do that?

3. You do a correlational study and find that the number of pets someone currently owns is significantly correlated with their anxiety level ($r = -0.89$). Here is the raw data you found:

Participant	Number of pets owned (X)	Anxiety level (Y)
1	5	2
2	2	8
3	1	8
4	4	4
5	2	7
8	6	4

Create the regression equation, then use it to predict what someone's anxiety level would be if they owned 3 pets.

Note the standard deviation of the X scores is 1.97 and the standard deviation of the Y scores is 2.51.

4. Find the standard error of the estimate, σ_{est} for the previous problem.

5. Interpret your answer to #4.

6. The higher the correlation between two variables, the _____ (larger or smaller?) the standard error of the estimate will be.

Solutions to questions and problems.

1) If you find (in a hypothesis test), that two variables are not significantly correlated, then knowing someone's score on one would not help you to predict their score on another. Thus, doing regression analysis, that is, creating a regression equation and using it make predictions, would not result in predictions which were any more accurate than just guessing. For example, if I told you Steve is 12 years old, could you predict what his family's annual income is any better than if you did not know Steve's age? No, because the *age of a child* is not correlated with that child's *family income*.

2) To predict Sophie's score on the Y variable, you'll need to know her score on the X variable. You'll also need to find the slope (b) and Y intercept (a) of the regression line based on those other 25 participants. With that, you can solve the regression equation for Sophie, that is, predict a Y score for her.

3)

Slope (b) = -1.13

Y-intercept (a) = 9.26

Regression equation: **Y' = 9.26 + (-1.13)(X)**

Predicted anxiety level (Y) for someone with 3 pets: Y' = 9.26 + (-1.13)(3) = **5.87**

4)

First, you need to make predictions on the Y variables (that is, find Y') for all partipants:

Participant	Number of pets owned X	Anxiety Level Y	(regression equation)	Y'
1	5	2	Y' = 9.26 + (-1.13)(5) =	3.61
2	2	8	Y' = 9.26 + (-1.13)(2) =	7
3	1	8	Y' = 9.26 + (-1.13)(1) =	8.13
4	4	4	Y' = 9.26 + (-1.13)(4) =	4.74
5	2	7	Y' = 9.26 + (-1.13)(2) =	7
6	6	4	Y' = 9.26 + (-1.13)(6) =	2.48

Next, apply the formula for the standard error of the estimate, σ_{est}, which gives you:

Participant	Anxiety Level Y	Y'	Y - Y'	(Y - Y')²
1	2	3.61	-1.61	2.59
2	8	7	1	1
3	8	8.13	-0.13	0.02
4	4	4.74	-0.74	0.55
5	7	7	0	0
6	4	2.48	1.52	2.31

$\Sigma(Y - Y')^2 = 6.47$.

$N = 6$.

$\Sigma(Y - Y')^2 / N = 6.47/6 = 1.08$.

$\sqrt{1.08} = \textbf{1.04}$

5) On average, we can expect predictions on the Y variable to be off by about 1.04.

6) smaller. Higher correlations result in more accurate predictions. And more accurate predictions mean a *smaller* average distance between your predictions and the actual scores. Note that some formulas for the standard error of the estimate, which of course get you the same answer as the formula you learned, actually include the correlation coefficient itself (but those formulas are more complicated).

Chapter 18
The chi-square goodness-of-fit test

Begin this chapter by considering the following research questions:

1. Do students have a preference for sitting in different rows of a classroom (e.g., the front, middle, back)?
2. Are males late more often than females?
3. Are people more likely to buy products they believe are scarce?

To answer the questions above, we would need to use a statistical test called a *chi-square* (X^2) *goodness-of-fit test*. None of the tests you've already learned will work, because there is an important difference between the research questions we asked before and the ones above. Can you see what it is?

The difference is that, in all the questions above, the variable being measured is not a *score*, such as reaction time or a score on a test, but is instead a *count* of *which category* something fits into, also known as a *frequency*. Look what's being measured:

1. how many students chose the respective rows (front vs. middle vs. back)
2. how many males, vs. females, were late
3. how many times subjects purchased scarce vs. not scarce products

Again, note we're not obtaining a score for each participant (and calculating means and such), but rather just counting. We will thus use the chi-square goodness-of-fit test[118] to answer all the questions above, starting with the first:

> *Do students have a preference for sitting in different rows (front, middle, back) of a classroom?* Note, as always, there are two possible answers to this: *yes* there is a preference, or *no*, there is not a preference.

In this study we would probably lead students into an empty room, one at a time, and record which row each of them chose to sit at. If we did this for a bunch of students, the results may look something like the following (next page):

---

[118] Chi-square is also denoted X^2, X being the Greek letter *chi*.

Chose front row	Chose middle row	Chose back row
17	20	23

The values in the table above are *frequencies,* since they represent *how many times* the events fit into the various categories. They are further called *observed* because they are the *findings*—what you *observed* in the study. The data collected in this type of study are thus called observed frequencies (f_o, for short).

> The **chi-square (X^2) goodness-of-fit test** *is used when frequency data is collected.*

The chi-square test is an example of what's called a *non-parametric* test, meaning that you do not have a distribution of scores. All the tests you've learned before this point were *parametric* tests. For example, in the independent samples t test, you compared two means (e.g., $M_1 = 32$ vs. $M_2 = 45$), but those means were each calculated from a distribution of scores, which you use to compute how much error you have. You cannot do this in a non-parametric test, so non-parametric tests tend to have less power than parametric tests.

By now you should know you must decide whether the research findings represent a *chance* occurrence that only *looks* like it may be a real relationship/effect, or represent a *real* relationship/effect. You should also know the procedure requires finding a *critical statistic* and then comparing that to an *obtained statistic.*

In order to calculate the obtained statistic for the chi-square goodness-of-fit test, designated X^2_{obt}, you need to figure out what you would have expected your findings to look like if there was no effect/relationship, that is, if the Null Hypothesis (H_o) is true. Those are called the *expected frequencies* (f_e).

> The **expected frequencies** *are the frequencies predicted by the null hypothesis—what would happen if there was no effect.*

Based on the definition of expected frequencies—*the frequencies you would expect to get if there was no effect*—try to fill in the blanks on the table on the next page. Note the null hypothesis, H_o, is: *Students do not have a preference for sitting in different rows* (and the alternative hypothesis, H_1, is: *Students have a preference for sitting in different rows*).

	Chose front row	Chose middle row	Chose back row
Observed frequencies f_o	17	20	23
Expected frequencies f_e	___	___	___

There were 60 participants altogether (17 + 20 + 23), each of which could choose one row to sit in. Therefore, if there was no preference, about 1/3rd of the 60 participants (that is, 20 of them) would choose the front row, about 1/3rd of the participants (20) would choose the middle row, and about 1/3rd of the participants (20) would choose the back row:

	Chose front row	Chose middle row	Chose back row
Observed frequencies f_o	17	20	23
Expected frequencies f_e	20	20	20

* * *

Now that you are familiar with observed and expected frequencies, you are ready to think of the question like this: *Do the observed frequencies basically match, or fit with the expected frequencies? Or, alternatively, do they differ significantly from, or not fit with, the expected frequencies?*

Below are two example cases so you can see what a good and a bad fit look like:

A seemingly good fit:

	Category 1	Category 2	Category 3
Observed frequencies f_o	23	24	28
Expected frequencies f_e	25	25	25

A seemingly bad fit:

	Category 1	Category 2	Category 3
Observed frequencies f_o	11	24	40
Expected frequencies f_e	25	25	25

See the difference? Now, we always need a statistical test before we can decide what the results mean—in this case whether we should call something a good or bad fit.

Nevertheless, we can safely say the second example is a worse fit than the first, and therefore we'd be more likely to decide there is a real effect in that one if we did X^2 tests for both.

Question: What would indicate there *is* a preference for rows chosen, a *good* fit between the observed and expected frequencies, or a *bad* fit between the observed and expected frequencies?[119]

*   *   *

Though it is important to be able to eyeball the results and decide whether an effect *appears* to be present, we need a way to *objectively quantify* how well the f_o's fit with the f_e's, so we can make a more confident decision. The X^2 formula does just that:

$$X^2_{obt} = \sum \frac{(f_o - f_e)^2}{f_e}$$

As with solving any formula, you must follow the order of operations. The steps to calculate X^2 are therefore:

1- Find $(f_o - f_e)$ for each category.

	Chose front row	Chose middle row	Chose back row
Observed frequencies f_o	17	20	23
Expected frequencies f_e	20	20	20
$(f_o - f_e)$	-3	0	3

2- Find $(f_o - f_e)^2$ for each category (square the values just obtained).

	Chose front row	Chose middle row	Chose back row
Observed frequencies f_o	17	20	23
Expected frequencies f_e	20	20	20
$(f_o - f_e)$	-3	0	3
$(f_o - f_e)^2$	9	0	9

---

[119] A *bad* fit would indicate a preference. A bad fit means that the results do *not* look like what you would expect to happen by chance (i.e., if there was no effect). And, as always, if the results don't look like chance, you conclude they are not chance.

A couple points about the first two steps.

- A relatively large discrepancy between the observed and expected frequencies (e.g., $f_o = 2$, $f_e = 10$) would result in larger values ($2 - 10 = -8$; $-8^2 = \mathbf{64}$) while a relatively small discrepancy (e.g., $f_o = 23$, $f_e = 25$) would result in a smaller value ($23 - 25 = -2$; $-2^2 = \mathbf{4}$).

- The frequencies themselves (f_o and f_e) don't determine the outcome here. Rather it's the *discrepancy* between them that matters: more discrepancy = worse fit = more likely it is there's an effect.

3- Divide by f_e for each category.

	Chose front row	Chose middle row	Chose back row
Observed frequencies f_o	17	20	23
Expected frequencies f_e	20	20	20
$(f_o - f_e)$	-3	0	3
$(f_o - f_e)^2$	9	0	9
$(f_o - f_e)^2 / f_e$	9/20=0.45	0/20=0	9/20=0.45

Dividing by f_e puts the (squared) discrepancies from the previous step into context. That is an important point, so it's worth your time to take a minute to understand it better.

Do you agree that a discrepancy of 4 means one thing if f_e is 6, but means something entirely different if f_e is 100? For example, doesn't the finding [$f_o = 10$, $f_e = 6$] *feel* different than the finding [$f_o = 104$, $f_e = 100$]? In the first it seems the observed value was quite different than the expected—you might have an effect there. In the second it seems the difference could easily just be chance/sampling error and thus there is no effect. Yet, in both, the result of the first two steps is the same:

- First one: $(f_o - f_e)^2 = (\mathbf{10 - 6})^2 = 16$
- Second one: $(f_o - f_e)^2 = (\mathbf{104 - 100})^2 = 16$

That's why we need this step— to put those values above into context. Look what happens when we divide the above by f_e.

- First one: $(f_o - f_e)^2 / f_e = 16 / \mathbf{6} = 2.67$
- Second one: $(f_o - f_e)^2 / f_e = 16 / \mathbf{100} = 0.16$

Now that seems right: The difference between 10 and 6 (first one, 2.67) is effectively larger than the difference between 104 and 100 (second one, 0.16).

4- The last step in calculating X^2 is to sum (Σ) the values just found. This tells you the discrepancy between the observed and expected frequencies across all the categories (which you can also think of as how well the observed frequencies 'fit' with the expected frequencies).

	Chose front row	Chose middle row	Chose back row
Observed frequencies f_o	17	20	23
Expected frequencies f_e	20	20	20
$(f_o - f_e)$	-3	0	3
$(f_o - f_e)^2$	9	0	9
$(f_o - f_e)^2 / f_e$	9/20=0.45	0/20=0	9/20=0.45
$\Sigma (f_o - f_e)^2 / f_e$		0.45 + 0 + 0.45 = 0.90	
$X_{obt}^2 =$ **0.90**.			

* * *

Note X_{obt}^2 is always a positive number because the last part of finding the numerator is squaring, and when you square a number you end up with a positive value. The denominator is a frequency, so it's always positive too (the lowest frequency you can have is 0). A positive number divided by a positive number equals a positive number. Since a chi-square test can only go in this one direction (the positive direction) it is always a one-tailed test.

As in any inferential statistical test, the *obtained* value must be compared to a *critical* value to determine whether or not the result is statistically significant.

Finding a critical value always requires a table, in this case the chi-square table (Table 5 in the back of this book). To find the critical statistic, X_{crit}^2, on this table we need to know 1) the level of significance we chose (let's say α 0.05 for this one), and 2) the degrees of freedom (df). For the chi-square, the formula for df is:

$$df = C - 1$$

      C is the number of categories.

With this information, try to find X_{crit}^2. Below is a small portion of the chi-square table.

df	0.05	0.01
1	3.841	6.635
2	5.991	9.210
3	7.815	11.345
4	9.488	13.277

Since df = 2 and α = 0.05, X^2_{crit} = **5.991.**

Of course, if the obtained statistic is larger than the critical statistic, you reject the null hypothesis (H_0), which says, as always, that there is no effect. Otherwise, you retain H_0 (decide there is *no effect*).

In this example, **X^2_{obt} (0.90) < X^2_{crit} (5.991),** so we *retain* H_0: There is no preference among students for the front, middle, or last row. The discrepancies between the observed frequencies and the expected frequencies were not statistically significant.

Our conclusion, including the APA-formatted statistical results, is:

> We found there is not a preference among students for different rows in a classroom, $X^2(2, N = 60) = 0.90, p > 0.05$.[120]

---

[120] Notice the APA statistical report for a X^2 test includes the total number of participants, in addition to the degrees of freedom.

Problems.

1) Are female students more likely than male students to show up for an appointment on time? Assume equal numbers of males and females had scheduled appointments. *Use α 0.05.*

	Late females	Late males
Observed frequencies f_o	21	36

2) Are people more likely to buy products they believe are scarce? Four products are put on a shelf, with different labels (see table below) and the number of times the products were purchased was recorded. *Use α 0.01.*

	"40 more in stock"	"30 more in stock"	"20 more in stock"	"10 more in stock"
Observed frequencies f_o	34	40	48	54

3) (Same as question #2, but with some different parameters) Are people more likely to buy products they believe are scarce? Four products are put on a shelf, with different labels (see table below) and the number of times the products were purchased was recorded. *Use α 0.05.*

	"40 more in stock"	"30 more in stock"	"20 more in stock"	"10 more in stock"
Observed frequencies f_o	10	15	21	30

Solutions to problems.

1)

- Figure out the expected frequencies.

	Late females	Late males
Observed frequencies f_o	21	36
Expected frequencies f_e	28.5	28.5

- Find the critical value: $X^2_{crit} = 3.84$ (α 0.05, df = 1)

- Calculate X^2_{obt} (see table below)

    A. find $(f_o - f_e)^2$

    B. divide by f_e

    C. repeat first two steps for each category

    D. sum the resulting values

	Late females	Late males
Observed frequencies f_o	21	36
Expected frequencies f_e	28.5	28.5
$(f_o - f_e)$	-7.5	7.5
$(f_o - f_e)^2$	56.25	56.25
$(f_o - f_e)^2 / f_e$	1.97	1.97
$\Sigma(f_o - f_e)^2 / f_e$	3.95	

X^2_{obt} **(3.95)** > X^2_{crit} **(3.841)** (Reject H_o)

Males and females differ in how often they are late for appointments, $X^2(1, N = 57) = 3.95, p < 0.05$.

2)

	"40 more in stock"	"30 more in stock"	"20 more in stock"	"10 more in stock"
Observed frequencies f_o	34	40	48	54
Expected frequencies f_e	44.00	44.00	44.00	44.00
$(f_o - f_e)$	-10.00	-4.00	4.00	10.00
$(f_o - f_e)^2$	100.00	16.00	16.00	100.00
$(f_o - f_e)^2 / f_e$	2.27	0.36	0.36	2.27
$\Sigma(f_o - f_e)^2 / f_e$			5.27	

$X^2_{obt} (5.27) < X^2_{crit} (11.345)$ (Retain H_o)

People are not more likely to buy products they believe are scarce, $X^2(3, N = 176) = 5.27$, $p > 0.01$.

3)

	"40 more in stock"	"30 more in stock"	"20 more in stock"	"10 more in stock"
Observed frequencies f_o	10	15	21	30
Expected frequencies f_e	19.00	19.00	19.00	19.00
$(f_o - f_e)$	-9.00	-4.00	2.00	11.00
$(f_o - f_e)^2$	81.00	16.00	4.00	121.00
$(f_o - f_e)^2 / f_e$	4.26	0.84	0.21	6.37
$\Sigma(f_o - f_e)^2 / f_e$			11.68	

$X^2_{obt} (11.68) > X^2_{crit} (7.815)$ (Reject H_o)

People are more likely to buy products they believe are scarce, $X^2(3, N = 76) = 11.68$, $p < 0.05$.

Chapter 19
Estimating with confidence intervals

Nearly all of the inferential statistics presented in the book so far have involved a *decision*. In all cases, the researcher's goal was to decide *whether or not* the results they found are statistically significant.

Some types of inferential statistics do not involve such a yes-or-no decision. In this chapter, you will learn about one of them: Making an estimation by constructing a confidence interval. An important thing to know right away is that estimation is only done if the researcher first decided the result is statistically significant. You can thus think of estimating as an optional follow-up that is done only when a significant effect is first found in the hypothesis test.

In Chapter 10, you learned the procedure for deciding whether the result from an experiment involving a single sample of participants was significant—the single sample t test. To be a bit more specific, you determined if a sample mean, M, was significantly different from a population mean, μ.[121]

Consider the main example from that chapter:

> *Is a person's spending in a store affected by how scarce the items appear to be? In an attempt to answer this question, you set up two mock stores. One has many of each item available while the other has just one of every item. Will participants spend a different amount of money in the store where items appear to be scarce? You give each of your 25 participants $100 to spend, and measure the average amount they spend in the scarce store. You find the participants in the sample spent an average of $55 in the scarce store.*
>
> *The sample standard deviation, s, is 8. Using α 0.01, decide whether the results suggest that we are affected by the apparent scarcity of items.*

If you decided the sample mean of $55 *was* indeed significantly different from the population mean of $50 (again, that's the mean you'd expect if there was no effect of *scarcity*), then you could follow that up with another important question: Although I found my sample of participants spent a mean of $55 in the scarce store, what mean would I expect to find if I could somehow test the whole population?[122]

---

[121] Remember, the population mean, μ, is what you *expect* your sample mean to be if there is no effect.
[122] You should know by now that we can never actually study the population, so we could never get a *definitive* answer to that question. But, we can *estimate* it, which is what we're going to do in this chapter.

What do you think? Would you expect, if you could have the whole population go into your scarce store, they would also spend an average of exactly $55? In other words, do you think µ would also turn out to be *exactly* $55? No, of course not![123]

But you will soon learn how to use a formula which will provide an *estimate* of what µ would be. And by *estimate* we mean a range, or an interval, within which we are pretty confident the *true* population mean—the mean we'd get if we *could* somehow test the whole population—would fall.

But before learning the formula to create such an estimate, you need to understand how estimating works. The first thing to clarify is that larger intervals mean less precision, and smaller intervals mean more precision.

> *Larger ranges/intervals are less precise and smaller ranges/intervals are more precise.*

For example, say you guessed a stranger's age is between 14 and 24, and your friend guessed that same stranger's age is between 18 and 20. Your friend is giving a smaller range of ages and is therefore being more precise, while you are giving a larger range of ages and are therefore being less precise.

With that idea clarified, let's consider what factors might influence how precise our estimate would be in a research situation such as our scarcity study. Could you name one—one factor that would influence how precisely we would be able to make estimations of what a true population mean is, based on our sample mean?

If you said the *sample size*, N, you are correct:

> *The larger the sample size, the more precise the estimate.*

And if you knew that the *amount of variability* in the sample also affects the precision of our estimate, you are really on the right track. Specifically, more variability leads to less precise estimates.

> *The more variability in the data, the less precise the estimate will end up being.*

---

[123] Because of sampling error, of course.

The other factor in determining the precision of our estimate is the *level of confidence* we wish to have. The rule Is as follows:

> *The higher level of confidence we wish to have, the less precise our estimate will end up being.*

*   *   *

Although the impact of sample size and variability are somewhat particular to research, the impact of confidence on a confidence interval can be illustrated with an everyday example.

Think of the example above, where *you* gave a larger range of ages than your friend when you were trying to guess a stranger's age. Remember, your range being larger means you were being less precise. But at the same time, because you were being less precise, you were more likely to be correct. That is, we can be more confident that the *true* age of the stranger is within your interval of 14 to 24 than within your friend's interval of 18 to 20.

To illustrate that concept, think about what the outside temperature is right now, wherever you are[124]. While it's true you cannot know the exact temperature just by guessing, you could estimate it. Do so by filling in the blanks below. Importantly, *be as precise as you can (that is, give the smallest range of temperatures possible)*.

You should start by taking your best guess about the actual temperature. You know this won't be exactly correct, but write down your best guess.

Next, build an interval around that best guess. But do it twice, under two different conditions.

1) Assume you want to be sort of confident, say about **50%** confident, you are correct—that the actual temperature, if we could measure it, would indeed be within the range you provide. Again, be as precise as possible but still be reasonably sure, about 50% sure, you're correct.

    The temperature outside right now is between _____ and _____ .

2) Next, assume you want to be *very* confident, say about **99.9%** confident, that you are correct—that the actual temperature, if we could measure it, would indeed be within the range you provide. Just like before, you want to be as precise as possible but also be very sure now, about 99.9% sure, that you are correct (and use the same starting point as you did for the first one).

---

[124] Pretend for this example that you do not have access to a thermometer (or the internet, etc.), so you could never find out the actual temperature.

The temperature outside right now is between _____ and _____.

There are no right or wrong answers, but your estimate in the first situation should be more precise (meaning a smaller interval) than your estimate in the second situation. This is because, in the second instance when you wanted to be more confident that the actual temperature fell within your range, you had to provide a larger range (be less precise).

Notice when you wanted to be more confident, which is good, you had to be less precise, which is bad. Or you could think of it the other way: If you want to be more precise, you must give up some confidence, and if you are OK with being less precise, you can be more confident. Consider the diagram below to help clarify that concept:

Confidence ━━━━━━━━━━━━━━━━━━ Precision

Think of the left end of that line as maximum confidence and the right end of that line as maximum precision. As you increase confidence (move toward the left), you get less precise. And as you increase precision (move toward the right), you lose confidence.

To summarize, the three factors that determine the precision of the estimate are:

1. **The desired level of confidence**— The more confidence you want, the less precise you will end up being (more confidence = less precision).
2. **The amount of variability in the data**— The more variability that is present, the less precise you will end up being (more variability = less precision).
3. **The size of the sample**— The larger the sample, the more precise you will end up being (more participants = more precision).

* * *

Now let's make an estimation, that is, construct a *confidence interval*, from our earlier study on the effect of scarcity. Recall we originally wanted to know if the *scarcity* of items affects how much money someone would spend in a store, but also recall we had already concluded, indeed, it does.

What we are doing now is taking the result we found in the sample, $55, and using it to estimate what result *we think we would get* if we could test the whole population. In other words, we're figuring out what we think the population mean would be if the whole population participated in our experiment—what the *actual* size of the effect is. Keep in mind the population mean we are talking about now does not represent what would happen if there was no effect, as it does in hypothesis tests. That was only considered to figure out if we had an effect. We already did that, and found that we *did* have an effect.

Even though we know the population mean, μ, would not be exactly the same as our sample mean of $55 because of sampling error, that same mean is nevertheless going to be our starting point for the estimate. And why not? Even though we know it's not perfectly accurate, it is still our best guess.[125]

Therefore, the formula for the confidence interval uses the sample result as its starting point. It will take the following general form:

the population mean = the sample mean, plus or minus some amount

or

$\mu = M \pm some\ amount$

How much that *some amount* is, in other words, how large our confidence interval will be, is determined by the three factors discussed earlier:

1. **The desired level of confidence.** Though you could pick any confidence level you want, the convention is to choose to be either **95%** confident or **99%** confident. Which you choose will affect the t critical score, t_{crit}.
2. **The amount of variability in the data.** This will be measured by the standard deviation of the sample and will influence the standard error, s_M.
3. **The size of the sample.** You will see sample size actually comes into play twice: when finding t_{crit} and when calculating s_M.

Given all of this, you should not be very surprised to learn that the formula for a confidence interval that follows up a single sample t test considers t_{crit} and s_M. The full formula is:

$$\mu = M \pm t_{crit} * s_M$$

  μ is the population mean you are estimating.

  M is the sample mean you found (the starting point of the estimate).

  t_{crit} is the critical t statistic, which is affected by the size of your sample (as measured by df = N − 1), and by the level of confidence.

  s_M is standard error, which is affected by the variability in your sample, as measured by standard deviation, s, and by the size of your sample, N.

_____

[125] Just like before when you began with your best guess about the actual temperature as a starting point to create your intervals.

Below is some information we'll need. This was given in the problem earlier.

- μ = $50
- M = $55
- s = 8
- N = 25

Although we are considering much of the same information that is relevant for a hypothesis test, we are no longer addressing *whether the results suggest people are affected by the apparent scarcity of items.* We already concluded in the hypothesis test that, yes, they are. Now we are following that up by constructing a confidence interval around our (significant) result of $55. To do that, we not only need the information just listed, but we also must decide how much confidence we want to have in our estimate. As specified above, we choose either 95% confidence or 99% confidence. For this one, let's go with **95%** confidence.

The formula again is:

$$\mu = M \pm t_{crit} * s_M$$

We can easily fill in the sample mean (the starting point of our estimate):

$$\mu = \$55 \pm t_{crit} * s_M$$

But clearly we need to also find t_{crit} and s_M to finish solving the formula. Which you find first makes no difference, so let's start with s_M. As you know, the formula for s_M is:

$$s_M = \frac{s}{\sqrt{N}}$$

Plugging in the information we need to solve that formula, s = 8 and N = 25, we get:

$$s_M = \frac{8}{\sqrt{25}} = \frac{8}{5} = 1.6$$

Next is t_{crit}. Even though we are looking this up on the t table in the context of a confidence interval rather than a hypothesis test, you still need the same 3 pieces of information. After all, the t table is still the t table, so to look up a t_{crit} you always need to know the number of tails, the level of significance (α), and the degrees of freedom (df).

Here's how to find this information for a confidence interval:

- *Number of tails:* Simple—always **two**. This is because you are going in both directions, plus and minus, from the sample result (M ± ...)
- *Level of significance, α:* If you want 95% confidence, use α 0.05 (5%) and when you want 99% confidence, use α 0.01 (1%).
  - o Think of it this way: Choosing an α of 5% means you want to make sure there is only a 5% chance you are wrong, and thus a 95% chance you're right (95% confidence). Choosing an α of 1% means you want to make sure there is only a 1% chance you are wrong, and thus a 99% chance you're right (99% confidence)
- *Degrees of freedom, df:* df = N - 1

In this case, we are doing a 95% confidence interval, so we use α 0.05, and our sample size is 25, so degrees of freedom = 24. And remember, the confidence interval is always two tailed.

With that in mind, find t_{crit}:

One-tailed	0.05	0.025	0.01	0.005
Two-tailed	0.1	0.05	0.02	0.01
df				
1	6.314	12.71	31.82	63.66
2	2.92	4.303	6.965	9.925
3	2.353	3.182	4.541	5.841
23	1.714	2.069	2.5	2.807
24	1.711	2.064	2.492	2.797
25	1.708	2.06	2.485	2.787
26	1.706	2.056	2.479	2.779

t_{crit} is **2.064**. If you did not come up with 2.064, be sure to note your mistake before moving on.

And as we know from our earlier calculation, s_M = **1.6**. Plugging all this into the formula and solving it, we get:

$$\mu = M \pm t_{crit} * s_M$$

$$\mu = \$55 \pm 2.064 * 1.6$$

$$\mu = \$55 \pm 3.30$$

And since $55 – 3.30 = **$51.70** and $55 + 3.30 = **$58.30**, the confidence interval is:

$$\mu = \$51.70 - \$58.30$$

There are more practice problems for you to work out, but it's just as important, if not more important, to understand what the answer actually *means*. So, here is what all of this means in the end:

> Our *sample mean* was $55. We are 95% confident that *the true population mean*—the result we'd get if the whole population took part in our study—is somewhere between $51.70 and $58.30.[126]

You could actually calculate a confidence interval after any type of statistical test, not just the single sample t test. You could even create a confidence interval around your prediction in a regression analysis. Although we will not go through any such applications, it may be helpful to look at the formulas, noting the similarity in structure among them. If you look carefully you can see they all have the same three parts: 1) what is being estimated, 2) the starting point for the estimate (i.e., the sample result), and 3) the terms that determine the interval (the critical statistic and the standard error).

You already know the formula for a confidence interval after a **single sample t test** is:

$$\mu = M \pm t_{crit} * s_M$$

The formula for a confidence interval after a **z test** is:

$$\mu = M \pm z_{crit} * \sigma_M$$

The formula for a confidence interval after an **independent samples t test** is:

$$\mu_1 - \mu_2 = M_1 + M_2 \pm t_{crit} * s_{M_1 - M_2}$$

And the formula for a confidence interval after a **related samples t test** is:

$$\mu_D = M_D \pm t_{crit} * s_{M_D}$$

In all cases, the formulas take the sample result, and then build an interval around it, where the size of the interval is determined the same way: by multiplying a critical value

---

[126] That also means there is a 5% chance the true population mean is *outside* that range. Had we done a 99% confidence interval, there would be a 1% chance the true population mean is *outside* the range we calculated (but of course the interval would have ended up being larger/less precise).

(determined by sample size and how much confidence you want) by standard error (determined by sample size and the sample(s) variability). Naturally, all of them are thus influenced by sample size, variability, and confidence level.

Questions and problems.

1) You conducted a study to see if empathy increases after people watch live theater. You found an empathy test online, and had a group of subjects take the test right after watching a play. Their average score on the test was 42, which you determined in a hypothesis test to be significantly higher than the population mean. The standard deviation of the sample (N = 36) was 13. Construct a 99% confidence interval around your sample mean.

Interpret your answer (What does "μ = __ to __" mean?).

2) You conducted a similar study to see if cognitive speed increases after people watch live theater. You found a cognitive speed test online, and had a group of subjects go to a play and then take the test. Their average speed on the test was 440 milliseconds (ms), which you determined in a hypothesis test to be significantly higher than the population mean. You studied 49 subjects and the standard deviation of the sample was 75ms. Construct a 99% confidence interval around your sample mean.

Interpret your answer.

3) You create another mock store, which has exactly one of all item (items were very scarce). This time you wanted to see if scarcity of items influences customers' *satisfaction* with their purchases. You used a standard test of consumer satisfaction and found that your sample of 25 subjects had an average of 5.1 (the average level of satisfaction was 5.1), with a standard deviation of 1.7. Construct a 95% confidence interval around your sample mean.

Interpret your answer.

4) Another group of researchers read about your study, created a mock store of their own, and measured their participants' satisfaction. They found somewhat similar results (their sample mean was 5.4 and s was 1.9). They had 100 subjects. Construct a 95% confidence interval around their sample mean.

Interpret your answer.

5) If you were to decrease the sample size in the study described in #4 above, the resulting confidence interval would be _____.

6) If you were to perform the study described in #1 above again using the same sample size, and the same level of confidence, but you found more variability in the sample the second time around, the resulting confidence interval would be _____.

7) If you were to re-compute the confidence interval in the study described in #2 above, this time using a lower level of confidence (e.g., 95%), the resulting confidence interval would be _____.

Solutions to questions and problems.

1)

t_{crit} = 2.75 (remember, when the exact df you want is not on the table, go to the next *lower* df)

$$S_M = \frac{13}{\sqrt{36}} = \frac{13}{6} = 2.17$$

$$\mu = 42 \pm 2.75 * 2.17$$

$$\mu = 42 \pm 5.97$$

$$\mu = 36.03 - 47.97$$

Interpretation: We are 99% confident that the true population mean is somewhere between 36.03 and 47.97.

2)

t_{crit} = 2.704

$$S_M = \frac{75}{\sqrt{49}} = \frac{75}{7} = 10.71$$

$$\mu = 440 \pm 2.704 * 10.71$$

$$\mu = 440 \pm 28.96$$

$$\mu = 411.04 - 468.96$$

Interpretation: We are 99% confident that the true population mean is somewhere between 411.04ms and 468.96ms.

3)

$t_{crit} = 2.064$

$$S_M = \frac{1.7}{\sqrt{25}} = \frac{1.7}{5} = 0.34$$

$$\mu = 5.1 \pm 2.064 * 0.34$$

$$\mu = 5.1 \pm 0.70$$

$$\mu = 4.4 - 5.8$$

Interpretation: We are 95% confident that the true population mean is somewhere between 4.4 and 5.8.

4)

$t_{crit} = 1.99$

$$S_M = \frac{1.9}{\sqrt{100}} = \frac{1.9}{10} = 0.19$$

$$\mu = 5.4 \pm 1.99 * 0.19$$

$$\mu = 5.4 \pm 0.38$$

$$\mu = 5.02 - 5.78$$

Interpretation: We are 95% confident that the true population mean is somewhere between 5.02 and 5.78.

5) larger (less precise)

6) larger (less precise)

7) smaller (more precise)

Statistical tables

Table 1. The z table

z	0	0.01	0.02	0.03	0.04	0.05	0.06	0.07	0.08	0.09
0.0	0.5000	0.4960	0.4920	0.4880	0.4840	0.4801	0.4761	0.4721	0.4681	0.4641
0.1	0.4602	0.4562	0.4522	0.4483	0.4443	0.4404	0.4364	0.4325	0.4286	0.4247
0.2	0.4207	0.4168	0.4129	0.4090	0.4052	0.4013	0.3974	0.3936	0.3897	0.3859
0.3	0.3821	0.3783	0.3745	0.3707	0.3669	0.3632	0.3594	0.3557	0.3520	0.3483
0.4	0.3446	0.3409	0.3372	0.3336	0.3300	0.3264	0.3228	0.3192	0.3156	0.3121
0.5	0.3085	0.3050	0.3015	0.2981	0.2946	0.2912	0.2877	0.2843	0.2810	0.2776
0.6	0.2743	0.2709	0.2676	0.2643	0.2611	0.2578	0.2546	0.2514	0.2483	0.2451
0.7	0.2420	0.2389	0.2358	0.2327	0.2296	0.2266	0.2236	0.2206	0.2177	0.2148
0.8	0.2119	0.2090	0.2061	0.2033	0.2005	0.1977	0.1949	0.1922	0.1894	0.1867
0.9	0.1841	0.1814	0.1788	0.1762	0.1736	0.1711	0.1685	0.1660	0.1635	0.1611
1.0	0.1587	0.1562	0.1539	0.1515	0.1492	0.1469	0.1446	0.1423	0.1401	0.1379
1.1	0.1357	0.1335	0.1314	0.1292	0.1271	0.1251	0.1230	0.1210	0.1190	0.1170
1.2	0.1151	0.1131	0.1112	0.1093	0.1075	0.1056	0.1038	0.1020	0.1003	0.0985
1.3	0.0968	0.0951	0.0934	0.0918	0.0901	0.0885	0.0869	0.0853	0.0838	0.0823
1.4	0.0808	0.0793	0.0778	0.0764	0.0749	0.0735	0.0721	0.0708	0.0694	0.0681
1.5	0.0668	0.0655	0.0643	0.0630	0.0618	0.0606	0.0594	0.0582	0.0571	0.0559
1.6	0.0548	0.0537	0.0526	0.0516	0.0505	0.0495	0.0485	0.0475	0.0465	0.0455
1.7	0.0446	0.0436	0.0427	0.0418	0.0409	0.0401	0.0392	0.0384	0.0375	0.0367
1.8	0.0359	0.0351	0.0344	0.0336	0.0329	0.0322	0.0314	0.0307	0.0301	0.0294
1.9	0.0287	0.0281	0.0274	0.0268	0.0262	0.0256	0.0250	0.0244	0.0239	0.0233
2.0	0.0228	0.0222	0.0217	0.0212	0.0207	0.0202	0.0197	0.0192	0.0188	0.0183
2.1	0.0179	0.0174	0.0170	0.0166	0.0162	0.0158	0.0154	0.0150	0.0146	0.0143
2.2	0.0139	0.0136	0.0132	0.0129	0.0125	0.0122	0.0119	0.0116	0.0113	0.0110
2.3	0.0107	0.0104	0.0102	0.0099	0.0096	0.0094	0.0091	0.0089	0.0087	0.0084
2.4	0.0082	0.0080	0.0078	0.0075	0.0073	0.0071	0.0069	0.0068	0.0066	0.0064
2.5	0.0062	0.0060	0.0059	0.0057	0.0055	0.0054	0.0052	0.0051	0.0049	0.0048
2.6	0.0047	0.0045	0.0044	0.0043	0.0041	0.0040	0.0039	0.0038	0.0037	0.0036
2.7	0.0035	0.0034	0.0033	0.0032	0.0031	0.0030	0.0029	0.0028	0.0027	0.0026
2.8	0.0026	0.0025	0.0024	0.0023	0.0023	0.0022	0.0021	0.0021	0.0020	0.0019
2.9	0.0019	0.0018	0.0018	0.0017	0.0016	0.0016	0.0015	0.0015	0.0014	0.0014
3.0	0.0013	0.0013	0.0013	0.0012	0.0012	0.0011	0.0011	0.0011	0.0010	0.0010
3.1	0.0010	0.0009	0.0009	0.0009	0.0008	0.0008	0.0008	0.0008	0.0007	0.0007
3.2	0.0007	0.0007	0.0006	0.0006	0.0006	0.0006	0.0006	0.0005	0.0005	0.0005
3.3	0.0005	0.0005	0.0005	0.0004	0.0004	0.0004	0.0004	0.0004	0.0004	0.0003
3.4	0.0003	0.0003	0.0003	0.0003	0.0003	0.0003	0.0003	0.0003	0.0003	0.0002

*For any z > 3.49: p < 0.0002

Table 2. **The t table**

df	One-tailed 0.05	Two-tailed 0.05	One-tailed 0.01	Two-tailed 0.01
1	6.314	12.71	31.82	63.66
2	2.92	4.303	6.965	9.925
3	2.353	3.182	4.541	5.841
4	2.132	2.776	3.747	4.604
5	2.015	2.571	3.365	4.032
6	1.943	2.447	3.143	3.707
7	1.895	2.365	2.998	3.499
8	1.86	2.306	2.896	3.355
9	1.833	2.262	2.821	3.25
10	1.812	2.228	2.764	3.169
11	1.796	2.201	2.718	3.106
12	1.782	2.179	2.681	3.055
13	1.771	2.16	2.65	3.012
14	1.761	2.145	2.624	2.977
15	1.753	2.131	2.602	2.947
16	1.746	2.12	2.583	2.921
17	1.74	2.11	2.567	2.898
18	1.734	2.101	2.552	2.878
19	1.729	2.093	2.539	2.861
20	1.725	2.086	2.528	2.845
21	1.721	2.08	2.518	2.831
22	1.717	2.074	2.508	2.819
23	1.714	2.069	2.5	2.807
24	1.711	2.064	2.492	2.797
25	1.708	2.06	2.485	2.787
26	1.706	2.056	2.479	2.779
27	1.703	2.052	2.473	2.771
28	1.701	2.048	2.467	2.763
29	1.699	2.045	2.462	2.756
30	1.697	2.042	2.457	2.75
40	1.684	2.021	2.423	2.704
50	1.676	2.009	2.403	2.678
60	1.671	2.00	2.39	2.66
80	1.664	1.99	2.374	2.639
100	1.66	1.984	2.364	2.626
120	1.658	1.98	2.358	2.617

Table 3. **The F table**

df within (denominator)	df between (numerator)									
	1	**2**	**3**	**4**	**5**	**6**	**7**	**8**	**9**	**10**
2	18.51	19.00	19.16	19.25	19.30	19.33	19.35	19.37	19.38	19.40
	98.50	99.00	99.16	99.25	99.30	99.33	99.36	99.38	99.39	99.40
3	10.13	9.55	9.28	9.12	9.01	8.94	8.89	8.85	8.81	8.79
	34.12	30.82	29.46	28.71	28.24	27.91	27.67	27.49	27.34	27.23
4	7.71	6.94	6.59	6.39	6.26	6.16	6.09	6.04	6.00	5.96
	21.20	18.00	16.69	15.98	15.52	15.21	14.98	14.80	14.66	14.55
5	6.61	5.79	5.41	5.19	5.05	4.95	4.88	4.82	4.77	4.74
	16.26	13.27	12.06	11.39	10.97	10.67	10.46	10.29	10.16	10.05
6	5.99	5.14	4.76	4.53	4.39	4.28	4.21	4.15	4.10	4.06
	13.75	10.92	9.78	9.15	8.75	8.47	8.26	8.10	7.98	7.87
7	5.59	4.74	4.35	4.12	3.97	3.87	3.79	3.73	3.68	3.64
	12.25	9.55	8.45	7.85	7.46	7.19	6.99	6.84	6.72	6.62
8	5.32	4.46	4.07	3.84	3.69	3.58	3.50	3.44	3.39	3.35
	11.26	8.65	7.59	7.01	6.63	6.37	6.18	6.03	5.91	5.81
9	5.12	4.26	3.86	3.63	3.48	3.37	3.29	3.23	3.18	3.14
	10.56	8.02	6.99	6.42	6.06	5.80	5.61	5.47	5.35	5.26
10	4.96	4.10	3.71	3.48	3.33	3.22	3.14	3.07	3.02	2.98
	10.04	7.56	6.55	5.99	5.64	5.39	5.20	5.06	4.94	4.85
11	4.84	3.98	3.59	3.36	3.20	3.09	3.01	2.95	2.90	2.85
	9.65	7.21	6.22	5.67	5.32	5.07	4.89	4.74	4.63	4.54
12	4.75	3.89	3.49	3.26	3.11	3.00	2.91	2.85	2.80	2.75
	9.33	6.93	5.95	5.41	5.06	4.82	4.64	4.50	4.39	4.30
13	4.67	3.81	3.41	3.18	3.03	2.92	2.83	2.77	2.71	2.67
	9.07	6.70	5.74	5.21	4.86	4.62	4.44	4.30	4.19	4.10
14	4.60	3.74	3.34	3.11	2.96	2.85	2.76	2.70	2.65	2.60
	8.86	6.51	5.56	5.04	4.69	4.46	4.28	4.14	4.03	3.94
15	4.54	3.68	3.29	3.06	2.90	2.79	2.71	2.64	2.59	2.54
	8.68	6.36	5.42	4.89	4.56	4.32	4.14	4.00	3.89	3.80
16	4.49	3.63	3.24	3.01	2.85	2.74	2.66	2.59	2.54	2.49
	8.53	6.23	5.29	4.77	4.44	4.20	4.03	3.89	3.78	3.69
70	3.98	3.13	2.74	2.50	2.35	2.23	2.14	2.07	2.02	1.97
	7.01	4.92	4.07	3.60	3.29	3.07	2.91	2.78	2.67	2.59
100	3.94	3.09	2.70	2.46	2.31	2.19	2.10	2.03	1.97	1.93
	6.90	4.82	3.98	3.51	3.21	2.99	2.82	2.69	2.59	2.50
120	3.92	3.07	2.68	2.45	2.29	2.18	2.09	2.02	1.96	1.91

unshaded cells α 0.05
shaded cells α 0.01

Table 4. **The r table**

df	One-tailed 0.05	Two-tailed 0.05	One-tailed 0.01	Two-tailed 0.01
2	0.900	0.950	0.980	0.990
3	0.805	0.878	0.934	0.959
4	0.729	0.811	0.882	0.917
5	0.669	0.754	0.833	0.875
6	0.621	0.707	0.789	0.834
7	0.582	0.666	0.750	0.798
8	0.549	0.632	0.716	0.765
9	0.521	0.602	0.685	0.735
10	0.497	0.576	0.658	0.708
11	0.476	0.553	0.634	0.684
12	0.458	0.532	0.612	0.661
13	0.441	0.514	0.592	0.641
14	0.426	0.497	0.574	0.623
15	0.412	0.482	0.558	0.606
16	0.400	0.468	0.542	0.590
17	0.389	0.456	0.528	0.575
18	0.378	0.444	0.516	0.561
19	0.369	0.433	0.503	0.549
20	0.360	0.423	0.492	0.537
21	0.352	0.413	0.482	0.526
22	0.344	0.404	0.472	0.515
23	0.337	0.396	0.462	0.505
24	0.330	0.388	0.453	0.496
25	0.323	0.381	0.445	0.487
26	0.317	0.374	0.437	0.479
27	0.311	0.367	0.430	0.471
28	0.306	0.361	0.423	0.463
29	0.301	0.355	0.416	0.416
30	0.296	0.349	0.409	0.409
35	0.275	0.325	0.381	0.381
40	0.257	0.304	0.358	0.358
50	0.231	0.273	0.322	0.322
70	0.195	0.232	0.274	0.274
100	0.164	0.195	0.230	0.230

Table 5. The chi square (X^2) table

df	0.05	0.01
1	3.841	6.635
2	5.991	9.210
3	7.815	11.345
4	9.488	13.277
5	11.070	15.086
6	12.592	16.812
7	14.067	18.475
8	15.507	20.090
9	16.919	21.666
10	18.307	23.209
11	19.675	24.725
12	21.026	26.217
13	22.362	27.688
14	23.685	29.141
15	24.996	30.578
16	26.296	32.000
17	27.587	33.409
18	28.869	34.805
19	30.144	36.191
20	31.410	37.566
21	32.671	38.932
22	33.924	40.289
23	35.172	41.638
24	36.415	42.980
25	37.652	44.314
26	38.885	45.642
27	40.113	46.963
28	41.337	48.278
29	42.557	49.588
30	43.773	50.892
40	55.758	63.691
50	67.505	76.154
60	79.082	88.379
70	90.531	100.425
80	101.879	112.329
90	113.145	124.116
100	124.342	135.807

Made in the USA
Middletown, DE
09 January 2018